THE ENTERTAINERS

1992-1997

KEVIN KEEGAN'S LEGACY

WRITTEN BY WILL SCOTT

Mojo Risin'
Publishing Ltd

Published in 2024 by Mojo Risin' Publishing Ltd
www.mojorisinpublishing.com

British Library Cataloguing in Publication Data:
A catalogue record for this book is available from the British Library.

ISBN-13:
978-1-7394265-1-4

Cover design
Robert Maltman

Layout
Neil Jackson, Media Arts
www.media-arts.co.uk

Printed & bound by Mailing Guy Ltd
Proudly published Up North.

Also by Will Scott:

Pavel is a Geordie
Black and White, no Grey Areas
Scoop – The Truth Only Gets in the Way of a Good Story
The Rafalution

Contents

Foreword

When people talk about The Entertainers they generally want to talk about David Ginola, Rob Lee, Peter Beardsley, or the signing of Alan Shearer, but there wouldn't have been The Entertainers without the likes of Brian Kilcline. Killer was the start of it all.

When I went to the football club there was no leadership at all. There were a lot of players there who weren't big enough for the club and they knew it and felt the pressure of it all. I told the chairman (Sir John Hall) I was going to buy a player who won't play every week and eventually won't play at all as we go forward but we needed someone at the time to lead the dressing room while we got on with running the football club. The players needed leadership and someone they could respect and that was Killer. He was a fantastic player for us on and off the pitch in that short period of time. He helped us escape relegation and set the foundations for us to kick on and get promotion.

A lot of the fans understood where we were at the time, Killer's role and what he did for us. Had we not stopped up then I would have gone, as would a lot of the staff and players. Killer played a massive part in us all coming back after we survived. Newcastle fans get that. They are a lot more knowledgeable than other fans and they could see what we and he did at the time. They appreciate a player who pulls on the shirt and gives his best even if he isn't the most skilful or the best. They know players don't need to kiss the badge. They know when players care about their football club.

Some of the players I signed weren't 100 percent of what I thought I was getting. Some were 99 percent, some were 50 but Killer was 100 percent of what it said on the tin and he was one of my best signings. I wouldn't have been able to make all of those great signings later on without him. He made my job easier because I was putting good players into a good team. When Killer came that was not the case. I put Killer into a poor team lacking in confidence and leadership. We were in such a perilous state at the time. Players were washing their own shirts and we had to travel to away games on the day of the match. We weren't able to stop in a hotel the night before. That's how bad it was at the time. The board were of the attitude at the time, 'Why should we put them in a hotel if they're that bad?'

Killer didn't need to leave because I had a coach's role in mind for him but he wanted to play more games and I couldn't guarantee that. I was happy to take him on as staff because he was a leader. The players loved him, particularly the younger players. When they stepped out of line, Killer would look and tell them they shouldn't be doing that. I understood that he wanted to play. I was the same, as are most players, they want to play for as long as they can.

Killer went live on a barge shortly after he left us. He wasn't your typical footballer and that's what I loved about him. His signing caused a problem at the time if you remember. The money was there and then it wasn't. Everyone remembers my line, 'It wasn't like it said in the brochure' but it was simply because there was a power struggle behind the scenes that I wasn't fully aware of. Then we kicked on. One minute we're fighting relegation to the old Third Division, now League One, and then we're challenging for the Premier League.

Things happened so fast at the time that maybe we didn't appreciate what we had. I think maybe Killer's role might be forgotten and it shouldn't. He was as important as any of the signings we made after him. We wouldn't have signed the Rob Lee's and Andy Cole's without him. I remember the day we signed him in the old board room at St James' Park looking across the car park and the old club shop. We were sitting, trying to thrash out a deal when he stood up and said, 'I can't do anything until I talk to my wife. She's in the car.' He then got up and disappeared for about 25 minutes. Sir John and the other guys in the room were like, 'Are you sure he's a leader?

He's just gone and asked his wife if he can sign.' I said, 'Yes, he's a leader. He's gonna sort out the dressing room and take us to the next stage. He's just not the boss in his house.'

Kevin Keegan

A Word From The Publisher

I have supported Newcastle United Football Club since 1984. My first match was Kevin Keegan's last. It was a testimonial/benefit match for the club, not Keegan, against Liverpool dubbed 'Auf Wiedersehen, Kev,' after his two-year stint in Germany and the famous television drama about three Geordie bricklayers. This was the first time I had seen Kevin, and as he flew off in the helicopter, even at a young age, I felt he would be back.

Supporting our club has never been easy. Like our near neighbours Sunderland, we have always been a club that has promised so much and delivered very little in return for the wonderful, unconditional support from the terraces. We were known as a yo-yo club by the media. Perennial strugglers in the top flight usually lead to relegation. Often amongst the runners and riders in promotion races but also spending a fair bit of time in mid-table treading water. So, let me ask you this: When you think of the 90s what does it remind you of? Britpop? Blair? Blue ice pops at a rave? Maybe it's Sir Bobby and Gazza and Italia '90 and what might have been. For me though, it's Kevin Keegan and the rise and fall of The Entertainers, his entertainers. It started with the great escape from relegation, to a rip-roaring promotion season, and then an unforgettable first year with the big boys in the newly formed Premier League.

We went from mid-table mediocrity in the old Second Division to Premier League title contenders, playing a style of football that had the 'sold out' signs up at St James' Park prompting the owners to extend and redevelop the ageing stadium.

Transfer windows were a joy to behold. No longer a selling club but a club that broke the world transfer record to sign local hero and England captain Alan Shearer.

It was a great time to be black and white. Our games were televised most weeks and we were everyone's favourite second team, apart from those on Wearside of course.

Pavel, Tino, Ginola, to name a few became household

names whilst our own class of '91-92 Clark, Watson, Howey and Elliot flew the flag for the academy.

All we were missing was that elusive trophy. That piece of silverware that we hadn't held aloft since the Fairs Cup win in 1969 with Bobby Moncur and the lads doing Joe Harvey proud in Hungary. We had the manager and we had the players. So, what went wrong? Well, read on and find out.

Steve Wraith

Chapter One: Malcolm Dix

Sir John Hall rightly receives plaudits for crossing the Rubicon in an unprecedented move to remove the old Patrician order at St James' Park. Yet, without the revolutionary zeal of Malcolm Dix, the ascension of Kevin Keegan, the birth of The Entertainers, world record-breaking transfers, Alan Shearer, swashbuckling soccer, tears, tantrums, triumphs or even Sir John for that matter, would have remained a mere pipe dream for Newcastle's long-suffering supporters.

Dix, founder of the rabble-rousing Magpie Group, alongside local business stalwarts John Waugh, Alan Rooney, and Peter Ratcliffe, was the original enemy within. He was a rebel with a cause, embodying a Trotskyite fervour, fuelled by a righteous grudge against the machinations of the old guard. He embarked on a fervent mission to dismantle the entrenched old aristocratic hold over the club. Through his periodical, The Supporter, he waged a relentless war of words, holding the club's hierarchy to account and igniting a revolution that reverberated through generations, inspiring a legion of future dissenters.

Ironically, the Dix family were one of the original shareholders, when Newcastle East End and Newcastle West End merged to form Newcastle United in 1892. He inherited his father's shares after he died. Those shares were in the original possession of his grandfather, Walter. Disillusioned by decades of inertia and betrayal, the Newcastle businessman decided to infiltrate the bastions of power and join the Magpies' board to bring it to its knees.

After years of struggle at the helm of the Magpie Group, however, Dix recognised the need for reinforcements. Turning to the allure of new wealth and the patronage of Sir John Hall, he forged an alliance that would reshape the destiny of Newcastle United, forever.

Rebel with a Cause

My dad died in 1973 and that's when the shares were handed over to me. I didn't really want to become a director, even though I had enough shares to become a director. One of the old directors, Fenton Braithwaite, a canny old character, said the board needed some fresh, young blood because the average age of the directors at that time was about 75.

Take old Stan Seymour, the original Mr Newcastle. He would have two whiskeys and fall off his chair. Stan and the others had been wonderful guys for the club in their time but their time was over and it was a time for change. Gordon McKeag was the youngest on the board in his 50s and I was in my 30s then. I remember an old Journal headline from a director called Jimmy Rush who said, 'We don't want any whizz kids on the board.' I was the whizz kid.

I formed The Newcastle Supporters Association, the NSA, which was if you like, the first ever fanzine before fanzines became popular. I approached the Evening Chronicle and Journal but they weren't interested so I went to the Gateshead Post and they agreed to publish it. I managed to get some advertising before we set it out, which paid for the publication with eight pages in newspaper form. We called it The Supporter. We launched it just after the club's extraordinary meeting, where Bobby Rutherford called me all sorts of names under the sun but we had the board on the run from that first edition. The Supporter continued for 21 editions

We worked from what is now the Irish Centre but it was once the Number 9 bar. I bought it for £65,000 from Crawfords the printers. Directly opposite was Newcastle Breweries' head office. I remember Paul Nicholson, the chairman of Vaux Breweries, came to see me because we wanted money to develop the place. He looked across towards the Newcastle Breweries' head office and said, 'Where do I sign?' He wanted a Vaux sign facing straight across from Newcastle Breweries. They paid for everything. We handed it over to some people to run, although they didn't run it particularly well. In the end, because I'd signed all the forms to be a guarantor on everything, I got hit with all the debts and I had to sell the place to the Irish. Before that, we opened the Number 9 bar, which Jackie Milburn opened for us. We managed to get seven or eight former Newcastle No.9s from all over the country and we went to Balmbra's Music Hall on the ninth of June, a significant date as all Geordies know, got a coach and drove up to the No.9 bar. It was very theatrical back then. When that club closed, we transferred the bar to the supporters' club, where Malcolm MacDonald opened it. When that closed, we took it down to a pub in Walker, where Mirandinha opened it. Then that place closed.

I'd had various battles with the Newcastle board, Lord Westwood, Rutherford and Gordon McKeag. We had general meetings and high court actions and it was becoming silly because it was costing me a lot of money. The Newcastle board had the bailiffs outside my door at one stage. They were not very nice people. My wife rang me and handed the phone over to the bailiff, who happened to be the chairman of Berwick Rangers. A nice bloke. He said, 'We haven't met Malcolm but I know all about you. I'll give you a 24-hour stay of execution if you can get in touch with your bank to help you out, which they did, thankfully. Newcastle treated me with absolute contempt. It was dreadful.

I realised I couldn't go any further forward. We needed somebody with financial clout. Sir John was the man we wanted to help us. He was the man of the moment, if you like, and came across as a genuine person who had the best interests of the people, Newcastle and the surrounding area. To be honest, it didn't take too much persuasion to get Sir John on board, despite what he says. He liked a bit of publicity and publicity doesn't do anybody any harm when you're building a huge shopping complex (the MetroCentre) in Gateshead. They both went well together. We had some right battles between us all because not everyone agrees with each other but then when we got the share issue sorted it was all very positive and things moved forward from there.

Sir John Hall had great trust in the various members of the Magpie Group. He gave us signed cheques. I had three signed blank cheques from Sir John in my wallet and I could use each one up to £500,000. That was a hell of a thing. I should have kept one, shouldn't I? We had to eliminate those shareholders because they had no interest in the club.

One of the great successes for me, which gave me tremendous satisfaction, having endured the constant knockbacks and insults, was buying the family shares of Lord Westwood in his son, Gavin's house, after several gin and tonics. Bobby Rutherford was a golfer and a keen cricket fan who occasionally came to the matches. His family inherited the shares. He wasn't interested in Newcastle United. Lord Westwood was interested to be fair. He was the chairman of the Football League and Vice Chairman of the Football Association.

There was lots of small corruption going on at the football club in those days. Nowadays it involves millions of pounds but back then some people at the club were getting their houses refurbished, extended or done up at the expense of the football club. This was because the directors didn't get paid. There was a directors' turnstile at St James' Park. The money collected from that turnstile was collected and divvied out between them all. This was their kickback if you like. Getting rid of those people and bringing in real business people to run the club gave me a great deal of satisfaction.

Sadly, Malcolm died in November 2021 at the age of 79. His good friend, Sir John, provided a beautiful eulogy at his funeral.

"If Malcolm had never fought the first battle, we would never have won the war. What Malcolm did not just for the football club but for this city must never be forgotten."

It never will.

Chapter Two: Sir John Hall

Sir John Hall needs no introduction to fans of Newcastle United. There aren't enough adjectives or eulogies to describe the enigmatic Ashington-born entrepreneur and what he did for the Magpies. Sir John was a visionary. His impact on the club was nothing short of miraculous, almost fairytale-like. As a pioneering businessman and passionate football enthusiast, Sir John's influence left an indelible mark on Newcastle, propelling it into a new era of success.

When Sir John took full control of Newcastle in 1992, the club was languishing in the depths of the old English Second Division, far removed from its glorious league title and FA Cup-winning past. His arrival marked the dawn of a renaissance for the Magpies. Recognising the potential of the club and its passionate fanatical following, Hall embarked on a mission to restore United to its former glory.

One of Hall's most significant contributions was the astute managerial appointment of Kevin Keegan. Bringing Keegan back to St James' Park as manager in 1992 was a masterstroke. Keegan's charismatic leadership and attacking football philosophy resonated deeply with the fans and reinvigorated the team. Under Hall's stewardship, the club experienced a remarkable ascent, earning promotion to the Premier League in 1993 and subsequently challenging for the title in the mid-1990s.

Hall's vision extended beyond the football pitch. He was instrumental in developing the club's infrastructure, ensuring that Newcastle United had facilities befitting a top-tier team. His investment in the St James' Park stadium, transforming it into one of the most iconic and modern grounds in English football, underscored his commitment to the club's long-term success.

Sir John's influence was not confined to the club alone. He played a pivotal role in revitalising the entire Tyneside region. His initiatives brought economic growth and a renewed sense of pride to the community, intertwining the fortunes of the football club with the city's broader aspirations.

Sir John's tenure at Newcastle United was characterised by bold decisions, substantial investments, and an unwavering belief in the club's potential. His legacy is evident in the enduring strength and ambition of Newcastle United, a testament to his extraordinary influence on the club's history and future. He described the Keegan years as 'the happiest five years of my life.'

Aside from a brief resurgence under Sir Bobby Robson, it was no coincidence that the club's fortunes flagged after both he and Keegan stood down in 1997.

Black and White Knight

The Magpie Group wasn't my idea, it was Malcolm Dix's idea. Malcolm, Peter Ratcliffe, John Waugh, and Alan Rooney had been fighting the club long before I got involved and made significant progress but they had hit a stumbling block. If they were going to take the club on, they needed more cash. That's when I got involved.

I am an Ashington lad and I've always been a Newcastle fan. I first came to watch with my dad when I was eight years of age in 1941. We stood on the Popular Stand. If you got in early you got to stand on this plank of wood beside the pie shop, which ran the length of the Popular Stand. If you got there late you were passed down to the front so you could see the game. My love for the club has always been there. I used to look across the pitch to the West Stand and the wooden directors' box, never thinking one day I would be there.

I started as a mining surveyor in the pit, became a chartered surveyor and then a property developer building up my own business. Malcolm Dix came to see me when I was building the MetroCentre. He knocked on my second-hand portacabin door with his entourage. They asked me to get involved. At first, I said I couldn't because I had too much on my plate. I said, 'I don't have time to take on the old board.' They kept coming back and I kept saying

I didn't have time but then they pulled a dirty trick on me. They went to see Bob Cass at the Mail on Sunday.

I remember it was the end of a difficult week. It was raining and Bob came to the portacabin. I asked him what he wanted and he repeated what Malcolm and the Magpie Group had already said. I told him I wasn't interested. I'm not a whiskey drinker but I always keep a bottle close by. Bob loved a drink. By the time we'd finished the bottle I said, 'OK, I'll put half a million pounds on the table to put towards a consortium.'

I never wanted to own a football club. I was a businessman building things in the construction industry. Football wasn't part of my scene. Yes, I was a supporter standing on the terraces and supporting the team, and yes, shouting 'sack the board' like everybody else. I always wanted that privilege but not owning the team or the club. So, I told Bob, I'd put down half a million pounds and told him the consortium needed to find another £1.5 million to force the board to put some shares on the market. I always felt it was a people's club and I wanted to democratise it. I wanted the people, the fans, to own it, not me.

Bob ran this story the following Sunday about how John Hall wants to save the club and is looking for other saviours. We had a bit of a problem because running a story from Sunday to Sunday wouldn't work. We needed people to carry the story daily rather than on a weekly basis. Malcolm then went to see John Gibson with the story. Gibbo then went to see the Chronicle owner, Graeme Stanton, and they threw their weight behind us. It was tremendous. That's how the Magpie Group took off. We got the share issue sorted on the dining table at Wynyard Hall with Minkoff's Solicitors. Malcolm had done a lot of work before I came on board and I don't think he got the credit he deserved. He had breached the damn if you like and he just needed someone to step in.

We wrote to the club and asked them to put shares on the market. They refused at first. Newcastle United

Football Club epitomised a lot of businesses in England at that point. In the Victorian era, there were entrepreneurs, like myself, who built up a business and then spent the money. Newcastle was the same. It had been built by the entrepreneurs, bringing together Newcastle East End and Newcastle West End. They then issued shares between the families of the entrepreneurs but they didn't have the wealth to take things forward. For a long time, they wouldn't do anything. We decided we needed to buy some shares to get a foot in the door. This is where the Magpie Group came into its own because they knew every family who had shares of Newcastle United. They also knew those who wanted to sell their shares.

At one stage, my son, Douglas said, 'Give me a million pounds and I'll go and get control.' I said, 'No! We're going to do it properly.' That decision cost me a lot of money because a lot of families wouldn't sell at first. However, we eventually got hold of 40 percent of the shares, which meant we, Cameron-Hall, were the biggest shareholders in the club. We put a manifesto together of what we were going to do.

Douglas and I were invited to the old boardroom. Jim Smith was the manager at the time. Jim walked out of the meeting saying, 'I won't sit here with these people.' This was because I challenged him. He wanted to sign a player past his best. The player was Roy Aitken, former Celtic and Scotland captain. Jim and I became friends later on but we were at loggerheads back then.

In our first board meeting, we said the fans must be able to buy shares in the football club. We put up a million pounds in shares for the fans and it was one of the biggest disappointments in my life. The fans didn't take them up. We sold about £100,000 worth of shares. When the share issue failed, the other board members laughed at me. Had the fans taken up the offer, I would have got my million quid back, the club would've been democratised and I wouldn't have had to take over the club.

After the share issue failed, I decided to have a holiday. I hadn't had one for years. Thomas Cook was celebrating the 150th anniversary of his death, I think it was. It was a trip, flying around the world for a month for £21,000. I went down to London to sign up for the trip and they wheeled in Alan Whicker. He did a programme on the holiday. It's been on television about 1,000 times and we never got paid.

Anyway, we're staying in this hotel in Repulse Bay in Hong Kong. We're in the middle of dinner and a waiter asks if there's a Mr Hall in the room because there is a phone call for me. I'm thinking, 'Who the hell knows I'm here?' It was Freddy Shepherd and my son, Douglas. I said, 'What do you want?' My son said, 'Dad, the club is going bust.' I said, 'That's impossible.'

Douglas told me that Barclays Bank was pulling the plug on the club. I said, 'OK, I'm back next week, we can sort it out then.' He said, 'No, it has to be today, we have to put £845,000 into the club.' The rest of the board members weren't going to put their money in until we, Cameron-Hall, put our money in.

When I returned from my holiday, I discovered the club had an overdraft of £1 million. Part of the deal with the bank was that it would remain that way as long as they didn't buy any players to push it above that. The club had gone out and bought a player for about £300,000. I can't remember who it was. I was furious with the board for their stupidity. That was when we launched the takeover and lads from the Magpie Group came in again to help.

The price of the shares had gone up but we managed to buy 90 percent of the club and had complete control. I didn't want to own the football club but as a businessman, you either back it or lose your money and I'm not in the habit of losing money. When I found myself in these positions in the past I went for the jugular.

If you're gonna do something you have to do it right and become something of a dictator. When companies become huge, you need boards to manage the divisions. But when you're a family business, like the old Newcastle United, you've got to be single-minded to drive it through. I was the person who decided how we were going to take it forward. The Magpie Group was a tremendous help and I couldn't have done it without them.

The Magpie Group then went out tracking or looking for shares. Then one would come back and say, 'I've got one.' Another would come back and say, 'I've got another,' until we got 96 percent of the shares. Then I cleared out the old board. We didn't have a clue about running the football club. I'm a businessman but not a businessman of sport. I couldn't run the team, plan tactics or anything, that was Keegan's job. I was the guy trying to get money and keep a tight rein on that.

About the same time as the takeover was going on, I got the go-ahead to build 900 houses in Wynyard and the business park. It was a multi-million-pound development but I couldn't do that and run Newcastle United. I had to put the building work on hold. It took ten years to come back to it. The council fell out with me because I didn't build it fast enough. It didn't help that they were Middlesbrough supporters down here. So, as I was taking Newcastle forward there was a lot of ill feeling down here.

Wynyard Hall became the bank and we had to put a load of money into Newcastle, about £10 million. Then it was cash in, loans getting repaid and then we took it forward. By the way, we have to raise a glass of Brown Ale to Scottish and Newcastle Breweries. They said they wanted to help us. Former Newcastle Breweries Managing Director Alastair Wilson says I know a fellow who can help you. He's just left Glasgow Rangers. It was Freddie Fletcher.

We got on well and he agreed to come in with us. If it wasn't for him, we wouldn't have managed to pull a team together. We were going down with Ossie Ardiles in charge. Freddie said, 'We need to get rid of him.' I asked how do we do that? He said, 'Leave it to me.' He went and knocked on Ossie's door the following day at 7.30am. Ossie invited him in and asked what he wanted. Freddie said, 'You're sacked.' It was that simple.

I asked, 'Who do we bring in?' He said, 'Keegan!' I said, 'But he's been out of the game for ten years.' 'That doesn't matter,' Freddie said. 'He's in Spain and he's bored.' He might have been out of the game but he was keeping an eye on things so, he hadn't lost his touch for the game if you know what I mean.' So, Freddie, Douglas, and Freddy Shepherd went out to see him in Marbella, Spain. He agreed and the guys brought him back with them. We were lucky to find him and he was lucky to find us. We found somebody with nothing to lose. With things like that you've just got to drive things through. I was the motivator.

I went around all the clubs throughout Newcastle and the North-East to talk to the fans. Clubs don't do that now. We told them what we were going to do and we got them on our side. We told them it would take time and wouldn't happen overnight. The fans understood and we had a tremendous reception wherever we went. We even went into the Strawberry for drinks. I was one of them anyway. I was a fan.

Freddie Fletcher was a tremendous chief executive for us. He knew everyone in the game. He was a leading force. He knew Jack Walker very well. He said to him, 'Let us know if you're ever going to sell Alan Shearer.' Sure enough, Freddie got a call from Jack telling him Manchester United had put a bid in but in Jack's words, 'I don't want to sell him to them. They've bid £15 million. Do you want him?' I'm thinking, 'Jesus, £15 million!' I said, 'Yes, we'll buy him.' We looked to where we could get the money from. Then we scrambled around to get the money together. Within an hour we said,' Yes.'

If you're looking for role models and professionals, dedicated to the game, and for children to look up to, then

Alan Shearer and Johnny Wilkson were two of the best. I would watch Wilkinson kick ball after ball after ball after ball while he was perfecting his game. That is why he was a world-class player. Shearer was the same. What a tremendous day when we signed him. There were about 12,000 people inside the ground.

My favourite game? Man United at home where we won 5-0. I still dream about it. They were all great goals but that one from Ginola, where he cut inside and curled it into the top corner, and Philippe Albert's chip. The stuff that dreams are made of. The 3-2 home game against Barcelona runs it close mind you.

I've got many favourite players over my lifetime but my all-time favourite was Bobby Mitchell, twinkle toes. He could just dance around players. But each generation brings something special like Malcolm MacDonald. What a centre forward he was and Tony Green, what a beautiful player. The one player that surprised me was Peter Beardsley. I didn't want him. I thought he was too old. I rang Malcolm Dix and said, 'Kevin wants to sign Beardsley. We'll not get any money back from him because of his age.' Malcolm told me that he'd do a great job for us and he did.

Kevin approached us about the Andy Cole transfer and said, 'I've been approached by Manchester United, they've offered £6 million and Keith Gillespie. I want us to move on without Andy Cole.' The way I looked at it, Kevin was the MD (managing director) of one part of the business and I had to back him. If I, or anyone else, started to interfere with that side of the business then you're in trouble. He told us he had someone in mind he wanted to buy, which is business common sense. Andy Cole, and Les Ferdinand, were great people by the way. Two of the nicest people you'd ever meet. So, Andy left and there was hell on but Kevin made the decision and we backed him.

We had to redevelop the ground as it was as tatty as hell. We sat down and spoke about it and John Waugh had some plans to develop a 60,000 fan stadium. I was doubtful. I didn't think we would get 60,000 fans but in hindsight I was wrong and he was right. Parking in the city centre was always a problem. These were the types of things we were looking at.

We asked ourselves, 'Were there any sites outside of the city centre? Then there was Leazes Park but there were some old mine workings there and it was freeholders' land so I didn't think we would get permission. Then we thought, what about Gateshead? We were having problems with the planners at the time. We also had problems with Newcastle City Council. They weren't very sympathetic to what we were trying to do despite the business we were bringing to the city. I wanted to move the stadium to Gateshead. The council then said the Tyne Bridge wouldn't be able to take all of the traffic and they would fight us on that issue. So, we said, 'Let's just try and redevelop the ground with what we can afford. At the time that was 32,000 fans.

I remember when we finished the first redevelopment feeling very proud of myself. I got to the ground early, walked around and saw this fan, sitting in the Gallowgate End, now the Sir John Hall Stand, in floods of tears. I approached and said, 'You all right, Jack?' He said, 'Oh, Mr Hall, I'm so happy.' I said, 'Happy, you're in tears.' 'I've been coming here 40 years and never thought I'd have my own seat here.'

It was at that moment I realised people lived their lives through soccer. I didn't realise how much responsibility we had over people's lives. It was quite frightening to have that. It was a bit of an epiphany if you like. We'd redeveloped it to 32,000 but we had 14,000 fans on a waiting list for season tickets. We had a lot of complaints we didn't go far enough. So, we had to go again and managed to increase it to 52,000. You could still do a bit more, around the Gallowgate End, and get 60,000 in. We have a great football ground with a fantastic atmosphere and left our legacy with that.

Football is adrenaline. I've got hundreds of little stories from my time as Newcastle owner. The game at Grimsby where we clinched promotion in 1993. I had the Bentley at the time. I drove me and my wife down the M62 on a beautiful spring evening. We stopped at a Little Chef at the end of the M62. As my wife and I had finished our coffees, a clapped-out, battered old transit van pulled up and splattered to a stop. About 15 got out and had a run-off, or a sprint race. They hadn't seen me. I shouted, 'Give me the number of your season tickets!' They couldn't believe what they were hearing. They ran back to the van to get them. They lined up in front of me with their heads bowed, apologised profusely and explained what had happened. They had crates of Brown Ale and no service station would allow them to stop. They'd reached the point where they couldn't go on any further for the toilet. I jokingly said, 'Don't do it again! I won't forget any of you lot and I'll have your season tickets off you.' My wife, Lady May, added, 'I won't forget you either but it won't be because of your faces.'

Another time I had a complaint from a service station on the A19 when Freddie (Fletcher) and I were in the office. They sent us video footage of them. We called the supporters in. They came and apologised and we sent them back to pay for what they had taken. That was the power of the season ticket. No one wanted to lose them.

There was another time when we played Peterborough away. We won 1-0. We got the train down. After we got off the train we looked to get a taxi. A fan said, 'The stadium is only there, just walk it.' So, we walked it. Some fans asked if they could walk with us. I said, 'Of course you can.' Next thing, there are about a thousand following us. They're coming out of the pubs and clubs and I felt like the Pied Piper. Then we come to a road. One of our fans stepped onto the middle of the road and stopped the traffic. He said, 'Stop! Wor chairman is crossing the road.'

Another time we were coming back from London on a Sunday night after a match. It was about 6pm-7pm. We got in the first carriage. Next thing two fans get on and we start talking. Another two followed and then more and more piled in when they found out I was there. In the end, everyone who booked tickets in our carriage had to move into the carriage next door. Some fans were lying in the racks as we talked football for three hours. There were queues down the train. They were shouting, 'Ask the chairman this.' Another would say, 'And ask the chairman this.' So on and so on. We had a great rapport with the fans and Keegan.

We backed Keegan to the hilt. I think we gave him about 60 million for players and mind, he knew how to buy players. It just took off and it was one of the most exciting times of my life, the Keegan years, the wonderful football we played. We had a wonderful rapport at the time but then things changed.

When the pressure came, Keegan couldn't take it at times. He walked out after the Swindon game and went home to Southampton. Next thing I know the press are on to me. They were telling me he had gone. It was my wife, Lady May, she said to me, 'Look, he's waiting for you to phone him. Just phone him.' At first, I said, 'I'm not picking up the phone.' Then Malcolm Dix said the same. So, I called him. It's been well documented what I said, that 'There are only two people who can save Newcastle and we're both speaking to each other on the phone.' It worked and he came back.

We never interfered with his team. I used to go down to the dressing room and wish the players luck, which he didn't like, but I used to invite the players and their families down to Wynard twice a year for a bit of bonding. Kevin threatened to quit a couple of times after that. In the end, I thought, employees can't keep blackmailing their employers so I got Freddie Fletcher to draw up a resignation letter for the next time he threatened to quit with no date on it, which he did. We had his resignation letter ready and we said, 'We know how you feel. Just sign here.' He signed it and he's never spoken to me since.

When Keegan went, we made a couple of mistakes with managers. I still don't know why Liverpool reappointed one of them. Then there was Souness. To this day I still don't know why we paid £8.5 million for Boumsong. Apparently, Alan Curbishley (Charlton manager) offered £650,000 for him. He'd heard we offered £850,000 for him. When someone told him it was £8.5 million he fell off his seat laughing.

We heard that Elsie, Bobby Robson's wife, wanted to come home. So, we arranged a meeting with Bobby at his home in Spain. He was one year into a two-year contract but Barcelona wanted Van Gaal to take over and push Bobby upstairs. We shook on a deal that Bobby would be coming home. I rang him a day later to make arrangements for him to come back and I could tell in his voice he wasn't coming. He actually wouldn't believe us that Barca was going to put him upstairs. Had that happened, we wouldn't have made those mistakes on the managers before him.

Would I have done anything different in my time? Maybe trying harder to convince Bobby Robson to come to the club after Keegan had left. I think that is the one mistake I made. I didn't push hard enough to get Bobby in earlier. I should have jumped back on the plane and been more convincing. He was at the peak of his time back then and after Keegan, he was our most successful manager in the modern era. He would have provided stability and we would have won leagues. We've avoided success for so long, always the bridesmaid, never the bride.

Chapter Three: Lee Clark

Kevin Keegan described Lee Clark as having the "best touch of anyone there (at the club), probably as good as any I have seen. It is his control that is world-class." High praise indeed, from Keegan, a two-time Ballon d'Or winner, a former England captain who had played with and against the very best the football world had to offer during the golden years of the 1970s and 1980s while playing for Liverpool, Hamburg SV, Southampton, and Newcastle.

The United playmaker was a footballing prodigy, sought after by nearly every top-flight club in the English Football League. The Walker-born attacking midfielder's talent was so precocious that Sir Alex Ferguson personally knocked on the Clark family door in the middle of a full English breakfast, making it known he was keen to take the talented teenager to Old Trafford. Likewise, Liverpool, then the dominant force in the country under Kenny Dalglish, offered Newcastle £250,000 for the 15-year-old England schoolboy captain, a sum worth more than any member of the Magpies' squad at that time.

Despite the tempting offers, Clark, rooted to his hometown and somewhat of a homebird, wasn't interested in joining two of the nation's biggest football giants. His ambition was solely to don the black and white stripes of his beloved hometown club and follow in the footsteps of the former greats who graced the hallowed turf of St James' Park. He did it with aplomb.

Black Or White, No Grey Areas

You always felt like you were in the presence of someone great. He had magnetism, an aura and an awe-inspiring magnitude of charisma. He had this characteristic without even saying anything. And when he did speak, you listened. He was a fantastic footballer in his day and spoke a lot of sense. And, when Kevin became manager, he made us feel like giants.

Keegan's instillation as Newcastle manager captured the imagination of the city, its fans and the players. We had no idea he was going to take over from Ossie Ardiles. We, like the supporters, got our information through the media. We were excited because of the impact he'd made at the club during his time as a footballer. We'd all watched his career closely and it was almost a fairytale story. The early rejection, working in a factory and playing in the old Fourth Division was later swapped for a glittering career with Liverpool, Hamburg, Southampton and Newcastle.

He won titles in England and Germany, the FA Cup, UEFA Cup and the European Cup as well as being a double European Footballer of the Year winner. Not only that, he had the honour of captaining his country, England. Kevin was arguably the first modern-day footballing superstar. There was glitz and glamour as well as the tears and tantrums. His life was played out in the full glare of the public spotlight but he handled it brilliantly, unlike a lot of footballers today, and became a role model for thousands of wannabes.

Keegan got accused of being out of the game for too long, that he'd be out of touch because he'd spent eight years on a golf course in Marbella. But, when you have the knowledge and experience, picked up as a player, at some of the biggest clubs in the world, it doesn't matter how long you've spent away from the game. It's not rocket science. Kevin had an amazing eye for a player and how he wanted his teams to play. The club could have chosen another superstar manager and it might not have worked out because not all big-name players become top managers but with Kevin, Newcastle and the Geordie fans, it was perfect. All the pieces of the jigsaw fit perfectly. They had a special relationship with him as did all who played under him.

Despite what I've just said, my career appeared to be in the balance on his arrival. I clashed with him almost immediately. I was a regular in the side under Ossie but that changed under Kevin after a practice match on the Thursday before his first game in charge, at home to Bristol City. I had, what the lads will tell you, one of my many infamous outbursts on the training pitch. On this occasion, Alan Neilson was at the sharp end of my tongue and boot. Alan is a good friend of mine, not that this mattered, as my mates will tell you. Kevin pulled me to one side and said words to the effect, that I, was, 'A talented footballer but no good if you're a hothead. We need people with calm personas.' Consequently, I was left on the bench for the visit of City and started only four of our remaining 15 matches that term.

Subconsciously, losing my rag, if you like, might have been a reaction to the fact that Ossie had gone. I'd lost an ally in our Argentine manager and I was hurting for his sacking. He believed in me so much and we had a great relationship. It is hardly surprising I was pumped up in training. Yes, I was excited Keegan was at the club but at the same time confused about my mentor leaving. Looking back, my frustrations were probably all a part of my adolescence, growing up, dealing with becoming a young man and footballer. As a young man, there are rarely any grey areas, you deal in black or white when arranging your lifestyle decisions, choices and opinions. Eventually, the team got the results we needed to stay up so you could say Kevin was vindicated in his selection. He achieved what he set out to do in staving off relegation.

You could feel the tension going into our last game of the season at Leicester. We had won six, lost seven and drew two of Kevin's subsequent 15 games in charge. The initial feel-good factor had been replaced by a lot of trepidation and uncertainty. Newcastle was on the verge of going into the third tier of English football for the first time in their history. Nothing less than a victory would do. As it turned out we could have lost and still survived but we weren't to know that on the pitch.

Those were the days of the transistor radio. That's how fans found out what other teams were doing. It seems a bit prehistoric now but there were no mobile phones, Twitter or instant access to Facebook or social media. Still, it was great to win our last two games and get six points to ensure we would stay up. I remember the bus journey back from the midlands and the sheer relief of staying up was tangible. There was no party or champagne but we certainly had a few beers on the trip back to Tyneside.

We weren't sure whether the gaffer was going to come back for the new season. His classic quote, 'It's not like it said in the brochure,' had us all worried. That was an absolute vintage Keegan line. Only he could've come out with that but we loved him. Everyone at the club wanted him to come back after he kept us up. There was a danger it wasn't going to happen though.

Later on, Terry Mac told me how they jumped in the car and headed home to their families with no purpose of coming back. At the start of the negotiations between KK and the United board, he wasn't getting the vibes the team were going to challenge for promotion to the Premier League. Keegan was never going to come back and be a manager for a team just treading water. Yet something changed during the summer and he got the finances to start the process.

It seemed as if there was a great weight lifted off us when we returned for pre-season training ahead of the 1992-93 campaign. Doom and gloom had been replaced by optimism and belief. There was a bounce in everyone's step and we were all feeding off Keegan's ebullience and enthusiasm. John Beresford, Paul Bracewell and Barry Venison joined us for pre-season training. They may well have been the only three signings Keegan made in the summer of 1992 but they were all experienced players who had a lot of ability and football to offer. This was proved when we embarked on an 11-game unbeaten run at the start of the season. Bez could've signed for Liverpool. We'd seen how good he was in a successful Portsmouth team that got to the FA Cup semi-final in 1992. We may have struggled to stop up in the term before but we knew we had some good players: Micky Quinn, David Kelly and Gavin Peacock all had quality, as well as the sprinkling of precocious youngsters in the group. It was a perfect blend.

I was handed a free role, almost, as the new campaign got underway, with Brace or Liam O'Brien sitting in for me while I got forward to help out the attack. It was their unselfishness that allowed me to do that. The pressure was then on me to create goals for the team or score myself, because I'd left them alone in the middle of the park, under the vulnerability of a counterattack. This was how we felt when David Ginola joined us. He was a bit of a liability defensively. That part of the game didn't come naturally to him but we didn't mind doing that little bit of extra work because he was a match-winner. He could turn nothing passes into a goal or a chance for one of his teammates.

Kevin helped Ossie's early development of Steve Howey. He didn't just become a centre-back, he became a majestic centre-half. He was big, strong and could compete in the air. Howey could play football as well. Sometimes when teams were dropping off, he would carry the ball forward, pick a pass, score from open play or score from a set play. Becoming a top-class defender was a natural progression for him.

Venners and Brace were a massive influence on me and the younger lads. They were senior players, trained well, spoke articulately and led by example with their performances. They were the catalyst for success in our promotion season. Pound for pound it would be very difficult to find a more consistent player at the club in Venners' time, whether it was at right back, centre half or the holding midfield player.

The introduction of Venners, Brace and Bez was the beginning of KK raising the bar for the team, in terms of the quality he started to bring in. Rob Lee, Scott Sellars, Andy Cole and Mark Robinson followed soon after. Robinson was a perfect example of this because he never became a first-team regular. He was a quality player who was a warning to those in front of him. They had to perform at a high standard because he was breathing down their necks. He may not have been in the first team but he contributed in a different way to the squad.

I wasn't a defender but we had some great ones at St James' Park in my time. I could reel them all off: Beresford, Venison, Kilcline, Howey, Watson, Albert and Peacock. What used to nark me and the other players were the accusations that we couldn't defend as a team. It was nothing more than lazy journalism because we were always in the top four in the defending stats for goals conceded. I feel critics took that game at Anfield as a stick to beat us with. It wasn't like that. We didn't lose or win 4-3 every week under Keegan. I'd be surprised to find more than two or three of those scorelines in his five-year reign. It was harsh and I felt for our defenders and goalkeepers because of it. They got pigeonholed that they were letting the team down. This was far from the case. It was derogatory. It became an urban myth and once it got drummed into the football-supporting, reading psyche, it was hard to believe anything else. You heard or read about it every time you picked up a newspaper or watched Match of the Day and Sky Sports: 'Great going forward but can't defend!' Absolute bollocks!

Robert Lee came to us in the early autumn of our promotion season and was in a different class. He might have been a bit of an unknown to Newcastle fans when he signed for us but we knew all about him from his Charlton days. He was always the Addicks' stand-out player. We were always concerned about him every time we faced him. He was a pass-and-move midfielder and when he moved from the right of midfield to the centre, it was never a problem for him. He did have a couple of tricks but he was more of a, get the ball into a striker's feet and get the return or second ball, or the old one-two.

Rob for me, was one of our blue-chip players because

he could play numerous positions at a very high standard. Like Venison, his consistency levels were phenomenal. He was a very humble man, likeable and bought into the Geordie/Newcastle way of life, as did his family. He loved it up here. I got on really well with Rob and he was one of the best players I've played with. He had the whole package. I had no problem when our roles changed in the side and he became the attacking midfielder while I became the holding player. He was capped by England and was playing well. Sometimes you have to hold your hands up and admit you can't compete with that.

The standard of training increased tenfold when Kevin came in, quite simply, because of the high rank of senior player he was bringing in. It was ridiculous, unbelievably high and phenomenal. They were not only good players but great professionals. The bar was being raised all the time and we had to step up to the mark or get left behind and the likes of Elliott, Watson, Howey and I did. Both myself and Watto got called up into the full England squad while Howey got several caps and was part of the Euro 96 squad. I'm sure he would've got more had it not been for injury.

Keegan would take the odd coaching session but it was mostly left to Derek Fazackerley. The boss was more of a motivational coach. KK would give them a heads-up to whether it was a defensive or attacking format, depending on the opposition we would be facing that weekend. Chris McMenemy did the same when he took over from Faz. The sessions ran like clockwork because the coaches had good players. Keegan was always on hand giving advice when we were playing because he was a quality player in his day.

Terry McDermott, on the other hand, had a good rapport with all the players and was like a buffer between the lads and the manager. He made them feel good about themselves. He was great at lifting the spirits of everyone, even those not involved in the team. It's tough when you're not in the starting 11 and you don't feel as if you're contributing. Terry Mac was always excellent at making you feel you're still part of the bigger picture. I say he was a buffer but Keegan didn't need one because he was always approachable. You could always go to him about anything, whether it was football matters or family-related. But there were occasions when you didn't want to talk to the gaffer and you'd seek out his assistant. Of course, there were things that the boss didn't need to know or, rather, you didn't want him to know. Terry Mac was perfect for that.

Arthur Cox was another good one to go to see. The former Magpies boss was as straight as a die. There was very good chemistry between all of Keegan's staff but the boss was an especially inspirational man. Everyone was prepared to run through brick walls for him. He was honest, open, and emotional. Terry Mac would try and keep us bubbling along with his humour when there were low periods or when we were having the odd blip and we rarely did have the odd blip. We were always used to winning. There weren't many times we lost at home. When we did it affected everything: your home life, social life, and work. This is when the KK's No.2 came into his own.

Terry Mac's worst job was on a Saturday afternoon before kick-off. We'd be in the changing room and when he popped his head around the door, we used to keep our heads down trying to avoid any eye contact. The lads knew he was there to tell a player the bad news, in that, he wasn't playing. The players turned this around and made a bit of a joke about it. We used to sit with towels wrapped around our necks because we called him the custard pie machine and didn't want to get our clothes dirty from the custard pie he was chucking! He didn't enjoy that part of his job but when we got the nod, we knew Keegan wanted to see us to explain why he wasn't picking us for that game.

I was very much like the gaffer, in a lot of respects,

because I couldn't hide my emotions very well. When he told me I was being left out, for whatever reason, I didn't agree with it. I always thought I should be in the team. We never had a shouting and screaming match. I respected the gaffer too much for that. He was honest enough to discuss his reasons for leaving me out of the side.

I won North East Footballer of the Year and just about swept the board with the entire Player of the Year awards in our 1992-93 promotion season. The North East Footballer of the Year Award was special because of the luminaries who had won it before, like Keegan and Peter Beardsley. And when you think about all of the quality players I was playing alongside, it made it all the more surreal. It was the first time I'd been to a black-tie dinner. I am a Walker lad, remember, so yes, before you ask, it was a clip-on tie.

After we won promotion, the whole team had an end-of-season trip to Cyprus. It was the famous or infamous holiday where Killer's ponytail was sheared off and his moustache got mutilated. Everyone thought it was me. In fact, everyone was sure it was me. Even I was convinced it was me – but it wasn't!

Watto, Tommo and I were having a few beers in Ayia Napa Square. The rest of the lads had stayed, either, around the apartments where we were stopping or relaxing by the pool. We came back and saw Killer lying asleep and witnessed in astonishment that half of his tache had vanished and mane of hair had disappeared. His ponytail was stuffed in a wine glass on a table by his side. Surreal wasn't the word. It was almost like a Biblical scene from Samson or the Lion, the Witch and the Wardrobe, where the evil White Witch had cut off Aslan's mane. Killer's hair was his pride and joy. It was clear he was sleeping off the intoxicating effects of an afternoon session because nobody would've dared to do it while he was sober. While the three of us stood there observing the horrific scene with an overpowering sense of foreboding, one of the lads told us we'd better watch ourselves because we'd cut Killer's hair.

Tommo, Watto and I, looked at one another, turned on our heels and immediately legged it away from the apartments and scene of the crime. After about 500 yards of running breathlessly, I stopped and said, 'Hang on lads, what are we running for? I know we've had a few beers but we didn't do it. We weren't even there.' The three of us knew we weren't guilty but somehow the lads had convinced us we'd done it. I was a mischievous lad, who played pranks, but then so did the rest of the team. I was generally in amongst the high jinks and tomfoolery when it was going on but not this time. We returned and protested our innocence.

Venison, Bracewell, Sellars, Fazackerley, Youth Development Officer, John Murray and John Carver were all in the firing line. To say he was upset is an understatement. It all kicked off! Tommy Wright and O'Brien jumped in to try and calm him down because Killer went berserk! He was knocking people out left, right and centre. It was like a Popeye cartoon! It was pure carnage! The same happened to those who knocked on his bedroom door and tried to protest their innocence. I heard a few were seen scuttling down the corridor on their arses! But the lads who did it took their medicine and realised they'd taken the joke too far. They must have, foolishly, drunk several pints of Dutch courage! Killer knew it wasn't us. He saw how upset and worried we were about it. Who were the guilty culprits? One or two of those named above. I'll let Killer name and shame them.

Killergate aside, Keegan assembled a magnificent spirit in our squad. There were some great footballers in there and even better characters. I can't remember one bad egg KK brought to the club during his tenure. I never wanted to leave the place. Even on our day off, we couldn't wait to get back to work. I loved it. I think it showed in the way we played. It demonstrated the togetherness we had as a group. We were all best pals and all got together with our partners. It was hard to replicate what we had as a group. The love and respect we had for each other was limitless. No one was left out of the group activities, from the youngest to the most senior player; we were all in this together. This transpired on the pitch. When one of us wasn't playing well, you had a mate who looked after you and pulled a rabbit out of a hat to win the game.

There were other great guys behind the scenes as well, like Keith Beverage. I remember when we played Athletic Bilbao in the UEFA Cup away. Our doctor/physio was known to enjoy a cheeky drink or two. The night before the game he asked the barman for a brandy. The bartender handed Keith one of those big goldfish bowl-type glasses and replied 'Yes sir, just tell me when to stop.' Keith had turned away to talk to someone at this point and the barman just kept pouring until, before you know it, the glass was full to the rim. Yes, he did neck it all.

Keith was certainly eccentric and a joy to be around. We all loved and respected him. He had been at the club a long time and was a big Newcastle fan. He walked into a patio door when we were in Northern Ireland to play in George Best's testimonial. Thankfully there wasn't much damage, other than to the door. On another occasion when we were playing Metz in the UEFA Cup, Keith was trying to stitch a wound to David Batty's head while drinking a can of McEwan's at the same time. It was belly-achingly funny. Batts just shook his head and laughed. Beverage was certainly a perfect surname to suit his persona.

I've heard a lot of stories about certain football teams being a drinking club but that was never the case at Newcastle. We all did go out together in the Keegan era, not so much before then. The young lads knocked about together but it wasn't such a massive thing when we were kids coming through. I wasn't a big socialiser anyway until I was about 20. My focus was to become a professional footballer before then. I never saw any players breaking any drinking rules.

You weren't supposed to drink 48 hours before a game but most players would have their last drink on a Tuesday if there was a match on a Saturday. The one time we broke this rule was the night we got promoted at Grimsby. We'd all had a good skin-full after the game and we had to play at home against Oxford two days later. We were awful. In fact, we were that bad Keegan said he was disgusted by our performance and walked out of the changing room at half-time. We rallied after the break and managed to win 2-1 with me and Andy Cole on the score sheet. The press wanted to know where the boss had gone. Terry Mac spun the line that Keegan's wife, Jean, was ill and left for that reason and not because we were rubbish. It was enough to put the press off the trail and kick us up the backside and play better in the second half.

We generally socialised on a Monday night if we didn't have a midweek game. You would enjoy your Saturday night after a win, sometimes a Sunday, but we trained on a Monday still. It wasn't accepted by any of the pros if you trained poorly because you were suffering from a hangover. Fortunately, that never happened with us.

Our Christmas nights out became the stuff of legends though. We all went out in fancy dress one year. I was Barney Rubble and off the top of my head: Derek Wright was a pink fairy, Alan Shearer was dressed as Terry Mac, with the tashe and curly perm and John Murray was Fabrizio Ravanelli. We started in the Black Bull by the ground and then walked into town and got as far as the Monument. All of a sudden, a ball appeared from nowhere and we got in a circle and played one-touch. Within minutes there were hundreds of people surrounding us when they realised who we were. It was crazy. Big Les always laughs every time I see him because I staggered out of Legends with Barney Rubble's head under my arm and stumbled down Grey Street.

At Maiden Castle, where we used to train, we didn't

have one big changing room, there were several in the corridor which could only hold between five and six players. We had loads of fun down there. Faustino Asprilla was always a victim of having his socks, shirts and clothing cut up. You would often hear Tino screaming, 'Fuck you! Fuck You!' He didn't speak much English but he could swear with the best of them. Moments later we'd see our Colombia international walking down the corridor in shredded clothes trying to find the culprits. The finger was always pointed at Shearer but Tino bought into that camaraderie.

Tino was great fun to be around. He was a bit of a fruit loop and used to go and buy his clothes from the Walt Disney or Warner Bros., shop. He'd wear t-shirts with Mickey Mouse, Donald Duck or some other Disney cartoon icon. Watto and I went around to his house in Darras Hall one Sunday to see if he wanted to come out for a drink. It was bizarre. His father was in the lounge, playing the bongo drums and Tino was nowhere to be seen. We found him in his bedroom lounging around. 'Get a beer boys,' he'd say. I kid you not. He had an enormous fridge in his en-suite full of beer! He'd also take out a bottle of Tequila when we were on one of our social evenings. He'd hide it in his inside jacket pocket and take sneaky swigs when we weren't supposed to be looking. Me and a couple of the lads got wind of it and had a taste. It was like rocket fuel, about 90% proof and he'd be necking it like pop! Crazy!

Tino used to have a chauffeur when he first came to Newcastle before he learned to drive. We all got sponsored vehicles and I remember the day he got his first car. He pulled out of St James' Park and you could hear the roar and screech of the motor as he tore up Barrack Road like an F1 driver. Moments later we heard an almighty crash and sure enough, our maverick Colombian striker shuffled back into the ground, walked up to the guy who was dealing with the cars, dropped a set of keys in his hand and said, 'Tino needs new car!' He'd only written it off! This was around the same time I was given an XR3i as a club car. It was a proper fanny magnet! I made the mistake of tearing past KK and Terry Mac one day. After a short inquest, they found out it was me and I was downgraded to a Vauxhall Vectra. After that, the lads were calling me 'taxi driver.' It went from being a fanny magnet to a fanny repellent!

On a more serious note, I honestly thought my career was finished after clashing with the boss at Southampton. It's fair to say that after my reaction to getting hooked at The Dell, I was hanging on for dear life. I didn't think there was a way back but I was prepared to do anything to regain his confidence again, even if it meant I had to wash his car, clean his shoes, do his laundry or make his tea. Ironically, I was one of the few players praised by the boss at half-time while a couple of the senior players were on the sharp end of his tongue. That was why I was surprised to see my number raised after the break. That's why I reacted the way I did. I nearly broke my toe in the process. It was a steel bucket that was kicked in anger. I was in agony but didn't want to limp and double the shame and embarrassment of behaving like a spoilt child in front of the television cameras. I was off down the touchline towards the tunnel but Keegan got up and dragged me back into the dugout. It was a proper humiliation in front of the armchair-viewing football world. It was like being smacked on the bum by my dad when I was a kid.

We eventually lost the Southampton match 2-1, a memorable game in its own right for those two brilliant Matt Le Tissier goals. Le Tissier seemed to do that every time we played the Saints, home and away. When we got into the dressing room after the match had finished, I got an absolute battering from Keegan. Then there was the seven-hour-plus drive in the coach back to Newcastle. I had plenty of time to reflect on my actions. Those long trips home aren't nice at the best of times but this was the worst of my Magpies' career. Fifteen minutes before we hit Durham, Terry Mac came down the bus and told me, 'The manager wants you to go to Leicester tomorrow night and play for the reserves.' My head was swimming with all sorts of scenarios, most of them bad. I slept on the events of the previous day and realised I'd made a massive error of judgement.

I went to Maiden Castle, where we trained before I set off for the game against Leicester hoping to talk to the manager. I knocked on his door and waited nervously for him to let me in. When I asked whether I could have a word Keegan rebuffed my advances saying he wasn't prepared to talk to me. He told me to go and play for the reserves, do my best and that he needed time to think about what he was going to do. I knew it was serious. I was in trouble and had to do something about it. I thought I'd kicked the last ball for the club.

Knowing my career was hanging on a thread I hastily arranged a press conference in front of the TV cameras and apologised to my teammates, staff, supporters and more importantly, the manager. This got me back in the game, as you might say. Had I not done that I reckon I would've been kicked out of the club. I had disrespected the manager and the club in front of the television cameras, although at the time I did it out of frustration. I hadn't realised the gravity of the situation. As a player, you are selfish, to a certain extent, and you're just thinking about yourself. You sometimes don't see the bigger picture. I certainly didn't at the time.

I was left out of the club's League Cup tie at Wimbledon a few days after Bucketgate, which is famous for Andy Cole going AWOL. Barry Venison and Paul Bracewell were rooming together ahead of the Wombles clash and they called me. Venners said, 'I see your mate has backed you up like the good trade unionist he is.' I hadn't a clue what had happened or what they were talking about.

'Coley's fucked off and no one can find him.'

Although Brace and Venners were taking the piss,

they were right, Coley had backed me up and told Keegan my punishment was too severe. They had trained in the morning and Andy wasn't in the best of moods. He had a few words with the gaffer on the training pitch. Keegan told him, in less kinder words, that if he wasn't in the right frame of mind, he could re-evaluate himself. Coley did just that and buggered off. I know I was his pal but he would've done that for anyone if he thought it was wrong. That's the type of guy he is.

I'm not sure whether Coley's stand and subsequent actions had any influence on KK's thinking but we were both back in the side for the following fixture. Keegan pulled us both into his office and asked whether we were prepared to play. Obviously, we were and, as these things work out, ironically, it was against Wimbledon at home, the team who had just knocked us out of the League Cup. The boss informed me I was playing but not in my usual position. I had to play on the right of a midfield four. There is no way I could play there as a winger because I didn't have any pace but I was prepared to play anywhere. I was just happy to be back in the team.

By the way, Coley doesn't get the credit he deserves for his time on Tyneside. I think it was simply because he went to our biggest rivals at the time Man United. The club could have turned it down but they didn't and let him go. He hit the ground running at St James' Park. I don't think it sunk in or he understood what the No.9 shirt meant when I first told him but he embraced it and scored an incredible 68 goals in 84 appearances. If they're not the stats of a goalscoring legend then nothing is.

There has been a lot of mud slung in Cole's direction throughout his career: being arrogant and selfish are two of the biggest. I know him better than most but I wouldn't use either of those words. He never forces himself on anybody he doesn't know. He is polite and respectful to those people. Anyone who gets his back up, he tells them in no uncertain terms. He doesn't suffer fools gladly at all.

He has his opinions but deep down he's a shy unassuming lad.

I remember Coley calling me this one day and said, 'You fancy helping me move into my new house?'
'Aye, of course, mate. Where is it?'
'Crook.'
'Where the fuck is Crook?'
'It's in County Durham. You're from this area, you should know it.'
'You're right, I am but I've never fucking heard of Crook.'
Anyway, I helped him move and around lunchtime we decided to go to the local pub for a sandwich. It was a Saturday afternoon as it happens and we didn't have a game for one reason or another. When we walked in it was one of those classic moments where everything just stopped. Pints went down, music switched off and people stopped talking to stare at the pair of us. I looked at the regulars, Coley looked at the regulars, I looked at Coley, Coley looked at me and we're both thinking, what's just happened? It's as if two aliens were standing in front of them. Obviously, Andy is a black man and I'm not sure they'd seen any black men up there at that time. We couldn't get out of the pub quickly enough.

At training on Monday morning, I pulled Terry Mac and said, 'What the fuck are you doing putting him out there?' To be fair, you can't blame the club for this one because Coley had asked for something outside of the city centre, away from the hustle, bustle and hassle of everyday life. It was eventually resolved and the club got him an apartment opposite Jesmond Cricket Club. Later on, Andy and I both bought an apartment in Greystoke Park, Gosforth, and lived on either side of each other. This being the case we shared lifts into training each morning. It was his turn one day and generally, we would go in quite early. So, I waited and waited and he hadn't turned up. He wasn't answering his phone. I even knocked on his door and there was no answer. I thought, 'fuck this, I'm not getting fined for being late' so I jumped in my car and set off to training. Didn't think that much about it because he regularly had family up from Nottingham or people from London and vice versa. Just as I pulled into Maiden Castle, I got a call from him.

'Hi Lee, you OK mate?'

'Am I OK? I've nearly got a fine for being late, how do you think I am?'

'Sorry mate but I've had to keep this top secret but I'm signing for Man United.'

I couldn't believe it. I was shocked, to say the least. Several things were going around in my head but at the top was: 'We're losing our talisman.' You'd struggle to get a better pairing than Cole and Beardsley in the top flight at that time. Pedro's vision and first time passing and Coley's running. They were perfect for each other, moulded together. When our £7 million striker was on a run, he didn't even have to think about scoring goals because it came so naturally to him.

We lost Cole to our nearest rivals but I thought Keegan handled it brilliantly. It was typically unique of him the way he confronted supporters on the steps of St James' Park to explain his actions. He understood the consequences but, knowing the gaffer, he always had something up his sleeve. Les Ferdinand was lined up, as it happens but it took longer to get him over the line than he thought. The boss tried to get Big Les in while Coley was still with us. He wanted to play them together. KK and Terry Mac took him to Anfield to watch Ferdinand in action for QPR and asked whether he could play with him. Cole never left Newcastle because he was unhappy. He left because it was Man United. It's different for other players. For Geordies, it's a no-brainer, there's no other club you want to play for. Look at Alan Shearer, he could've signed for Man United.

There is a bit of bitterness from people about Andy because he was a star on Tyneside. He achieved legendary status for his goalscoring. He wore the No.9, took on the pressure of wearing the shirt and was successful. It is a shame he isn't held in the same esteem as our other famous No.9s. I'm aware he went seven games and two months without a goal. This wasn't because he was going through the motions or unhappy. He wasn't that type of man. Even accusations that he'd been found out weren't true or couldn't be true because it wouldn't matter if defenders knew what he was going to do, they still couldn't stop him. Maybe he was carrying an injury. He had problems with shin splints I seem to remember. It happened several times during his Newcastle career. The manager would never risk him if it was career-threatening but Keegan knew even a half-fit Andy Cole was worth having on the pitch because he could win a game out of nothing. He went on to win Premier League titles, FA Cups and a European Champions League winner's medal. He went on to become a better player.

Cole's sale was weird because we'd stopped becoming a selling club. We were a buying club then. Supporters were concerned we were going to go back to selling our best players like we did in the 1980s with Chris Waddle, Beardsley and Paul Gascoigne. This was never the case. Maybe KK thought Cole and Beardsley had run its course and wanted to freshen it up with Ferdinand. Big Les's partnership with Beardsley was just as successful but different.

I went down to watch Coley's debut at Old Trafford against Blackburn Rovers, which they won 1-0 thanks to an Eric Cantona goal. There was a gentlemen's agreement Cole and Keith Gillespie, the makeweight in the transfer, wouldn't play against their old clubs. But, as these things happen, we faced Man United the week of the transfer. I remember the game well, we drew 1-1. There's a great picture of Peter Schmeichel standing over me in the Black Bull opposite St James' Park, with my signed shirt for Pugger. I think I'm telling him to 'fuck off!'

It was a great game, the atmosphere was unbelievable, as it usually was, and there were two great teams doing combat. Mark Hughes put them ahead and suffered an injury thanks to a Pav challenge before Paul Kitson levelled. It was tough for Kitson because he had to step into Coley's shoes. It didn't matter who we got, it would've been tough for anyone to fill his boots. His goalscoring record was ridiculous.

I'm aware Cole was caught on camera singing an anti-Keegan song at the 1996 FA Cup final. I never saw it and was surprised when I heard the tale. Coley had nothing but respect for the boss and vice-versa. He loved his time at Newcastle. He would've instantly regretted it but probably got carried away with the moment. I would liken this to my t-shirt moment when I played for Sunderland.

Going into the 1994-95 season we were all full of optimism, of course. We finished third in our inaugural Premier League campaign and the team was confident we'd improve on that the following term and maybe win a trophy. I missed the final two months of the 1993-94 season, and you could say I was in rehabilitation ahead of the new term. I had broken a metatarsal bone in my foot. A metatarsal wasn't as famous or sexy back then until some fella, who played in Manchester, lifted the profile of the bone before the 2002 World Cup. I think my first game back after that injury was in the second leg of the UEFA Cup against Antwerp. We had a lot of serious injuries that term. We were without Philippe Albert, Barry Venison and Scott Sellars for long periods and then we sold Cole. They were all big important players for us. No team would've coped with so many of its big hitters being absent. It is little wonder our season ended in a whimper.

Philippe Albert was a fantastic guy and an unbelievable player. That goal against Man United in the 5-0 victory summed up what he was all about. He had the vision and ability of a number ten. Philippe took me out to this pub which sold all the foreign beers. Think it was called Beerrex, around the back of the Civic Centre. He had me on this Lucifer beer from Belgium. I can't remember getting home. I think he carried me.

Albert's signing summed up Keegan. Not only was he signing great players but bringing fantastic characters to the club as well. It's obvious that homework on a player was done before he brought them in. You can't get that lucky every time. We were just as excited as the fans when Keegan signed a new player. Marc Hottiger was another great lad and a smashing footballer he brought in. When you consider all of the different backgrounds we came from, it was staggering how well we all got on.

The debate, conspiracy theories and arguments of how we didn't clinch that elusive Premier League title in 1996 will go on forever. We all have our opinions or reasons why we didn't land the hallowed trophy of champions. I've heard them all and have my own, of course, but it goes without saying, that it still hurts to this day that I don't have a Premier League winner's medal in my collection.

There was a definite air of expectancy that enveloped the club as Kevin Keegan invested £14m supplementing our already gifted squad with the considerable talents of Les Ferdinand, David Ginola, Warren Barton and Shaka Hislop. We were also aware our nearest rivals at Old Trafford had allowed Mark Hughes, Andrei Kanchelskis and Paul Ince to leave. That was a lot of experience, although it has to be said we never underestimated Man United. While we respected the Red Devils it was all about us and what we could do and, on our day, we blew everyone away.

Our style of play captured the imagination of the nation and installed us as the country's second-favourite team. The gaffer wasn't one for the traditional pragmatic approach and we relished being part of that. It was a breathtaking paradigm of fluent, eloquent, one-touch football where attack became the best form of defence. This was no more personified in Ginola, our new £2.5m signing from Paris Saint Germain. The British footballing public had not witnessed his like before. Never mind that, we had never seen his like before. Most footballers seem to flourish when they have time and space. Our charismatic Frenchman, on the other hand, seemed to relish being heavily marked with his back to goal and with little room to manoeuvre.

With Ginola branding his unique style of wing wizardry on the left, Keith Gillespie providing a more traditional pacey role on the opposite flank, Peter Beardsley applying vision, awareness and ammunition in the hole and Robert Lee supporting a bludgeoning Ferdinand through the middle, we destroyed just about everyone who crossed our path in swashbuckling style. We led the Premier League table from the curtain-raiser and then it all went wrong in late March.

At the end of the 1994-95 campaign, and before pre-season training had begun, me and a few of the other lads used to go into St James' Park even when we were supposed to be on holiday. We just loved being around the place. We were sitting in the reception area of the Milburn Stand one day having a bit of craic. The gaffer happened to be in at the time. We weren't sure whether he'd had his holiday and was back trying to sign players or not. There was always speculation we were after this player and that player. Ginola hadn't been mentioned at this point. His signing had been quick and out of the blue. Keegan invited us into his office and offered us soft drinks and chocolate from his fridge. He pulled me to one side, away from the rest of the lads, for a one-on-one chat to talk about the forthcoming season. He discussed several tactical options: how when he played with two strikers, Peter Beardsley would drop deep and make up an extra man in midfield with Lee and Gillespie etc. Keegan also confessed my exclusion from the side on several occasions was undeserved. KK explained he only did so to accommodate players with a bigger stature, such as

Beardsley and Lee, who were both full internationals. So, when he suggested whether I would be interested in this new defensive midfield role it came out of the blue.

In essence, when we returned for pre-season training, Keegan wanted me to take on the role in small games, whether it was six-a-side; eight-a-side, keep ball session, or a tactics session and take it from there to see if I was suited to it. The suggestion was a shock but all I wanted to do was to play for my beloved club. If that was the only way it was going to happen, I was going to do it. The way we played anyway, meant I was going to have a lot of the ball and that suited me down to the ground.

We started the pre-season build-up and it was working well. I was on the ball more than I ever was in my former attacking role. I relished the new position and it became easy for me. I had the option of knocking the ball to the feet of Ginola on the left, hitting one over the top for Gillespie on the right, punching little ones down the side of the centre-halves or sliding it in the spaces between the midfield and defence for Beardsley and Lee to get on the ball.

I have to say, Ginola was an incredible player and another great addition to the group. When he first came to Newcastle he was stopping in the Gosforth Park Hotel. Being two very important members of the social committee, Steve Watson and I, decided to take him out to sample some Geordie culture. We didn't go as far as buying a Greggs' pasty or a ham and pease pudding stottie but we took him out for a few beers in some of the city's local hostelries. We started in the Three Mile Inn. After a couple of hours, and one or two libations, our flamboyant Frenchman decided it was time to go back to the hotel for a sauna and massage. We weren't having that. The rule was that once we were out, we were out for the day! And by God didn't our France international suffer the following day in training? He was blowing through his arse while Watto and I kept up with the leaders. It is fair to say he was staggered by our appetite for a good time and the fact we didn't suffer in training the following day.

Big Les was another one happy to live a quiet life. Our new No.9 confessed on his arrival that he never used to drink before he came to Newcastle. The Toon Social Committee can take credit for that one as well. Our £6m striker bought Andy Cole's old flat next to me when he moved to Tyneside. There was one night when the Paparazzi got a sniff that he had the famous model and television personality Dani Behr stopping over at his. Les asked if she could stop with me for a short time while he got rid of the photographers. I was delighted to help out a friend and his damsel in distress. I said, 'Not a problem Les, but I'm not too sure she'll be happy stopping with me knowing what I've got and knowing what you've got to offer.' Dani turned up at one of our home games and it was pissing down. Newcastle supporters got wind of it as well and started singing a suggestive song about her and Les. We didn't take the piss too much.

Ferdinand never wanted to leave Newcastle and although we've never spoken about it, I'm sure he was hurt by the way it happened and how it was handled. The club agreed to sell him and then Shearer got injured but he'd already given his word to Spurs. Big Les wouldn't go back on his promise. He was a man of honour and integrity. He was given the nickname 'Sir Les', by the press and fans and it was fully justified. He's a total gentleman, one of the nicest fellas I've ever had the pleasure of knowing in football. He was a magnanimous man and an unselfish player and what a footballer he was by the way.

I missed only two or three games through injury up until that fateful home clash with Man United at St James' Park when we were 12 points clear. Man City away was my last game and I never started another that season. There were 11 games left and I was an unused sub in seven of them, coming on sub in the last three.

There are several theories as to why we blew our

12-point lead. The main catalyst for destruction, seen by many, was Keegan's decision to splash £7m on Colombian international Faustino Asprilla from Parma. Another popular theory was the capture of David Batty. The boss believed we needed some defensive cover to protect the rich vein of attacking wealth and invested £4m capturing Blackburn's midfield enforcer as a consequence.

What do I think? I believe Keegan shouldn't have changed anything up to that point. The stats back me up. They tell you I shouldn't have been dropped. There are various conspiracy theories and I certainly believe the boss should've just left Big Les and Beardsley up front and used Tino like he did at Middlesbrough that day as an impact player. He came on and changed the game when we were flat and needed a spark. Subsequently, we beat Boro 2-1.

I'm guessing Keegan looked at the Man City game, where we drew 3-3, and thought we weren't solid enough defensively, that's why he brought in Batts. If you look at the fixtures before he came in, from the beginning of January, we won five, drew one, lost one, scored 12 and conceded five. In the 11 games that followed without me: we won five, drew two, lost four, scored 14 and conceded 12. We'd only lost four in the previous 27 Premier League games so why try and change something that isn't broke?

Batty was a magnificent footballer. We got on very well personally. I never had a problem with Keegan signing anyone, Batty especially. He was top quality, an England international, had experience, been there, done it and got the t-shirt. I never held a grudge and my respect for Keegan remains to this day, in fact, it still goes through the roof.

Rumours were flying around in the media we were going to sign Batty before he came in, as these things do. Batts turned up on one of our Monday nights out, down Julie's nightclub. Beardsley stayed behind and brought him to the Quayside to meet us. It was the first time I'd met him. He was, and is, a good lad. We had a few beers together and all of the lads were taking the piss about him coming in to take my place. It was all good craic and banter.

Batts and I became close friends, or as close as you could get to him. He lived in Wetherby and was a real family man. He was a funny lad, with a real dry sense of humour. It never affected our relationship and I admired him as a footballer. You talk about two-footed players and he was up there with the best of them. He could ping passes over any range with two feet but he played the defensive midfielder role differently from me.

As the title was slipping away from us, or we were losing games, I never witnessed a lack of fizz or enthusiasm in the training camp. We'd never been in that position before or experienced it. There was only Beardsley who had won a title before Batts turned up. Venners and Brace had gone by this stage. We all felt the defeats and were hurting as a group. If we lost a game on a Saturday, Sunday or Monday, the following training session we would be low because we were unhappy about the defeat. There would be no laughing and joking then but then we would pick it up again after a couple of days.

Did the boss's mood change at this time? What you see is what you get with Keegan. He can't hide his emotions. You know when he is unhappy or happy. I am the same. You can tell within seconds of seeing me what my mood is like. He was our leader and when he felt low so did we. There was never a time when teammates were having a pop at each other during the run in that season.

Towards the end of the 1995-96 campaign, there were a few players who had a crisis of confidence because results weren't going our way. Players weren't playing to the same level and self-belief dropped, which is natural. When you're a player of a certain level, a lot of the time, it's what's going on between your ears. Your self-belief and confidence go. You certainly see it with goalscorers.

I've been lucky that I've played with some fantastic forwards in my career who were phenomenal strikers. When they're in a rich vein of form it's instinctive and they don't think about it. If they have a lean period, it's weird, because they tend to overthink things or try too hard, if that makes any sense. So, when things aren't going for you the way they were and the goals and wins start drying up, you do have a few doubts and question your ability.

After the Spurs game at the end of the season, we didn't want to come out on the pitch and do a lap of honour. The only reason we came back out was to show some appreciation to the fans. It was never a lap of honour. We were so close yet so far and we could've added to that. We were deflated. We felt flat.

We had a very vocal dressing room and, although we were all low, several players tried to rally us saying it was a great effort, we should be proud of our season and we'll come back and have another go next term. We thought, 'Yes, it makes perfect sense. We've had this experience and we're better equipped now.' It didn't mask how low we all were. It was a fantastic achievement. We knew once we got back for pre-season training the boss and Terry Mac would be lifting our spirits to go again after our break. I heard Keegan had offered to resign at the end of the season and it wouldn't have surprised me if he did. He was an emotional guy and a bit impulsive at times. We never got wind of it though. He was desperate to win the title. Maybe he thought he had failed. No one else connected with the club thought that: the players, staff and supporters. I bet he thought that. Second to him wasn't good enough. That was his nature but he came back after the summer refreshed, signed Shearer and his enthusiasm was back tenfold.

We were on our way to Thailand and Singapore for a pre-season tour in the summer of 1996. Just as we boarded the plane and the doors were about to shut the manager jumped up, grabbed his carry bag and disembarked.

We knew something had happened but didn't know what. Keegan then joined us in Thailand a day or so later. We'd heard and read the speculation we were in the running to sign Shearer. But rumours surrounding the club were rife so we didn't know how true it was.

The boss got the squad together on his arrival in the Far East and said, 'If you don't realise that we're one of the biggest teams in Europe and the world, you will now. We've just broke the world record transfer fee to sign Alan Shearer.' Shearer then joined us a couple of days later. It was a wow moment. I think deep down we weren't that surprised because, as I've said a dozen times already, Keegan continually did this with the standard of player he kept bringing in. Every season the players were bigger, better and more high profile. We were excited all the same. The squad was confident it could win the title without Shearer coming in but his signature made us stronger. Sir John Hall, his son Douglas and Freddy Shepherd need to take a lot of credit as well. They were always looking to expand the brand. They travelled all around Europe and the world looking for innovative ways to take the club to another level and sign the best players of course.

There's been a big deal made of Shearer demanding Ferdinand's No.9 shirt. It was written that the incumbent holder of the jersey was widely upset about having to hand it over. I can't comment on whether that was true or false, although if I had to guess I'd say it was incorrect. He was more upset about taking my number ten than giving up the No.9. Being the gentleman, and all-round good guy, that he is, Big Les wouldn't take it at first. He said, "It's Nash's number." It didn't sit well with both Les and me at the time but the club insisted he wore the shirt. He took it badly, as I did. Shearer and Ferdinand got on like a house on fire, on and off the pitch. But it is impossible not to like Big Les; everybody loved him.

I was at a bit of a crossroads in my career at the end of the 1996 season after being pushed out of the first team picture. I'd had chances to go to other clubs before but never contemplated it. Celtic with Tommy Burns, who was the manager, was interested in taking me as was Brian Little at Aston Villa. They went through the correct channels and I spoke with Keegan about it. There was never any official meeting.

Thinking back, he was probably sounding out my feelings on such things but I didn't want to give up the dream of playing for my home club without fighting for a place. As much as I was frustrated at the end of the campaign, I wanted to prove my worth. I knew I was good enough. Keegan knew I was never going to let him down, whether coming off the bench or being recalled to the side in place of someone else.

It only hit home that I'd have to leave when Keegan left. I remember coming on as a sub when we beat Tottenham 7-1 and playing a big part in it. We blew them away like they were a lower-league club when they were one of the best teams in the country. We did the same against Leeds United a few days later. That was 3-0 against one of the best young sides in the Premier League. I wasn't aware he'd tried to resign after the Boxing Day game at Blackburn, where we lost 1-0 but when we went to a bitterly cold Charlton Athletic and drew 1-1 in the FA Cup, I remember the manager getting on the bus and keeping his woolly hat on. We're thinking, 'What's going on there?'

The day after the draw at Charlton Terry Mac called a meeting at Maiden Castle. It was quite emotional. He told us Keegan had left and that he and Arthur were taking charge in the short term. We were devastated. If Keegan hadn't brought us to the club, he would have nurtured and developed the young lads that were already there when he joined. We all ran through the proverbial brick wall for him. We never felt like he'd let us down.

Stories broke soon after about having to balance the books and we began to understand. The club had become a PLC and he'd stopped enjoying being the manager because of what that entailed. Apparently, he had to raise between £5m and £6m before he left. In essence, it was the sale of Big Les. He was fine about moving lads on to bring in new players but having to sell players to balance the books wasn't what he was about. He wanted the club to be different. He didn't want the club to go back to selling a Waddle, Beardsley or Gascoigne. When Sir John Hall initially came, they didn't do that. They started buying players to compliment the best players rather than flogging them.

I was back in the side at this point, doing well and enjoying my football. I was playing as a narrow right midfielder, because let's be fair, I didn't have any pace. I provided the assist for Rob Lee to score against his old club at The Valley. We went to Villa, in the game after Keegan had left, and we went 2-0 up. I scored before it finished 2-2. I hit the post in the last couple of minutes which would've made it 3-2.

Kenny Dalglish came in and we'd gone from one former iconic player to another, who was also a fantastic manager. While we were all devastated Keegan had gone, the Scot coming in kind of softened the blow if you like. Shearer and Batts had both played under him and won the Premier League. He was very different to KK. You could read Keegan any day of the week whereas Dalglish would keep things tight and inside. He was very protective of the players even when their performances were poor. In private he was a funny man full of humour and liked a laugh. We were all in awe of him as a player for his achievements.

Dalglish's first game was the FA Cup Third Round replay against Charlton. Shearer and I both scored in a 2-1 victory. I was on a roll. Not only was I starting games but scoring as well. My confidence was sky-high. We then went to The Dell and I scored again before Newcastle United nemesis Matt le Tissier scored yet another wonder goal to draw 2-2. He must have loved playing facing us.

It always seemed to be a world class finish every time he played. Then we faced Forest at home in the next round of the FA Cup and the new boss pulled me into the office. He said, 'Look, wee man, I'm leaving you out today.' I asked for a reason. He replied, 'There isn't a reason. It's just because Peter Beardsley is fit and he's the club captain.' That was the definitive moment. In my heart of hearts, I knew, it didn't matter what I did on the pitch I was always going to be down the pecking order with Beardsley, Rob Lee and Batts before me, no matter how I was performing. This was hard for me.

I have no axe to grind with Dalglish over his part in the club's history. I know he wasn't very popular with supporters in his time at St James' Park but, as much as it hurt to see the team struggle, I'd gone and had my time. The club hadn't forced me out. It was my decision. I didn't feel as if I got a fair crack of the whip at times and I can back that up. I was an easy option to leave out for the so-called big-name signings. I was the local lad who wouldn't moan or sulk because I was just happy to be playing for my hometown club.

When I had to make the difficult decision to leave it was a wrench. I was giving up the dream of playing for my beloved team but I was a footballer who wasn't playing football and that is what I wanted to do, play football. There were three incredible footballers in Beardsley, Lee and Batty, playing in my position. There was no shame in being unable to dislodge them from the side.

I knew my time was up at Newcastle. It goes without saying, I left with a heavy heart.

Chapter Four: Steve Howey

As one of the rising stars of Ossie Ardiles' class of 91-92, Steve Howey was instrumental in sealing Newcastle's promotion to the Premier League in the 1992-93 season, playing a crucial role in transforming the side from a struggling tier two side into a flamboyant top-flight outfit, which ultimately led to international recognition with England. Prior to that, Howey's embryonic career at Newcastle United had a bit of a stop-start feel to it.

Initially signed as a striker by United goalkeeping legend Willie McFaul, the Wearside-born youngster was given his debut by Jim Smith in a 2-0 defeat at Old Trafford against Manchester United in the club's fateful 1988-89 relegation season. Howey might have thought this was the start of something special but it took another year before he got his boots dirty for the first team again.

When Ardiles replaced Smith as Newcastle manager in 1991, he saw Howey's potential and attempted to convert the talented teenager into a defender, recognising that he lacked the qualities to be a successful striker. Unfortunately, the popular Argentinian wasn't around long enough to develop Howey's burgeoning talent. It fell to the charismatic Keegan to complete his transformation into a fully-blown international defender.

Although Howey lamented Ardiles' sacking at the time, he acknowledged that a managerial change was necessary if Newcastle was to avoid relegation to the old Third Division and to rejuvenate the team's fortunes. This need for change was starkly highlighted by a surreal incident in training where Newcastle lost a practice game against... no opposition.

The Boy Done Good

We had a shadow play session under Ossie before our game on Saturday. He picked the starting XI who would play in that game. We're playing against no one and the idea is to pass the ball around, score a goal and then come back and start again. We kicked off, the ball was passed to Lee Clark, Lee passed it to Kevin Scott, which is bizarre in hindsight because we're supposed to be going forward. Kevin passes it to Steve Watson who passes it back to the goalkeeper Tommy Wright. Tommy was putting his gloves on in the back of the net. The ball goes in the goal and we're 1-0 down and we're not playing against any fucker. We were going through a really bad time back then. I looked at Ossie who was rocking on his heels with his head in his hands. He was going, 'Fucking hell boys, we're sheet!' That's how bad it was. So, while it was sad to see Ossie go, we needed a change and Kevin Keegan came in at the right time to save us and transform the club.

I started as a centre forward and I think everyone who saw me in those early days would tell you I wasn't a centre forward. In fact, my name wasn't Steve Howey in the first couple of years at the club, it was useless Mackem bastard. I was born in Sunderland, played for Newcastle, and now live in Middlesbrough and I've got a brother who is a twat. Guess I'm a glutton for punishment.

I was a home bird and didn't want to move away. I could have signed for Sunderland and other teams but during the school holidays, I would come to Newcastle. We had some really good lads there: Steve Watson, Robbie Elliott, Alan Thompson, Lee Clark, Matty Appleby, and Alan Neilson among others. I didn't mind trekking over at 6am. I'd get the bus into Sunderland city centre, the train to Newcastle and the number 38 bus through Beirut, I mean Benwell. You'd see loads of burnt-out cars as we were travelling up to the training ground. I liked the vibe. I could've gone to Sunderland but I think I made the right decision.

Jack Charlton was the manager when I first went to the club but I signed for Wille McFaul. The youth team manager was Colin Suggest. We didn't have any centre forwards at the time so me and Lee Clark played up front. We scored a lot of goals together in the youth team and in the reserves, which is long gone and has been replaced with the under-23s. We were playing against seasoned professionals in the reserves which was a big help as a 16, 17-year-old.

I made my debut at 17 at Old Trafford because we had a few injuries. I came on as a substitute. We lost 2-0 and we'd already been relegated to the second tier which was Division Two at the time. It was quite surreal because I had pictures of the Man United players from Shoot and Match on my wall. I then had to wait another year before I played another game.

Kenny Wharton asked if I'd like to play for some team in Winnipeg, Canada, around that time. Think there are more polar bears than people live there. I didn't fancy it and I made my full debut against Plymouth Argyle in a 2-0 win at home on the first day of the season. I struggled to get game time until Ossie Ardiles took over and I struggled as a centre forward because we weren't that good at the time. I think Ossie got rid of the experienced lads too early like Mark McGee and Roy Aitken. It was literally, boys and against men in most games because Ossie had put all of the kids in. I'm playing up front, wearing the famous number nine, and I was from Sunderland, which probably didn't fit well with a lot of supporters. It didn't help that I was shit at the time.

We were aware of the Sir John Hall takeover with the Magpie Group. Did it affect us? No, not really. As kids, we were just concerned about trying to get into the first team. With Kevin, everything just snowballed and there was an instant feel-good factor around the club. Everything was a breath of fresh air, to the players and fans.

Everyone across the country must have been thinking 'Where have these come from? They're playing ridiculous football.' We became everyone's second team. Before that though we were struggling and in a perilous position. We got the result at Leicester, although we didn't need it in the end as results went our way. After that, Kevin sat down with Sir John Hall and they said, 'This must not happen again.' We then saw players leave and big-name players arrive: Barry Venison, Paul Bracewell, John Beresford, Kevin Sheedy and training just got better and better and better. It was so intense. It was weird because we never worked on anything like set plays or shapes. Kevin was all about five-a-sides, crossing and shooting. He wanted players to enjoy training. The standard was so high that some of the new players coming in couldn't handle it and were sold on.

Brian Kilcline was almost the catalyst for the start of The Entertainers. Later on, when he wasn't playing as much, he was still there in the dressing room encouraging the lads and we absolutely loved him. He was great with me, giving me fantastic advice. At the same time, the lads would rip the piss out of him because of his gear. His clothes were horrific. He didn't care though, he was all for the boys.

At the end of his time with us, it all went a bit pair-shaped after we won promotion and went to Aya Napa for a holiday. Barry Venison is a nightmare. Venners often used to joke he was going to cut off his ponytail. You have to understand, Killer loved his hair. At the time I'd just moved into a new house with my Mrs and I didn't go. Venners and Brace were saying you have to go on these trips. They said, 'Winning titles and cups don't come along very often so we have to enjoy these moments together.' Dunno why I was humming and haring because we eventually got divorced. I should have just gone.

Killer would often take the ponytail band off and head-bang to some music with his hair flying all over the place. He could drink as well. He passed out on a sunbed and Venners was the catalyst behind cutting his hair. I don't know if he did it but he was behind it. Killer was hurt because no one stopped them from doing it. Derek Fazakerley was there, a great lad and a great coach. Killer had been tipped off that it was Faz and he went to his room and just knocked him clean out. When they came back you could tell things had changed. He wasn't the same which is a shame because he was, is, a lovely man.

We started with a 3-2 win at home in the pissing rain against Southend at St James' Park and it snowballed from there. It was ironic that our 11 consecutive game-winning streak ended against Grimsby with a 1-0 defeat thanks to a Jim Dobbin worldy because we then actually clinched promotion at Grimsby in a 2-0 win later on in the season. We then beat Leicester 7-1 to wrap things up on the last day of the season. That was ironic too. Leicester was the opposition on the last day of the previous season. We had to go to Filbert Street to win to stay up. It was amazing to beat them so convincingly because they were flying at the time. We demolished them. It just showed how good we were. I know a few of the Leicester lads who played that day and they said that they just couldn't get anywhere near us.

Then it was all change to prepare for the Premier League. Kevin was great at moving players on such as Ned Kelly and Gavin Peacock. He thanked them for their services and told them he'd get the best possible deal he could for them. Andy Cole was one of the players that came in. I remember playing against Coley in the youth team when he played for Arsenal. We beat them 1-0 as it happens and I scored. Then I remembered playing against him when he was at Bristol City. I told Kevin after the game that he was decent. He was quick and had two good feet. Did I think he'd come to Newcastle and do what he did? No. He struck up this partnership with Peter Beardsley which was fantastic. I still scratch my head at why Kevin sold him to them (Man United) but it is what it is.

We had some great players at Newcastle: Ginola, Tino, Rob Lee, Ferdinand, Shearer, but Beardsley was the best I ever played with and I played for England with the likes of Paul Gascoigne. His tongue was quite sharp in the dressing room at times but in training and games, he was ridiculous. He had that trick that everybody knew was coming but no one could do anything about. Kevin loved him and if he gave a shit pass it was never his fault. Keegan said it was our fault because we weren't on the same wavelength. Joking aside, he was superb and his partnership with Coley was frightening.

Philippe Albert was another great addition to the team. He was Belgium's answer to (blue comedian) Chubby Brown. He loved Sid the Sexist from The Viz magazine but what a great lad. He spoke like the French policeman out of the TV series 'Allo 'Allo! He'd just signed for us and I was in the players' lounge with my mam and my dad. My dad wanted to meet him so I introduced them to him, 'This is my dad, Norman, and my mam, Yvonne.' He just pied my dad off and turned to my mam, 'Allo Yvonne, I've 'eard a lot about you. I've 'eard you've had two lovers in your life, the army and the navy.' He basically called my mam a slag. On a match day, when the teams were in the tunnel raring to go, shouting at each other and geeing each other up. Philippe, who was always at the back as we were coming out of the tunnel, would shout, 'Lads!' We'd all turn around and he'd shout, 'Tits oot!"

We had great camaraderie in my time at Newcastle. We'd go out down the Quayside as a team on a Monday or Tuesday. We'd go to (Italian restaurant) Unos first, then onto Martha's Bar, Jimmyz and Julies. Kevin encouraged us to socialise together and then he'd have us in the next day for a roll count and to make sure there hadn't been holy hell the night before.

We'd all go upstairs before training for a cuppa and tell stories about the night before of who had been with this bird or that bird. Cough, that was the single lads of course. We were out one night and this really attractive girl came up to me and asked if she could buy me a drink. I said it was OK, 'I'll get you one.' The girl catches the eye of Philippe. He leans over and says, 'Well, 'ello, do you like chocolate?' She says, 'Yes.' He said, 'Well, suck my cock it's a Mars Bar.' Bez tried to check him, 'What the fuck you doing, Philippe?' He was going through his whole Sid the Sexist routine. 'Do you like flowers? Get your tulips around this,' 'Do you like jewellery? Suck me cock it's a gem.'

So, we're telling the tales and Bez pipes up, 'What about the big daft Belgian?' The stories are flying and Philippe is sitting there stretched out laughing. Kevin turned to him and said, 'Philippe, they're taking the piss out of you, why are you laughing?' He said, 'Because at the end of the night she sucked my master.'

Tino Asprilla was another one: absolutely nuts. Away trips were always pretty long for us so the likes of Bez would arrange games for us to play on the way. There'd be card games at the back for pretty big money. On my table, it would be me, Bez, Rob Lee and Scoot (Scott Sellars) and we'd play for pennies. Some of the other lads like Steve Watson would bring videos to watch on the bus. We didn't have any initiations for new lads, where players would have to sing on the table, but you had to bring something for the bus to keep us entertained.

Shearer had told Tino that he had to bring something. So, he puts this video on and it starts with Columbian music. It was diabolical. Ken, the bus driver, ejected it and said it was shit. The lads told him he must do better. Tino took this onboard and then on the next trip he brought another video. He put it on while we were waiting for the gaffer and Terry Mac. The video starts with a woman's foot in a high-heel shoe. The picture pans out and we see this stunning, beautiful woman, in sexy underwear looking out across the ocean from this luxury villa. There's a knock on her door, she opens it to a big hairy-arsed geezer, with a bushy beard, in work clothes, and a white vest, and within two minutes we're watching hardcore pornography. The bus was still standing. Mams and dads with their kids are outside the bus waving us off at Maiden Castle and we're playing hardcore pornography on the bus. The dads are trying to turn their wives and kids away while breaking their necks to have a closer look at what we're playing. Kevin climbs on the bus to a woman screaming in ecstasy. He screams, 'What the fucking hell is this? Ken! Get this off! We've got mams and dads and kids here.' Kevin is just about to eject the video when Tino runs down the bus shouting, 'No, no, no! You must leave this on, eets my new meesis!' Tino was dating a porn star from his time at Parma. Think he just should've brought her to the players' lounge but that was Tino.

David Ginola was gorgeous, wasn't he? I'm into women but there was a time when I thought he could probably turn me. He had such a physique on him too. Looking at him naked and thinking, 'That's not fair' (he looks like that and I don't). He could wear a bin liner and still look the dog's bollocks. He was shocked that we were sharing the showers with the university students. He thought they were reserves at first until we told him we were sharing the facilities with some students.
'Theese did not 'appen at Paris Saint Germain.' Nash (Lee Clark) shouted, 'Well you're not at fucking Paris Saint Germain anymore.' I think it was a bit of a culture shock at first. I remember we played Middlesbrough early in the 1995-96 season at St James' Park. A good friend of mine, Neil Cox, was playing right back for Boro that day. David tore him apart. I felt sorry for Neil. I felt like going over and telling David to back off torturing him, it was that brutal.

David was a model for Cerruti. I set him up once and although his English was very good, I told him a rude word and it got him in trouble with a woman when we were out one night. He swore he would get me back for that. I'd forgotten about it because months and months had gone by. Me and Bez went to this fashion show in London that David was doing with lots of Page 3 models, so we thought we were having some of that. We were struggling to get a cab to the gig so we asked David if he could help. He said sure, the limousine that is taking Mr and Mrs Cerruti has a couple of spare spaces so they'll be able to drop you off. He said when you get in the car say, 'Suce ma bite, salope, this to Mrs Cerruti, she'll love you for it.

We get in the car, they're talking to us in broken English. We're talking to them in the Steve McClaren way, in English with a French accent. Then as I got out of the car I turned to Mrs Cerruti and said, 'Suce ma bite, salope.' She was in shock. Her husband gasped too, then he started laughing. I said, did I say something to offend you? Her husband said, "You said, 'suck my cock, you bitch!" He then asked why I said it. I told him it was David. We all fell about laughing. That aside, and I probably deserved it, he was a great lad. He bought into the project like all of the big stars, such as Big Les, that came in. We made sure they knew what the club and area meant to us and the fans.

Keith Gillespie was another great lad. His nickname was Dizzy, not because he was thick but after the trumpet player. He was actually really bright. He had a bit of a ruckus with Shearer in Dublin on a trip one time but we managed to keep it quiet because Al had knocked Keith clean out. A week after the incident, me, Bez, Rob Lee, and Warren Barton did a Q&A gig at the Dunston Federation Breweries. A member of the audience asked Warren what had happened. Warren said he didn't know because he wasn't there but 'The Boy' was. 'The Boy' was my nickname, courtesy of Barry Venison. Kenny Dalglish was the manager but he wasn't flying with us. Terry Mac was looking after us, which was a pointless exercise. He was the fox looking after the hens. Terry Mac said the gaffer was getting here at 7pm make sure you're back for something to eat and then you can go back out.

To relieve the boredom, we would play childish games. This time we had a pint in the middle of the table filled with all sorts of horrible alcohol. It would be something like names of football clubs in alphabetical order, or airlines or flavoured crisps. It would go around the table and you couldn't repeat a name already said. If you got it wrong, you'd have to take a drink. Then it would be your turn to pick a topic. Keith was already pissed and in a bad mood because an hour or so earlier as he walking into a bar the door swung back and hit him. He couldn't stop it because he had his hands in his pockets. Keith always wanted to fight everybody and the irony of all this, he couldn't fight sleep.

Shearer is a massive windup merchant. If anything was going on, Shearer was generally behind it. As we're playing the game it's always stopping at Keith. Shearer's winding him up calling him a thick Irish bastard. Keith stood up and said, 'Listen, you baldy bastard, one more time and we're going outside.' I managed to calm him down and start the game again. I say, 'Flavoured crisps. To my left, salt and vinegar. Keith then repeats, 'Salt and vinegar.' I said, 'Fucking hell man, Keith!' I've got this champagne cork in my hand and I bounced it off the table in disgust at the same time. It could have bounced anywhere but it didn't, it hit Keith in the eye. Shearer, quick as a flash, said, 'Look at you, you're the only Irishman that doesn't know where Cork is!'

'That's it! That's it!' Me and you outside,' Keith shouts. Des Hamilton turns to me, 'You not going to stop them?' I'm like, 'I'm at the embryo stage of a drinking session, I'm going nowhere.' Thirty seconds later Des is back. 'He's hit him. He's only fucking hit him.' I go along the corridor and I see Shearer standing over Keith who is flat out on the floor with claret everywhere. I said, 'What you done?' He said, 'I hit him.' I said, 'I can see that but you've knocked him out.' He said, 'Well yeah, he went to punch me first.' I told Shearer to get himself away and I'd sort it out. I got an ambulance to sort Keith out. I thought he was dead!

So, I've told this story at the Q&A and Rob Lee, who I love by the way, is not only murder sometimes, he's always halfway up Alan's arse. He only phoned Shearer and grassed me up for telling the story. He passed the phone to me and the first words Shearer said was, 'You Mackem bastard! You told the story?' I said, 'Yes, the supporters loved it.' I said, '600 people stood up and started chanting 'Shearer! Shearer!' He said, 'Were they?' I said, 'Aye.' He said,' You keep telling that story, bonny lad.'

Chapter Five: Steve Watson

Steve Watson holds the distinction of being Newcastle United's youngest-ever debutant, having made his first appearance for the Magpies against Wolves in 1990 at just 16 years and 233 days old. The versatile Geordie, adept as a defender, midfielder, and striker, faced a significant setback a year before he was due to leave school when the club informed the underachieving teenager he was being released.

Undeterred, the Wallsend-born starlet knuckled down, worked exceptionally hard, proved the club wrong and earned an apprenticeship. Watson then established himself in the first team under former managers Jim Smith and Ossie Ardiles. However, everything changed during Kevin Keegan's first full season in charge. The United young gun suddenly found himself excluded from the squad as the Magpies surged up the Division One table and into the promised land of the Premier League.

Being left out only strengthened Watson's resolve to fight his way back into Keegan's plans. His determination paid off after a rigorous summer of training with his mentor, Stevie Black, earning him a place in the starting XI as United embarked on a swashbuckling Premier League adventure.

Young Gun Goes For It

I came through the Newcastle Centre of Excellence, as it was then, with the likes of Alan Thompson, Robbie Elliot, Lee Clark and Steve Howey. It was great that we all came through and got in the first team. It was very much like Man United's kids coming through, although we didn't have any trophies to show for it. I didn't have a position. I dotted about everywhere. In fact, I started as a goalkeeper.

I was at the Centre of Excellence from the age of ten and at the age of 15 I was told I wasn't going to be kept on. I was heartbroken at the time. It's one of the hardest things to do to a kid, tell him he's not going to be kept on, and it's one of the hardest things for a young kid to hear. I played all sports at school: basketball, cricket, tennis, and athletics. I was doing the high jump and triple jump, and I think Newcastle thought I wasn't focused enough on football, the way Clarky and Alan Thompson were. So, I screwed me loaf and got stuck in. In my last year at Wallsend Boys' Club, I was playing up front and I did well. The club then came back and said, 'You've done enough, we've seen a reaction.' They signed me as a striker and then five months later I made my debut at right midfield.

"It was, of course, an honour to be the youngest-ever player to represent Newcastle. Like most lads, I was a Toon supporter, watching them as a kid. Jim Smith was the manager who gave me my debut. I've witnessed things in that dressing room that would shock youngsters today. They'd probably think he needed arresting. When he lost his temper, tea cups and Jaffa Cakes would go flying but I'll always be grateful to Jim for giving me my debut. I was performing well in the reserves at the time.

Players all peak at different times, you only need to look at the likes of Jamie Vardy to see that. He didn't burst onto the scene until he was in his 20s. I was the last person from my teenage group to sign a professional contract but the first to play in the first team. I made my debut against Wolves. I'm not sure which is more memorable, that, or Lee Clark scoring a header. John Burridge was my roommate when we were travelling to away games. He'd be walking around naked with a pair of goalkeeper's gloves on. I'm not sure if a 16-year-old today would be exposed to something like that when you're talking about safeguarding young players. It was an eye-opener for sure. He'd often ask me to throw oranges at him so he could test his reflexes. It has to be said that it was a bit surreal rooming with him.

We had quite an ageing side when I broke through. There was Budgie, Ray Ranson, John Anderson, Mark Stimson, Roy Aitken, Kevin Dillon, Liam O'Brien, Mark

McGee, and Mickey Quinn. Aside from me, Clarky, and Steve Howey, who was knocking on the door then, most of those players were in their 30s. It helped have our energy around the place and I think the fans appreciated having a couple of locals in the side.

I've been a manager since and you're always sad to see a manager lose his job and I was sad to see Jim go. The only manager I wasn't sad to see go was Ruud Gullit. But I think it was time for Jim to go when he did. Ossie came in and should take a lot of credit for putting the youth in, to the detriment of results to be honest. He was very positive, on the front foot but didn't pay much attention to what would happen when we didn't have the ball. He kept some of the older lads that he thought could help us but ultimately, we couldn't get results.

The game against Charlton sums up Ossie's time at Newcastle. We were 3-0 at half-time and lost 4-3. Obviously, even though we were young we knew what we should and shouldn't do but I think that was the catalyst for the end of his time at Newcastle, even though it wasn't his last game as manager. I think that was against Oxford in the cup.

I know it's been said that a week is a long time in football but I remember Ossie pulling me and Lee Makel to one side and saying it is going to be tough from now until the end of the season. He told us he was going to get some of the seniors involved and help us get through it. He then said we probably wouldn't be used again until the end of the season. I was a bit deflated hearing that. Then, Ossie got sacked on the Monday, Kevin Keegan came in on the Tuesday and I played in the next game against Bristol City in a 3-0 home win in Kevin's first game in charge.

It was funny because I thought maybe that was it and my time was up at Newcastle but I think maybe the youth team coaches had told Kevin that I was better than the other players we had at the time. Funny enough, I was lucky enough to play in Kevin's first and last game. Kevin had a lot of success with Lee Clark and Steve Howey in the promotion season. Not so much myself, because I didn't play much in the promotion season.

Kevin was everyone's idol at the time because of what he did as a player with Peter Beardsley and Chris Waddle. I was always Chris Waddle in the street games with my mates. To see him and Terry Mac come in was breathtaking for me. As a young player, I was aware of the takeover behind the scenes but I was young at the time so didn't get the gravity of it. I will say that it doesn't get said enough about the gamble taken by Sir John Hall, Freddie Shepherd and Douglas Hall. Not just to take over the club but to take a gamble on Kevin who had never managed. It could have gone either way but as it happens it couldn't have gone any better. It was a ballsy decision and I don't think anyone other than Kevin could've had that effect, not just on the players, the team and the club, but the city as well. Everyone bought into what he was doing.

We've always had great support and will continue to do so but I remember it had gone flat at St James' Park just before Kevin had come in. Then, it's buzzing again when Kevin arrived. There were some games that adrenaline just got you through games back then. It became a bit of a soap opera until the end of the season and typical Kevin, it went down to the last game of the season. Only Kevin could have written that.

After we survived, his management, some of it was harsh and tough. David Kelly, for instance, had done fantastically well for us. He let David go and then he brought in an unknown in Andy Cole. He made brilliant decisions and wasn't afraid of making hard decisions. He was quite ruthless moving on players and bringing in better ones as we progressed.

Kevin brought in Brian Kilcline, who brought a calmness to the side, which is a strange thing to say because he looked like a lunatic. He was a proper leader of men and exactly what we wanted at the time. We were very much on the front foot and we needed Killer at the back. He was a good talker to the young ones, keeping them right and he was great around the training pitch. Killer had the same sort of respect from us as Peter Beardsley did when he came in. They had high standards and it was quality control in training.

I think he moved on Micky Quinn because he saw the dynamics of the team in the future. Quinny was an out-and-out goalscorer and wouldn't have fitted in with the way Kevin wanted to play. He was a bit old school, happy-go-lucky. He wouldn't have looked after himself the way Beardsley or Andy Cole did. So, he let him go. He did the same with Killer. It was almost as if he said, 'Thanks for your help, now we're going to go a different way.'

The promotion season was special. The open-top bus around the city, the holiday in Cyprus, and thankfully we all came back in one piece, unlike Killer's hair. Kevin didn't have a recruitment officer or a sporting director. All of the scouting was done in-house and the signings he made for little money were unbelievable. You just need to look at Rob Lee. Then there was John Beresford, Paul Bracewell, Barry Venison, and Scott Sellars. They all came in a did a great job. Kevin just made great signings. He always managed to bring in people who fit into the great camaraderie in the dressing room as well. We were all best mates. We always did things as a group.

A lot of attention seems to focus on how we trained and that it wasn't very sophisticated. That it was five-a-side etc, but that's what Kevin and Terry Mac did at Liverpool in the 1970s and 80s and they were arguably the greatest British team ever. Yes, I know Man U have had a spell when they were great and then there was the Arsenal Invincibles but that Liverpool team was special. We did ball skills and technique to make sure everyone could handle the ball but mostly it was highly intense five, six or eight-a-sides. Terry Mac never took any sessions because he wasn't a coach and he'll tell you that. He was Kevin's No.2 but we had a fantastic coach in Derek Fazakerley. A lot of the time Kevin was on the pitch with us playing and Faz was almost coaching Kevin as well. It seemed to work.

It was rare at the time for teams to have foreign players back then, certainly in the North-East, but Pav came through with Jim Smith. He was an unbelievable athlete who couldn't speak much English. He was something that we'd not seen before because he was so agile and flexible. He'd pull off saves you'd think were impossible. Then he'd make a mistake and you'd think, 'That was easy.' He came as a young man and was a very special keeper by the time Kevin got here. Football aside, he was one of the best blokes you'll ever meet. Geordies very rarely get it wrong and everyone took to him. Seeing him in that grey t-shirt, with Pavel is a Geordie written across it, after we won the Championship at St James' Park was great. We had great goalkeepers come in and challenge him, like Shaka Hislop and then Shay Given, who was probably the best goalkeeper I played with. But for a long time, Pavel was a very special member of our squad.

In our promotion season, I was probably one of the only ones that took a step back. Kevin ended up sending me back with the juniors. I played the odd game and didn't even play enough games to get a medal. That was probably the kick up the backside I needed at the time. I could've gone either one of two ways that summer. I could've sulked but I met a man who changed my life and career in Steve Black. He's trained champions like Glenn McCrory, Jonny Wilkinson, Danny Cipriani, Jonathan Edwards, and Joey Barton. I spent all summer getting into the best physical and mental shape I could with Blacky, Lee Clark, the Newcastle Falcons Rugby Club, and Glenn McCrory who was training to fight Lennox Lewis. I never really looked back from then. I got back in the squad and played the first game in the Premier League against Spurs and then played in every season after that. If I'd not met Blackie, I don't know where I would have been.

We did well in the Premier League when we went up because Kevin made us believe we could beat anybody. He told us we had nothing to fear. I know we lost our first game against Spurs but it was a tight game and Spurs were a top side. People talk about sports psychology as a modern facet of the game but Kevin was a master at it and I don't even think he knew he was doing it. We were so highly motivated that we weren't afraid of anyone.

Peter Beardsley was a great signing for us the second time around. I remember him in his first spell, or rather his goals. That one against Portsmouth away when he dribbled past everyone in the box and checked back before he scored. Then there was the goal where he chipped Joe Corrigan at St James' Park against Man City. Like Killer, his impact just wasn't on the pitch, it was also behind the scenes in training. He'd be maxed out in every session. He never had a lazy day or took his foot off the gas and he wouldn't let anyone else in and around him to do the same. He was such a special player. Andy Cole was phenomenal but I wonder how well he would've done without Peter around him. If you ask Les Ferdinand, Alan Shearer, Ginola, none of them would underestimate Pedro's impact.

I got a little put out at times when Kevin kept buying right-backs in Marc Hottiger and Warren Barton. He couldn't have thought much of me. Just as well I was versatile and I could get in the team in other positions. Hottiger was another good athlete, a good player. Philippe Albert came in around the same time. They both got it. They got the club and they got the city. Back then, we didn't have the technology to check out players. Now we can check out their lifestyles, characters and family situations. Kevin somehow managed to bring in players with good character who got the club and the city. After the first pre-season training session we all went out to Jesmond: Hottiger, Albert, Alex Mathie, Malcolm Allen and within a couple of days everyone was solid with each other as a group and got it. I have to say, they couldn't believe the Toon. They didn't know what hit them.

We had a great bond with the fans. I don't get it now, that the players don't mix with the fans, even if it is once a month. There is such a void between the fans and players. Back then we could go out after a game, have a pint and chat with the fans about the game. Kevin made us believe we were employed by the fans. If one of us had arranged a game of golf and tried to sneak away after training, Kevin would be pulling us back in. He'd be like, 'Sign autographs for everyone first and then you can go.' It wasn't an act by Kevin, he was a man of the people. All of the press were onboard as well. If they weren't, he was quite brutal and there was no way back.

Tino was a one-off. He didn't learn any English but he learned Geordie and he said everything in a Geordie accent. Everyone knows the story about how he got off the plane, had a glass of red wine with Kevin for his lunch and then the gaffa asked whether he fancied going on the bench against Middlesbrough away. He came on, twisted Steve Vickers inside out and crossed it for me to head in. I still had a lot to do there by the way, heading home from five yards. I remember putting my arms up to celebrate and everyone ran past me to celebrate with Tino. That was just the start and he was brilliant.

In the early days, he had an interpreter, a young lad, green as grass. We were in Julies this one time and Tino said something to him and then off he went. We saw him whisper something to some girl and the next thing she slapped him across the face. Tino just stood laughing his head off. He used to buy his clothes at Warner Bros in the Metro Centre. They were awful. One time he came in wearing a denim shirt and we're thinking, 'Well, that's not too bad.' Then there were other times he came out with us and he's got the Warner Bros., cast on the back of his shirt, like Tweety Pie, Bugs Bunny, Speedy Gonzales, the

Tasmanian Devil and Wile E. Coyote. He just didn't give a toss. His parties, well, they're not safe for work or family viewing, let's just say.

Tino was also a special talent. The game against Barcelona, not just his hat-trick, but his performance that night was out-of-this-world. They played with a back three and he occupied them all. For me, that was the greatest single performance I've ever seen from a striker and you have to bear in mind I've played with Alan Shearer, Les Ferdinand, Pedro and Wayne Rooney. Then you've got the other side of the coin where he was shocking, getting substituted at half-time against West Ham.

David Ginola was another mercurial talent. I saw him not long ago and he came and cuddled me. I was with my wife. After he walked away, she said, 'He's good-looking.' Yes, he is! Me and Clarky would always try and muscle in when David and Big Les were talking together when we went out. We were like a wicketkeeper and a slip fielder. David was 6ft 2, strong as an ox, two good feet, mobile, he could go either way. He didn't have much going for him, really, did he? He was a defender's nightmare because you couldn't show him anywhere. That first season he was unlike anything we'd ever seen.

It was a nightmare for John Beresford because he had to do two jobs. Every time Bez complained to Kevin, the gaffer just shrugged it off saying, 'Look, he'll win us more games than lose us games.' Shearer had a couple of rows with him because his standard had probably dropped a little by the time he came. He was the most talented player I'd ever seen. He was a gentleman and one of the best-looking bastards you'll see in your life.

On the other hand, Philippe Albert was the biggest pint drinker you'll ever meet in your life. Bear in mind I'm from Wallsend and I've met a few drinkers in my time. There was one time he arranged a night out at Bierrex, behind the civic centre. It was his turn to pick a venue and he wanted a night out on Belgian beer. There was one drink called Duval and another called Lucifer, they were about 8.5% to 9% in strength. We started drinking and then after a while, there were bodies lying everywhere. Newcastle United's first team lying on the lawn outside spewing up. Aside from his drinking prowess, he wasn't a bad footballer.

Me and Bez were quite advanced as attacking full-backs who could score goals but Philippe was the new breed of centre-halves back then, much to the disgust of Steve Howey and Darren Peacock. He would just pass it and go. Everyone bangs on about the Man United goal but there was a goal against Man City at Maine Road the season before: He played three one-twos with players and then slotted it in. You never see centre halves do that, ever! He was a great defender but ahead of his time as a forward-thinking defender.

Kevin made so many brave decisions but the bravest of them all arguably, was selling Andy Cole. And, he was even braver by going out on the steps to talk to fans about his reasons for selling him. Managers don't do that but that's what Kevin was all about. He thought the fans deserved to know what he was doing and thinking. He told the fans to trust him and don't forget we got Keith Gillespie as part of the deal. He was a bargain. I got Keith the move, thanks to me being a shit defender. He turned me inside out to score at Old Trafford just before he came to us. Then Kevin brought in Big Les which gave us a different dynamic for the Premier League.

Coley did well for himself when he left and he was the second top goalscorer in the Premier League before Harry Kane caught him. If you talk to Coley he'll tell you he had a great time at the club but it was probably the right time for him to move. I think he was a Man U fan. He struck up a great partnership with Dwight York and he went on to have a very successful career.

We didn't know about Kevin's 'I'd love it' moment. We'd just had a tough game at Leeds where we won 1-0 and we were getting on the coach. The press officer at the time was Graham Courtney and he followed us on the bus with Kevin following him. Graham kind of stopped for a moment, looked at us and then exhaled very loudly. Back then we didn't have Sky Sports on the bus so it wasn't until we got home that we found out. David Batty had memorised the whole rant and for the next two weeks after that, he'd go through it in training. Kevin used to laugh his head off.

By the way, what a player David Batty was. You'd hardly ever see him after training or a game. It was as if he hated football. As soon as training was finished, he was off back down the road to his wife and kids but he always put in a good session. Batty was probably underrated. He surprised me when he came to sign for us. I'd already made my mind up, he was like a crab, sideways passes and put the odd tackle in and get booked but no, he was a great player. He wasn't your typical footballer. He'd rock up to training with a pair of boots, in an Asics tracksuit, and then he'd be off home.

You'd never have to worry about what Kevin was thinking because he always told the truth. Fergie must've been sitting rubbing his hands at home thinking, 'We've got him.' But we loved him for his honesty. He didn't go down in our estimation. If anything, he enhanced it.

Two games pivotal in our run-in were against Liverpool and Man U and we lost them both. Against Man U we had loads of shots, and Philippe Albert hit the crossbar. Then there was Schmeichel who was the best goalkeeper of our era who saved everything. Was it average finishing on the day or brilliant goalkeeping? Everyone has their own opinion. Some things went against us as well, like Ian Woan hitting a worldy from 35 yards for Forest in a 1-1 draw at the City Ground. I don't think we got worse towards the end of that season it was just Man U went on a hell of a run. Man U deserved to win it. They won something like 16 of their last 18 games.

Should we have won it? Yes, we should have. There's not a day that goes by without thinking about it. And there isn't a day that goes by where I don't wish I had a Premier League winner's medal. Everyone seems to get blamed whether it's Tino, Kevin's defensive work, or lack of it but it's a collective game and we all take the blame. We all know how to play and shut up shop at times. It just wasn't to be.

I didn't see it coming at all, Kevin leaving. Alan Shearer had signed for us in the summer and we were still in Europe. We didn't have a brilliant start to the season but we were sitting pretty. I still don't know 100% why he left. I'm not even sure if he's been interviewed about it. I heard he'd said he'd taken us as far as he could. I was devastated he left. As a player, we're professionals, so we couldn't sit and sulk because there was always a game coming up.

We didn't want to lose Kevin but then Kenny came in. He'd won the league with Blackburn and Alan and David Batty had spoken highly of Kenny. Kenny was another idol from the 1970s and 80s so we thought, 'OK, Kevin has gone so we have to look forward to Kenny coming in and playing for another legend.'

Alan Shearer was the best around. I wouldn't say he single-handedly won the league for Blackburn in 1995 but he was phenomenal, unstoppable. He was different to what we had. Les Ferdinand was as strong as Alan, Peter Beardsley had a different skill set to Alan, Coley was like a goal poacher and Alan had this ridiculous knack of scoring goals. And, he wanted to be the top goalscorer in every game, whether it was training or in his back garden. He'd take his own goalkeeper's head off to score, Shay and Pav would testify to that. He was ruthless in his pursuit of goals and that was part of his personality. You could put a ball into him and it would stick. He wouldn't complicate the game. He would get it down, pass it and get in the box. He was the best in Premier League history about doing that. He made shit passes by fullbacks look good, which I was all for.

I had the best time in my football career at Newcastle. I grew up, came through the ranks and made my debut with some of my best mates. The whole Kevin Keegan era was amazing. Talking about memorable games: the 5-0 win over Man United springs to mind. People talk about the 4-3 games with Liverpool and I'm sure they were good games for the neutral to watch but not for someone playing in them if you lose. They were shit for us because we got beat. The game against Barcelona, 3-2, the game at Royal Antwerp. We won 5-0, Rob Lee scored a hat-trick of headers and I scored.

I'd played up front with Andy Cole for three games and scored a few goals, a couple against Southampton so I was looking forward to playing against Antwerp. Kevin pulled me in the hotel two hours before the game and told me he was putting me on the bench. I was gutted. I said, 'Gaffer, why?' He said, 'Peter's fit.' I said, 'Fair enough.' No arguments there.

The Barca game at St James' Park I marked Rivaldo, one of the Brazilian greats. It was a special night as were the trips to Wembley in the FA Cup finals. It was just a shame we didn't win any silverware. The most memorable goal? The one against Liverpool at Anfield in the League Cup. We won 1-0. I scored a few goals considering I was a defender. I scored a hat-trick for Everton once but that was the best, especially as I married a Scouser.

One of my regrets was leaving Newcastle under Gullit. Looking back, I would've handled it differently and stuck it out. I would've loved to play under Sir Bobby Robson. I wouldn't say I didn't enjoy my time at Villa but I just don't think I come to terms about leaving Newcastle.

Chapter Six: Pavel Srniček

Pavel Srníček arrived at Newcastle from Banik Ostrava in 1991 for a fee of £350,000 during the Bald Eagle, Jim Smith's reign on Tyneside. The Czech Republic native faced a myriad of challenges in his first year, adjusting to a new country, culture, and language because he couldn't speak a word of English when he landed at Newcastle Airport on that bitterly cold January morning in 1991.

Despite those early struggles, Srníček soon became a key figure under Ossie Ardiles as the Argentinian despatched the old guard before injury interrupted his brief time as the club's first-choice custodian ahead of John Burridge and Tommy Wright. After regaining full fitness, he fought his way into new boss Kevin Keegan's team as Newcastle swatted away all that stood before them on the road to the Promised Land of the Premier League.

The Magpies' final day thrashing of Leicester City at St James' Park culminated with local hero Lee Clark presenting Pav with a grey T-shirt sporting "Pavel is a Geordie" emblazoned across it, a gift from his Clarky's brother Michael and Mick Edmondson from The Back Page bookshop. The T-shirt unquestionably symbolised Czech's difficult journey and subsequent triumph over adversity. Srníček's confidence grew and grew on the back of it and his early errors and 'dodgy keeper' chants were quickly forgotten as he matured into a first-class goalkeeper. The Czech's agility, shot-stopping abilities, and commanding presence ensured legendary status among the Geordie Republic's fans. Srníček played a pivotal role as Newcastle challenged for the Premier League title during the 1995-96 season as he shared goalkeeping duties with Shaka Hislop.

Sadly, an acrimonious departure from the club, after a clash with new manager Kenny Dalglish in 1998, was followed by a brief return in 2006, much to the fans' delight. Srníček's love for the club and its people made him an adopted Geordie, leaving a lasting impact on Newcastle. His legacy is that of a loyal and talented goalkeeper who played a significant role in one of the club's most exciting eras.

Srníček suffered a fatal heart attack while on his way to his mother's house on December 20, 2015. He was placed in an induced coma at a hospital in his hometown of Ostrava. He passed away nine days later, on December 29, aged just 47 when his life support machine was switched off due to irreversible brain damage. Srníček's funeral was held in his hometown on January 4, 2016.

Gone but certainly not forgotten, the big Czech is fondly remembered by all who saw him play and had the privilege of meeting him. A true prince among men. Pavel is a Geordie, always.

Pavel is a Geordie

'Kevin who?'

'Kevin Keegan. You've never heard of him?'

'No, I don't think so.'

My interpreter went on to reel off a list of his achievements: two-time European Footballer of the Year, European Cup, UEFA Cups, FA Cup, titles in England and Germany and a former England captain. To be honest, it wouldn't have mattered whether he'd won a Nobel Prize, an Oscar or a Blue Peter badge. I still didn't know who he was.

It didn't take me long to get to know Kevin and understand what he was about. He changed my life and the lives of those at the club, forever. In my career, I have never come across anyone quite like Kevin Keegan. The way he talked and the ability he had to motivate players. He had such an enigmatic personality and was an extremely inspirational character, yet his team talks were very brief. There were never any long Churchillian, 'We will fight them on the beaches.' Most of the time he would come into the dressing room before a game and would talk to us for a couple of minutes. He'd name the team and say something like, 'This is the team you're playing today. Show me you're better than them.' Then he would walk out of the dressing room. After the game, he would return and say, 'Thanks lads, I would swap any of you for anyone in the world,' or words to that effect. In the five years he was at Newcastle it was always the same.

At Maiden Castle, where we used to train, he would stop and chat and sign autographs with fans. He was always the last one to leave the training field. He would stay until every supporter had gone or until every fan had got his signature. He certainly had charisma and charm. When he was talking on the television, he was always comfortable, spoke articulately and came across well. I know he lost it on TV, that time after we beat Leeds 1-0 at Elland Road, but that was a bit different. He was under intense pressure and felt strongly about what Sir Alex Ferguson had said about whether Leeds would raise their game against us in the same way they did with Manchester United. Everything about him and his actions spoke volumes about his passion and commitment.

The Newcastle fans gave me a bit of grief when I first broke into the team, with the 'dodgy keeper' chants. Admittedly, I wasn't playing very well but I was still coming to terms with the hustle and bustle of British football. I was determined to win over the supporters and some of our players who I felt didn't rate me either. I was still recovering from my knee ligament injury when Kevin arrived and only played one game for him that season, a 3-2 home defeat to Tranmere. Tommy Wright was back between the posts for the next game, a trip to Ipswich, which we also lost 3-2, and remained there for the rest of the season Kevin preferred Tommy to me at that time. I didn't quite get what all the fuss was about when he arrived as the new manager but I soon got caught up in it all and what he meant to the supporters.

I couldn't put my finger on it at the time but I did have a feeling something special was about to happen. Kevin had an aura around him. The club was skint yet he got £20 million to buy new players. No one else before him could get it. I was thinking, how is that possible? He must have some charisma to talk the chairman, Sir John Hall, into investing that money in the club.

He got all of the players together when he first arrived and introduced himself and Terry Mac to us. My English still wasn't great at this point so I didn't understand a lot of what was being said. When Kevin first joined us, he gave us a lot of freedom. Back then we did shooting practice followed by games of five, six, seven or eight-a-side. That's all. We did this every single day. Some days he would say, 'Right, we're going to pick four teams, with four goalkeepers, and we're going to play a mini-tournament.' Everybody loved it. There was little work on tactics. It would be, come in, warm up, shooting sessions and then a game. Kevin never spent much time with me when he first arrived. I think it was because I didn't speak much English. He did have a chat when I'd returned to fitness from injury. I didn't understand much of it, mind, but I think it was about giving both Tommy Wright and me a chance to prove ourselves.

If life was tough on the pitch, it was even harder off it because we got burgled inside our first year on Tyneside. Thieves got into our house one evening when I was playing a game for Newcastle, which didn't help. I had a friend over from the Czech Republic. I had just bought a brand-new television and video and set the tape for the match. I told my friend we would watch the highlights when we got back in. So, my wife, daughter, friend and I all went to the match. We returned home and I let my friend in first, and although it was pretty traumatic at the time, looking back, it seemed like a sketch from The Fast Show.

'Check to see if the match taped?' I shouted to him.

'No, it didn't tape,' he replied.

'How is that?'

'Because it didn't.'

'Why not?'

'Because there is no video!'

'What do you mean, there is no video'
'There is no video. You don't even have a television! You don't have a video or a television, Pav!'
I thought my friend was taking the piss. Then I switched on the lights and saw everything was gone. It was as if a plague of locusts had been let loose and they'd devoured everything. The house wasn't smashed up or anything but they took all of our clothes, TV and video, although the microwave was left in the middle of the garden at the back, next to a pair of socks. I think they were using the socks as gloves to hide fingerprints. I'm guessing they were still in the house when we came home and dashed through the back and over the fence. After that, my wife didn't feel safe in the house with our little girl, especially with me being out all day, so we bought a house at 2 Hownan Close, Gosforth.

It looked as if we were going to be relegated to the third tier of the football league for the first time in the club's history while Ossie was in charge. Kevin came in for the last 16 games of the season and the impact was immediate because we beat Bristol City 3-0 at home in his first game in charge. He then made Brian Kilcline his first signing and immediately installed him as club captain. Keegan later remarked that Killer was the most influential signing he had ever made for the club. He was an important signing for us because he was a big personality and crucial in saving the club from relegation and possible bankruptcy if some stories are to be believed.

Keegan built the team around Killer at the time. Killer would be shouting, screaming and bollocking people on the pitch and everyone took it because they respected him. He was an experienced defender, after all, who had won the FA Cup with Coventry. I didn't know who he was, but then again, I didn't know much about anything or anyone at that time. I lived in a Communist state for all but one year of my life.

Overall, the results weren't great. You could feel the

tension and atmosphere as the end of the season was closing in on us and we still didn't have enough points to stay up. We won seven, lost seven and drew two of those 16 games and just survived thanks to a dramatic last game of the season at Leicester, where we won 2-1.

David Kelly was a great friend to me. He was always asking whether I was OK or if I wanted anything. Kevin Sheedy was another new signing Keegan brought in to help us beat relegation. He was a terrific lad. He lived near me in Darras Hall and picked me up for training on several occasions. It must have been difficult for him trying to make conversation with someone who didn't speak the language, yet he tried. He would ask, 'You OK Pav? You fit?' and I would just answer everything with a, 'Yeah, yeah, everything good.' I can laugh about it now but it must have been difficult for him and the others. I have some nice memories of those lads. Yet the Special K show was nearly over before it started when Keegan walked out after we had beaten Glenn Hoddle's Swindon Town 3-1.

We felt we were just about to turn things around after a mixed bag of results under Kevin. Only four days earlier we had been down to Cambridge United and won 2-0. The home victory over Swindon meant we had won four, drawn one and lost only two since Kevin arrived. We were all shocked when we heard he'd walked out of the club. It turns out Kevin was trying to buy a player and Sir John Hall either wouldn't sanction it or couldn't raise the money. Some said it was Swindon's David Kerslake. After the Swindon game, Kevin walked into the dressing room and said: 'Good luck lads. This isn't about you.'

The chairman eventually resolved the problem, so he was back before we knew it. Rumours were flying around at the time that Kevin was always throwing a tantrum to get his way but we had never seen that side of him. Later on, Kevin had a fantastic position in the club with regards to getting what player he wanted. I believe that the walk-out episode strengthened that standing and worked in his favour. I think Sir John was maybe frightened he would walk out again, so he bought every player Kevin asked for. No more so, later on, than when he signed Andy Cole and then Alan Shearer for a world record fee of £15 million. This said a lot about Keegan. It was as if he was saying, 'You want me to stay? Then you need to go and sign this player and that player otherwise I will walk away.' He seemed to be a master at manipulating a situation. When he came back to training the following Monday nothing was said, to my memory. We just carried on where he left off although, not long after, our results started to suffer and take a turn for the worse.

We drew 1-1 away at Grimsby, and beat Sunderland 1-0 at St James' Park in the following two matches before five defeats in a row left us on the brink of relegation. A tremendous strike from Ned Kelly in a 1-0 triumph over Portsmouth, and my old boss, Jim Smith, gave us three valuable points. We followed up that with a nail-biting 2-1 victory over Leicester in the last fixture of the season to stay up. As it happens, we didn't need to win that day but we weren't to know the other results were going to go in our favour. Gavin Peacock put us ahead in the first half and the game just seemed to drag on from then. Steve Walsh equalised in injury time before putting one in his own goal only a minute later. It was Roy of the Rovers stuff. I didn't understand the gravity of the club's situation until later. It was a relief to stay up. Who knows what would've happened had we gone down?

At the end of the season, I still didn't know where I stood at United. I hadn't established myself as the club's No.1. A lot of other people would've just thrown in the towel and decided not to return for the following season but I was a proud man, proud of where I was from in the Czech Republic. I felt I was representing my nation and, if I had quit, I would've been seen as a failure by the people of my country. Also, I didn't want to let my family down.

There was no real hint of what was to come when we

returned for pre-season training. Kevin was giving interviews before the curtain raiser against Southend, stating he was confident Newcastle could challenge Manchester United for the Premier League title. When you consider we survived the previous campaign by the skin of our teeth that was an extraordinary statement. Anyone other than Keegan making statements like that you would think they'd been taking drugs! I thought maybe consolidation or a place in the play-offs might have been a more realistic target but hats off to the gaffer, it was champagne stuff all the way.

In pre-season Kevin signed Paul Bracewell from arch-rivals Sunderland for £250,000, and Barry Venison from Liverpool for the same fee. Venners was a steal at that price but he was deemed surplus to requirements by Anfield chief Graeme Souness, who was doing a similar rebuilding job on Merseyside to the one Kevin was doing on Tyneside. Keegan finally landed John Beresford, who had caught his eye during Portsmouth's run to the FA Cup semi-final the previous season. It had looked as if he was going to sign for Liverpool until he failed the medical. There was no problem passing a medical at St James' Park, if my experience was anything to go by.

It was a new-look side to the one which had flirted with relegation the previous season, and there was a good blend of youth and experience. Kevin converted Steve Howey from a striker to a centre half while Killer and Kevin Scott also provided experience at the back with Venners. Kevin Brock had a good head on his shoulders, while Kevin Sheedy had seen it all and got the T-shirt. Lee Clark was arguably the rising young star in the camp, with Robbie Elliott, Steve Watson and Alan Thompson also showing promise, while the veterans Brace, Sheedy and Liam O'Brien added their know-how in the middle of midfield. Up front, there wasn't a better front pairing in the division than David Kelly and Gavin Peacock. They dovetailed together beautifully. Gavin would drop deep into the hole while Ned was happily running in the channels.

Micky Quinn got his nose pushed out of joint and said some unsavoury things when he left but admitted later regretting saying them. I was aware of the problems he was having with Kevin because everyone was saying what a great player he was. He had a great record as a striker. Kevin moved him onto Coventry because Quinny wanted to play every week and wouldn't accept being a squad player. Keegan did the same with Franz Carr.

Ned Kelly was also moved on by Kevin the season after, which shocked me, given all he had done for the team. Ned came to see me and said he was leaving the club. This was unusual because players rarely confided in others they were leaving. One day they would be there, the next they were gone. There was no bitterness from Ned at all. He accepted Keegan's honesty that he would be buying bigger and better players to take the club on to greater heights. What a job he did for Newcastle. He used to bust a gut in every game. Keegan appreciated players like that, giving 100 percent for the cause. Ned was great with me. I appreciated everything he did.

Keegan seemed to have a knack for getting the most out of his players, and when he couldn't extract any more out of them, they would be shipped out. He was also preparing for life in the top flight and knew he had to keep refreshing the squad and adding better players. Kevin Sheedy did a great job helping to keep us up in 1992 and was instrumental in the great start we had in our promotion year. A younger model arrived in the shape of Scott Sellars and Sheedy left as well. Another surprise was the transfer of Gavin Peacock to Chelsea for £1.5 million. Keegan did this with Andy Cole as well. I reckon he was born with that instinct of knowing when it was right to get rid of a player but when a new player arrived at the club everyone got excited, even more so when it was an unknown like Coley.

Keegan paid £1.75m for him from Bristol City, a lot of

money for an untested talent. Yet Kevin never seemed to buy a bad player, so we knew he must have secured something special. You could see in training, immediately, that we had captured an exciting new talent. He was fast, had great movement and, of course, an eye for goal. Andy Cole was a fantastic player for us.

I got my head down during pre-season training and worked hard. I played in a couple of the friendlies before the new term but it was still unclear who would start the season. Tommy finished the last campaign in goal so I expected it would be him who would start the new season as the club's No.1. I remember talking to Kevin about a new contract after we got promoted to the Premier League. He said, 'We cannot give you more than what you asked for.' I can't remember what the number was at the time. I was disappointed with the offer, so asked why. He said, 'You and Tommy Wright are on a level pegging and I want the goalkeepers on the same salary.'

Tommy was the manager's preferred choice at the beginning of the season as we won the first 11 games. I felt like a passenger or an outsider. The team were playing fantastic football but I wasn't involved, so I felt a little left out. I didn't get a look in until a 0-0 home draw with Swindon in November. Tommy got injured in the 3-2 win at Birmingham in the previous fixture. It was the game where Kevin Brock went in goal because Kevin didn't put a goalkeeper on the bench. It was a time when you could have two substitutes. It was also the game where former chairman Stan Seymour had a heart attack and later died. There was no point banging on the gaffer's door demanding to play because, to be fair to Tommy, he did play well when we went on that fantastic run. He was unlucky to get injured. Despite that, I still hated being No.2.

The back pass rule came into effect in the 1992 season. It was brought in to discourage time-wasting and overly defensive play and to combat time-stalling techniques, which happened to stifle the 1990 World Cup in Italy.

Goalkeepers were no longer allowed to roll the ball and pick it up either. Once the ball was released to the floor you had to kick or pass it. You could only hold the ball for five seconds as well once it was under control. This may have speeded up the game but it made a goalkeeper's job more difficult. I came into my own when this rule was introduced because I was more comfortable with the ball at my feet than most goalkeepers. I remember a flattering comment made by Leicester manager Brian Little earlier that season. We had played City in the Anglo-Italian Cup and beat them 4-0 at St James' Park. The Foxes boss jokingly quipped he was thinking about putting a transfer bid in for me, as a striker! Little had been impressed with my footwork in the game.

Kevin made the unusual step of bringing in Jimmy Montgomery as the club's goalkeeping coach around that time. Unusual because Monty was a Sunderland legend and the Black Cats were our fierce rivals. It was typical of Kevin though. If you were deemed good enough to be involved with us it didn't matter where you came from. If I remember rightly, it caused more of a fuss on Wearside than it did on Tyneside.

Sunderland supporters were outraged their club couldn't find a role for their former hero yet their sworn enemies could. I enjoyed working with Jimmy. He was a Sunderland legend and rightly so. He used to talk about his playing days; in particular, the 1960s side he played for. We spoke about his famous save against Leeds in the 1973 FA Cup final and how good the banter was in his heyday. Monty used to drive me into training and supporters used to stand by the goal and watch us and listen to his patter. I used to love sharing the passion and knowledge we had with those supporters standing around watching us as well. It wasn't just about the 90 minutes on a Saturday because not everyone could get into the stadium. You have to give Keegan some credit for that. Jimmy wasn't with us very long because a role was eventually found for one of Sunderland's favourite sons. It must have been tough for those followers south of the Tyne to see one of their own help improve the team of their bitter enemies, while their fortunes floundered.

Monty was a great coach and I missed him when he left. I had a great season after that and claimed the first-team goalkeeper's jersey as my own. I kept 13 clean sheets in 32 games as we steamrollered most of the opposition who stood in our way and won the championship at a canter. We had fun, there was a great feeling we were doing something special and I thought I'd done more than enough to cement my place as the club's No.1 goalkeeper.

It was a great time for the team, the fans and the city of Newcastle. The camaraderie in the dressing room was incredible. It wasn't one person, although Ned seemed to be at the centre of a lot of banter. We all bounced off one another. One person would say something, another would add to it and then we would all fall about laughing. Not every club I played for had this togetherness. At the time, I didn't realise that this was as special as it was, until after I left the club. Credit must also go to Sir John Hall, as well, because he was the man with the money bringing in players. It was a great combination between Keegan and Hall. Hall trusted Keegan's intuition and instinct for players and he was rewarded for that.

Sir John used to come down into the changing room now and again, shake all the players' hands and wish us good luck. He would jokingly ask how the Czech currency was doing and added that I must be a happy man with the wages I was getting. There was never any pressure on the manager asking why this player or that player wasn't playing. It is different in Italy and the Czech Republic. The chairmen are buying the players and interfering with team selection. They want to know why their favourites aren't playing and why the team isn't playing a certain way. Sir John never did any of that. He trusted Kevin to get on with his job. You have to give him credit for that. Every year Sir John would have a party in his house for all the players and their families and it was great fun. I couldn't see the owners or chairmen of other clubs doing the same.

We played an open expansive game with flair and passion. Everybody was pulling in the same direction. We wanted the Division One title and no one was going to stand in our way until we got it. It was fantastic to be a part of that group. The confidence kept building up to almost unassailable levels. We felt invincible that season. With the crowd behind us, it was amazing. The passion and noise those 36,000 Geordies generated were astonishing. You could feel and almost touch the atmosphere when you ran onto the pitch in the stadium. The hairs on the back of my neck used to stand up. My heart would be pumping and it would get the adrenaline going. I used to thrive on it.

I remember reading somewhere that Killer said the favourite time of his career was at Newcastle, yet he lifted the FA Cup as captain of Coventry in 1987. Killer hardly played for us because Steve Howey was emerging as a fine young centre-half but Killer thrived on the banter. He loved coming into training every morning, he loved the lads and having a drink with them. He was always supportive of everyone who played. He had a fantastic attitude. There was a television interview a few days after we clinched promotion to the Premier League, with Keegan, Ned and a couple of others. Killer asked Kevin in front of the cameras if he could have a more comfortable cushion to sit on in the dugout for the forthcoming season. That was the measure of the man, always laughing and joking.

I remember when Sparta Prague played away at Chelsea when I was goalkeeping coach and the Blues' supporters were all quiet. The Sparta players were asking, 'How is this possible when Chelsea are the best team in England?' I would tell them that this isn't how it was when I played at Newcastle United. At Maiden Castle, between

3,000 and 4,000 fans were watching us every day. They would come with their sandwiches, tea and coffee and I would stay behind half an hour after training and shake most of their hands. It was the happiest time of my life.

I would teach the kids a little bit after training, if they wanted, or sign autographs. It was an absolute pleasure for me. When I tell people about this time at Newcastle they don't believe it. We had more supporters at training than going to games in the Czech Republic. Then we had a party against Leicester on the last day of the season. Ned Kelly and Andy Cole both bagged a hat-trick in our 7-1 triumph, with Robert Lee adding the other. That aside, I knew I had won the fans around after that game in particular. In the past, they may have shouted 'dodgy keeper' but not anymore. Instead, if I made a mistake, supporters got behind me rather than having a go. They were shouting, 'Pav, keep your head up,' and 'Come on, Pav, don't worry about it,' which was nice. I never heard it inside a stadium after our Division One championship win.

The Pavel is a Geordie T-shirt is a well-known story now. Lee Clark's brother, Michael, gave it to Clarky to pass on to me. Clarky said, 'Wear this and you'll be a Geordie legend.' Looking back, it is still a special moment for me, why? It was a symbol of acceptance from the Newcastle supporters. It seemed the fans chanted my name even louder when they saw me wearing it on the pitch for the customary lap of honour after the trophy was presented. I remember after the game, in the dressing room, we celebrated and had some champagne. Ned Kelly said to me, 'Come on, Pav, walk with me and go back on the pitch and let's enjoy this.' So, we went back on the pitch and it was a fantastic feeling but all of that season was special. When you take into consideration, that we were nearly relegated the season before it was a phenomenal achievement. It was a complete turnaround in fortunes. We more or less started with the same squad as the previous term. Venners, Brace and Bez were the only new signings before

Rob Lee came in October. Andy Cole, Scott Sellars and Mark Robinson were added later on to seal the title.

Barry Venison wasn't the greatest footballer but he had the heart of a lion, a great motivator and a first-class attitude. One of the best professionals I have ever played with. He will die for you on the football pitch. He'd do anything to win a game of football. I loved that about Venners. He was hard but fair and dished out bollockings when they were deserved but also gave praise when it was needed. He never got personal with you. It was for the greater good of the team.

John Beresford was a chirpy kind of chap. He was always laughing and joking and had a smile on his face. He was another good guy in the dressing room. We had a great team full of characters but there were no prima donnas or superstars. When we went out, for a meal or a drink, we all went out as a team. What a difference to when I first joined the club when there were little cliques all over the dressing room. We were all in this together, fighting for the same cause.

A couple of hours after the game, celebrations and lap of honour, my wife and I got in the car and tried to head off for home. I was heading down Percy Street and we stopped at the traffic lights opposite the Three Bulls pub, I think it was called. There were hundreds of supporters out on the streets, having a drink and celebrating. Then one supporter spotted me and shouted, 'It's Pav!' About 40 supporters ran to the car and started singing, 'Pavel is a Geordie,' while the traffic lights turned from red to green. We couldn't go because the car was surrounded by fans rocking and shaking the vehicle. They tried to lift it from the road and put it on the side. I opened the roof and tried to get the lads to stop and calm down. It was obvious, several drinks had been taken. They were dancing and singing and were in high spirits. Some of them poured drink into the car shouting, 'Pav, have a drink, man!' Pavla, my wife, and Vendy, my daughter, were in the car and were shocked, although they knew they weren't in any danger. The traffic lights changed about five or six times. There were cars backed up behind wondering what was going on before we eventually got away. No one stuck behind us complained. When they saw what was happening, they just laughed. It was great fun. Everyone was in a party mood.

I remember we had a big party at the Civic Centre a few days after we won the league. The streets surrounding the building were chock-a-block with supporters. Thousands of them had turned out to see the bus parade and it was pissing down. They had stopped buses and other traffic getting in and around the Haymarket. Never before had I seen anything like it. The supporters were singing in the rain, chanting all our names and I thought to myself, I've finally found my second home. I had a sense of belonging. I loved the city, the football club and, more importantly, the supporters, and they had taken me to their hearts. I remember thinking to myself, life is great, despite the hassle of getting home for a holiday. I had just won the league and established myself as the club's No.1 goalkeeper. I felt euphoric, on top of the world and excited at the prospect of playing in the Premier League, which had just been formed the previous season. We were a young team with several Geordies in the squad, which the fans always appreciated. St James' Park was being redeveloped and taking shape quite nicely off the field and we were ready for a new adventure. We were quietly confident we would do well in the top flight but never expected to finish quite as high as we did in our first season back in the big time.

In hindsight, the second season was harder because we weren't an unknown quantity anymore. We probably got away with a lot in our first season through our naivety. Yet despite all of the supporters' adulation, performing well and earning the right to be the club's No.1. There was talk of us signing Mike Hooper when we were back in pre-season training. Sure enough, Kevin signed him a month into the new campaign. Mike was not just brought in for competition for me but as the club's No.1 goalkeeper. This was the story of my life at Newcastle. It didn't matter how many times I got in the team and played well. I thought I was winning the fight but losing the war against Kevin because it seemed he didn't like to be proved wrong. When Mike arrived, I thought, Jesus, he must be some goalkeeper to be better than me. I'll have to try and up my game and be at my best.

No disrespect to Mike, because he was a good keeper, but I didn't think he was better than me. When I saw him in training, I thought he was overweight, he couldn't dive on the left side, but he was a strong kicker of the ball. Maybe Kevin thought Mike would be better at handling crosses than me, which wasn't one of my strong points when I first arrived in England. I liked Mike as a person. He was a good guy, polite and very helpful. He didn't cover himself in glory and soon after he arrived the fans were hostile towards him. He even spoke with me about it, put his hands up and admitted he wasn't playing well. He confessed he was relieved when he was eventually dropped because he let me know he was struggling like he'd never struggled before.

Mike was an unusual guy. He kept a menagerie of animals. He had bull mastiff dogs, snakes, tarantulas and other exotic spiders. He also had a Great Dane. I nearly shit myself when I first went to his house and I saw this dog with a massive head standing with his paws on the six-foot garden fence, looking at me. He let the dog in and it jumped up at me, paws on my shoulders. I'm saying, 'Mike, what's happening?' He says, 'Don't worry, Pav, he's a nice dog.' Well, I'm 6ft 2in, but the dog was taller than me when it stood on its two hind legs. The other dogs, I'm not sure if they were Bull Mastiffs, Bull Dogs or other fighting dogs. Mike said, 'Don't even look at the little one, he's a nasty little bastard.'

Mike was an incredibly intelligent man. I believe he had an English degree. He was always playing Scrabble with Keegan on the bus to and from away games. Mike never made a fuss or complained when he got dropped and couldn't get back in the side. When Keegan left him out of the team, Mike came to seek me out. He shook my hand and wished me good luck He was disappointed, you could see that but he was honourable with it.

I remember we played at Liverpool and won 2-0. I played well that day. A few days later he picked me up for training and he was very complimentary about my performance. He said, 'Pav, you were fantastic. You had a great game against my old club.' These words came from a man whose place I'd taken in the side not long before. He didn't have to say it but it says a lot about the man. He had integrity and grace. I liked Mike a lot. He was a nice man and had something special about him. I'm sorry his football career did not turn out the way he wanted.

I started the new season in goal but we lost 1-0 at home in the campaign's curtain raiser against my old boss, Ossie Ardlies, and his Tottenham side. The game was a bit of an anti-climax. We just didn't perform and Teddy Sheringham netted the only goal of the game. We then travelled to Coventry. I got sent off for bringing down Roy Wegerle and my old teammate, Micky Quinn, blazed the ball over the bar from the spot. We had taken a 1-0 lead after Liam O'Brien's free-kick was deflected in but goals from Peter Ndlovu and a header from Mick Harford gave them the three points. It is fair to say we had a stuttering start to life in the Premier League. A hard-earned point at Old Trafford against last season's champions was the start of our turnaround. Ryan Giggs put one past me with a 20 yards free-kick, which I got a hand too, before Coley levelled it for us.

We hadn't yet been christened The Entertainers but we were fast beginning to earn it. We seemed to be everybody's second favourite team and everyone loved the way we played our football, which was very exciting for us as a team and squad as well. I'm guessing the British public hadn't seen anything as refreshing as our style of football for a long time. We just kept the momentum going from the previous promotion season and carried it on during our first campaign in the Premier League. Kevin kept adding quality players to the squad as we went along and that helped, no one more so than Peter Beardsley.

I remember everyone questioning whether we should be paying £1.5 million for a player in his early thirties. Some of the tricks he would pull off, the little bits of magic and genius were a joy to watch. There was a buzz about the place when we knew he was returning home. It was a crushing blow to lose Peter on the eve of the season. He fractured his cheekbone in a friendly at Liverpool after a challenge from Neil Ruddock, who scored the winning goal in a 1-0 win. There was a lot of bad feeling because Beardsley felt the Reds centre half did it on purpose.

When Pedro returned to the side, he struck up an immediate rapport with Andy Cole. It was a fantastic strike partnership, almost telepathic. Pedro would drop off short, Coley would set off and he would find him with a slide rule pass, nine times out of ten. It was one of the best combinations, if not the best, I'd ever had the privilege to play with. Andy netted 41 times and broke the goal scoring record of Newcastle folk hero and legend Hughie Gallagher. Pedro, meanwhile, helped himself to 24 goals. None of Pedro's goals were tap-ins, either. They were from 20 yards, 30 yards, mazy dribbles, left foot and right foot. They were all different. It was exciting to watch. He always gave 100 percent, even in training. Pedro was a fantastic man, an incredible person and a dedicated professional. One of the best I've had the fortune to play with.

Budgie returned to us as well. It was great to see him back at the club. He acted as cover but mainly as a coach. He used to set up the sessions for the goalkeepers. I always got the feeling he was putting them on for himself, rather than for me, Mike or Tommy, who left for Nottingham Forest that term.

Andy Cole was having different problems settling in. I'm not sure how it worked out but the club found him somewhere to live in Crook. It was strange because it was a bit out of the way and none of the other players lived there. Andy was a proud man with a strong personality and felt intensely about his position. Kevin and Andy had had a few choice words in training which resulted in our record signing going AWOL. Andy wasn't the best trainer when he arrived at Newcastle. I think his performances on the pitch were the main thing and he always played well in general. Kevin was probably frustrated with Andy because he didn't give it his all in training as well. Mind you, Pedro always said the Newcastle training sessions were tougher than anything he'd ever encountered at Everton or Liverpool and he'd won trophies with them.

I never thought the situation with Coley or Clarky, when he was upset at being substituted at Southampton that time, would fester and cause problems in the future. It was all sorted out very quickly and we moved on. In general, we always had a happy dressing room. There weren't any bad eggs in my time there. In fact, other than seeing Budgie and Chris Guthrie, our kit man, going hammer and tongs at each other, I never saw a physical fight between any of our players. I'm not even sure what that was about, although Budgie could be a bit feisty at times.

I didn't want to cause any problems for the gaffer but I believed in my ability. No disrespect to any goalkeeper who arrived on Tyneside during my time at the club but I didn't think any of them were any better than I was. Looking back, maybe that's why Newcastle fans like me and call me a legend because I stood up for myself and proved doubters wrong. I am not saying I was the greatest goalkeeper Newcastle ever had, far from it, but I must have done something right. There are more famous and better players than me who have worn the famous black and white jersey, yet they haven't had the respect afforded to me on Tyneside. I think the United fans knew I was honest and hardworking and did my best for the club. It gives me a great deal of pleasure and satisfaction that they appreciate what I did. I have a great affection and bond with the people of Newcastle. I just wish I could've played 400 or 500 games for the club, won the supporters a trophy and maybe earned a bit more money, because all of these things go together.

After a slow start to our inaugural Premier League campaign, we picked up and were flying. It just took a while for us to find our feet, settle and get used to playing in the top flight. We never had many experienced Premier League players. We had Pedro, but he was a striker. We never had any seasoned defenders, other than Barry Venison, who would say 'slow it down' or 'tuck in and take it easy'. Kevin Scott and Steve Howey were good defenders but they were still kids. They didn't have the old-school know-how of a Steve Bruce and Gary Pallister. Darren Peacock had played a lot of top-flight football but he didn't arrive at the club until the following February, while Ruel Fox came to the club a month earlier.

A lot of the time the full backs were bombing on and we were being exposed at the back because of it. Then I would get criticised off Kevin because of the risks I was taking but I was playing as a sweeper as well. It was a Catch-22 situation: damned if I do take risks, damned if I don't take risks. I played the last 15 games of the season. I kept seven clean sheets and conceded 12 times as we finished the season on a high by claiming third position and a place in the UEFA Cup. I played 22 matches altogether keeping clean sheets in eight fixtures. I won the No.1 jersey again. Another season closes and I see off another goalkeeper. John Burridge, Tommy Wright and Mike Hooper, all challenged me for the No.1 jersey. As the season drew to a close, I remember thinking, 'I wonder if Kevin will sign another goalkeeper next season?'

Andy Cole's transfer was a massive shock not only to Newcastle supporters but to us players as well. It rocked the club to its very foundations. There was no hint or clue that he was looking to move. I know he had a fall-out with the gaffer before a League Cup tie at Wimbledon the previous season but we thought that was all water under the bridge. We had the best striker in the Premier League at the time. He had scored 41 goals for us in the last campaign and I'm thinking, who else is going to score the goals now he has left? I was at home when I found out. Andy was missing from training that day but that was nothing unusual. He often missed a training session. The squad worked out as normal that day, had lunch at the training ground and then we all went our separate ways, like we always did. I turned on the news later that night and I saw Kevin confront angry supporters on the steps of St James' Park explaining why he had sold Andy. The club received something like £7 million and got Keith Gillespie in exchange as well. That was a lot of money back then. It was the most expensive British transfer fee at the time.

I didn't know whether Coley was unhappy at Newcastle, Kevin was unhappy with Andy or whether there were some other politics involved. You could tell he wasn't right. His body language seemed all wrong and Andy hadn't scored a goal in nearly two months before the deal went through, his worst spell at St James' Park. When you think about all the flair players we had at the club, it was unusual. It wasn't the Andy Cole we all knew, that's for sure.

If you look at Andy's record at the beginning of the 1994-95 season he was banging in goals for fun; then they dried up. It was always said, or written, that we couldn't defend, yet a month before he departed games were very tight. There were three 0-0 score lines in four games before him leaving, while we lost the other 2-1 at Norwich. Notably, Ruel Fox netted from the spot against his old club that day. The same when we lost the title, everyone said we couldn't defend yet we didn't concede many more than Man U. The difference was they scored more goals than us. I can't remember anything in particular that was said at training the following morning. At the end of the day, most professional footballers are selfish and are only concerned about themselves. They are only interested in whether or not they are playing at the weekend.

We were all shocked but the gaffer had done this before with David Kelly, so we thought he must have someone else lined up to replace him. That was arguably the biggest surprise, in that Kevin didn't have a replacement. The gaffer tried to buy Les Ferdinand but QPR wouldn't sell until the end of the season. There were loads of speculation on who was coming to the club. Roberto Baggio, George Weah and Martin Dahlin were just three. Apparently, Baggio was seen at a chippy in Westerhope, Hristo Stoichkov was caught eating a Greggs pasty on Gosforth High Street, while Romario was supposedly drinking Newcastle Brown Ale in Rosie's Bar. It was that type of season.

Paul Kitson was signed earlier that term but I think supporters were disappointed because he didn't score as many goals as Andy. Paul was a different type of player anyway and hadn't been brought in to replace Andy. You always wonder how players would cope with coming to a bigger club. Newcastle was growing at a staggering rate and Paul had arrived from a smaller club.

Keith Gillespie was a good addition to the side. He was quick and had a bit of flair. He had a few problems after he ran up a gambling debt so high that Keegan had to step in and sort it out. The bookies threatened to go to the papers with the story. The gaffer intervened and told them if they went to the papers they wouldn't get a penny back. It did get out but, from what I believe, the club controlled the story so it wasn't as damaging. Keith was always telling me funny stories about his drinking adventures and exploits with women. I'm thinking, 'Fucking hell Keith, you need to calm down otherwise you'll find yourself in trouble.' He was like, 'Pav, I love the drink and the women.' But he was a young lad, only 19-years-old when he signed for us. Sometimes he would turn up in the clothes he had worn from the night before, the scruffy bugger.

He trained hard though and always gave 100 percent. He was a lovely lad, and wouldn't hurt you in any shape or form. Ironically, we played Manchester United the weekend after we sold Andy. There was a gentleman's agreement between the two clubs that neither Coley nor Keith would play in that game. The atmosphere was maybe more charged than normal considering the circumstances. Then again, the games we had against Man U were always passionate and feisty affairs. Mark Hughes and I collided as he scored early on and was stretchered off with a knee injury as a consequence. Straight after the game I went to Sir Alex Ferguson and apologised and asked if he would send my best wishes to Mark who had gone straight to the RVI hospital. The following day in training I mentioned to Barry Venison and a couple of the lads that I might go to visit Mark in hospital. Venners told me to leave it and said there was no need. They pointed out, I had already apologised to their manager and it was an accident after all. I wasn't convinced and still wanted to see if he was OK, until Venners said, 'How many times has he fucking knocked you out and never apologised? So, there's no need to feel guilty.' Venners was right, of course. Despite that, I still felt responsible. Mark was one of the toughest opponents I ever faced in my career.

After finishing third the previous term, expectations were higher than before. We were expected to do even better in the new campaign. We had a stronger squad; we had a Premier League season under our belts and we were quietly confident we could maybe win the league, or at the very least a cup competition. Yet, although we had a good side, that played open attractive football, I was always conscious we didn't have the experience of Manchester United. Even our boss, Kevin Keegan, didn't have the familiarity of Sir Alex Ferguson. He was still a relatively unproven manager despite how well he had sculpted Newcastle into a top Premier League side.

Kevin knew if we were going to progress every year and get closer to Manchester United you had to buy better players and make competition tougher for us each season. Phillipe Albert and Marc Hottiger were the two major signings brought in before the kick-off at Leicester City. They both played for their respective national teams but that was pretty much all I knew about them. However, if a player arrived at the club with an international pedigree, you knew he must be a first-class footballer. Nevertheless, you're always curious to see how the new arrivals respond to the surroundings and wonder whether they will be able to cope with the incredible passion generated by our supporters. It's no place for the faint-hearted and, with the foreign players, it seemed there was an unwritten law that they had to be better than their English counterparts. I knew how difficult it was to settle and adjust as a foreign player so I used to try and help out when new lads turned up at St James' Park.

Philippe Albert may have been an unusual centre-half to most football fans in England but his type was quite common in Europe. You generally have one centre-back who can play football, like Philippe, and another like Darren Peacock who could bash it away. Philippe was great at taking people on, had good vision, great shot and could score goals when he wasn't defending. He was a very good footballer.

We started the season well, unbeaten in 11, nine of them victories, and we were top of the league before tasting our first defeat, a 2-0 loss at Manchester United in late October. Gary Pallister and Keith Gillespie netted. Andy Cole missed the game at Old Trafford through injury. Ironically, we had just beaten the Red Devils 2-0, at home in the League Cup, three days earlier, thanks to late goals from Phillipe Albert and Paul Kitson. However, the two teams were radically different. Sir Alex played about eight of his kids in the cup game. The likes of Paul Scholes, David Beckham, Nicky Butt and the Neville brothers got a run out if I remember correctly.

The League Cup was a great night all the same. It was like we had issued a statement of intent. We were more than pretenders to the Manchester United throne. Yet looking back, that's all we were. After the defeat at Old Trafford, we had a difficult spell we never really recovered. Every team has a sticky patch, whether it is Man United, Chelsea or Liverpool. It is how you recover from a period of playing poorly and get out of it. With Man United it was maybe two or three games, with us it was longer. We only won one game in eight after the defeat in Manchester.

We crashed out of the UEFA Cup to Athletic Bilbao on away goals, won 3-2 at home, lost 1-0 away. We hoped to get the away goal that would take us through to the next stage of the competition but it wasn't to be. The two late goals we conceded in the home leg proved costly to us. We were coasting quite comfortably at 3-0 then the fans were doing a Mexican wave around the stadium and as Kevin said at the time, we got complacent and didn't finish the job. Then there were injuries to several of our key players, notably Barry Venison and Andy Cole, and we lost Phillipe Albert and Scott Sellars for more than half of the season. All of a sudden, our confidence was low and maybe our squad was not as strong as we first thought.

Most of our supporters remember our return to the UEFA Cup with a great deal of fondness. It was the club's first sortie in European competition since 1977 and we got off to a great start in the first round at Royal Antwerp. I know people will look at the 5-0 score and think it was a stroll in the park, but it was anything but that. We scored early on but I had to be at my best and made four or five saves to keep a clean sheet. It could've easily been 5-5. This was the game where Rob Lee scored a hat-trick and at the end, Keegan was on his knees in front of the cameras bowing to our goalscoring midfielder. Rob Lee was a great player for Newcastle. Kevin singled him out for exceptional praise all of the time. We all used to take the piss out of Rob, saying Kevin was his dad.

I started the season as the club's No.1 goalkeeper but it was always in the back of my mind Kevin would bring in someone else after it didn't work out with Mike Hooper. The gaffer then tried to sign the USA international Brad Freidel. There were several times in the past when one of the lads would open a newspaper at training and read that we were linked with a keeper. Understandably, they would take the piss. That is part and parcel of being in a dressing room. It would be something like, 'Hey, Pav, I see someone else is after your shirt,' or, 'I see you have another friend coming to keep you company.' That happened with all the players. Alan Shearer was always winding up the lads with stuff like this, although he wasn't there at this time.

I remember when we had The Entertainers' exhibition game against Liverpool at Kingston Park when we had all retired. One of the Liverpool players chipped me to score. After the match, Shearer came into the dressing room and said, 'Some things never fucking change, eh, Pav?' That was Alan, he always had a wisecrack for the occasion. I just laughed. Brad came to train with us midway through this season. He was a good goalkeeper and was with us for a couple of months but he couldn't get a work permit at the time because he didn't meet the criteria needed.
At the time you had to have played in 75 percent of the games for your national team. The team all went out for a drink down the Quayside one evening when Brad was training with us. Later on, the pair of us headed back up home, he said that I was the best goalkeeper he had trained with at the time. I returned the compliment because, to be fair, Brad was good. Had Brad managed to get a work permit, however, I knew he would've replaced

me as the club's No.1. I told him that. He acknowledged what I had said and recognised that I would be a tough challenger for the No.1 shirt.

I suppose when you think of Mike Hooper, he was in a worse position than I was because I had replaced him in the pecking order. If another keeper came in, he would be the club's third choice. Mike said to me in the dressing room one day, 'Pav, looks like I'm finished here now.' Every game I felt under enormous pressure because I thought if I made a mistake, then I would be out of the team. I got a lot of help from the players. They were always very supportive towards me in times like this but they didn't pick the team.

While our form in the league was faltering, we still fancied ourselves to win the FA Cup. We could beat anyone on our day. We were handed a tough home draw in the third round against Alan Shearer's Blackburn. It didn't look good when they managed to get a draw and take us back to Ewood Park. Even worse, Pedro was injured before the replay. Yet we managed to beat them 2-1 thanks to a late Lee Clark goal after Chris Sutton cancelled out Marc Hottiger's opener. It was a great result considering Rovers won the league that year. Paul Kitson bagged a hat-trick as we saw off Swansea at St James' Park in the fourth round before, we despatched Manchester City, 3-1, in yet another home tie. Keith Gillespie grabbed a brace and Bez netted the other.

We travelled to Everton in the sixth round as favourites but ended up losing to a scruffy Dave Watson goal. Everton was a tough, physical side, while we liked to get it down and play. It was a horrible game to play in. We just didn't get the rub of the green in that match in the same way we didn't get it against Bilbao in the UEFA Cup. We were disappointed to go out of the FA Cup but we still had things to play for. We were third in the league. The title was out of our reach because Blackburn and Man U were too far ahead, although we could still qualify for the

UEFA Cup.

A spectacular Peter Beardsley goal against Arsenal in injury time gave us three valuable points, after the Everton defeat but we couldn't quite build on it. We subsequently won only two and drew three out of our last nine games. Why did we collapse? The injuries to key players didn't help. But maybe there was a lack of belief and confidence in the camp. Whatever it was we couldn't put another consistent run together like we did at the beginning of the new season. It could have been the second season syndrome, where teams were a little bit wiser to us, while we struggled to adjust to teams finding us out. We finished sixth that season, which wasn't too bad when you think about it, but we didn't qualify for Europe. That was disappointing.

European competition was special for everyone. We had a taste of it and wanted more but it wasn't to be that year. But after the way we started the season, it felt like a failure. We were top of the league until mid-November and then gradually lost ground. I think there were a couple of games towards the end of the season which kind of typified our campaign. The home fixture against Spurs was one of those games. We took a 2-0 lead within ten minutes but then the game turned on its head and we were 3-2 down after less than half an hour. I got sent off for bringing down either Nick Barmby or Jurgen Klinsmann, I can't quite remember who it was because it happened so fast. Mike Hooper came on and saved the penalty and then Pedro equalised later on. Getting sent off cost me my place in the team for the start of the 1995-96 season because I was suspended.

I have to say Venners was fantastic that season. Kevin had switched Barry to the centre of midfield anchor role, with the arrival of Marc Hottiger at right back, and won two England caps in that position. He didn't look out of place in the Three Lions' lineup and played well in both games. It wasn't a great season for the team but I was reasonably happy because I had played every game except those fixtures when I was suspended. Barry Venison and I probably had our best campaigns for Newcastle in the 1994-95 season. I had established myself as the club's No.1. Yet I knew I was going to be suspended for the start of the new season and once again, wondered who Kevin was going to bring in to replace me.

I remember Bob Wilson offering his opinion in a newspaper article before the 1995-96 season. In it, he wrote off Newcastle's chances of winning the Premier League because, in his opinion, you couldn't win a title without a decent goalkeeper. In essence, he was saying I wasn't good enough. You often wonder why people, such as Wilson, are asked to give an opinion about a club or player when they have no connection with it. What was his motive? Had someone asked Ronnie Simpson, Willie McFaul or Mick Mahoney, then fair enough. They had a relationship, link or association with Newcastle. Wilson did not. He played all of his football in London with Arsenal. I felt something wasn't quite right and maybe there was a bit of a conspiracy going on. Sure enough, I later find out Wilson is Shaka Hislop's coach at Reading. It seemed he was pushing up the profile of his protégé. The last thing I want is to be disrespectful or criticise Shaka because he became a friend of mine and was a good keeper. I remember the pictures of Shaka and Kevin together and how the press made out he was one in a million, in that he was earning £1 million a year. Discovering that deflated me, being the club's poor pauper on £150,000 a year.

Another new season was upon us and there was fresh optimism, which, to be honest, was always the case every time we returned for preseason. We were installed as the Premier League favourites despite our meltdown in the second half of the last campaign. The gaffer went out shopping in the summer and spent £6 million on Les Ferdinand, £4 million on Warren Barton, £2.5 million on David Ginola and, of course, £1.5 million on Shaka. I was no different to the rest of our supporters. I was excited at the prospect of seeing them all in action. I played against Les when he was at QPR and he always seemed to do well against us. It was no surprise when we signed him. The newspapers were full of his imminent arrival on Tyneside. We knew what a good player he was. Football ability aside, Les was a fantastic man. I would love to have stolen some fashion tips from him but I couldn't afford the clothes he bought. He always looked smart, dressed well and was popular with the ladies and he wasn't called Big Les for nothing.

I remember one day, he was towelling himself down after he had come out of the shower and his crown jewels were on show. The gaffer said, 'Les, I don't want any of your money, your houses or your riches. I want to borrow that, just for an hour. I'll visit my wife and then you can have it back.' The comment had all of the lads in hysterics.

Unlike Les, we didn't know much about David Ginola when he first arrived on Tyneside. I remember a few players being put out when the sponsored cars were being handed out at the beginning of the season. We all got a Rover while Ginola got a big Range Rover. I remember Rob Lee taking the piss out of him, saying, 'Ah, you must be something special, eh? And we're shit because you get the big car and we don't.'

David was a great guy with an overwhelming amount of charisma. You don't get all of this special treatment if you don't have an exceptional talent. After I saw him in action, I realised that maybe he was worth all of the fuss. David was extremely intelligent and very knowledgeable about music and fashion. I used to love listening to him talk about music, whether it was jazz, rock or pop. He was passionate about the subject. He was a fascinating man as well as a fantastic footballer. He had flair on the pitch and was just as flamboyant off it. He lived in St Tropez, where his house was built into a rock. He lived in a different world to the majority of us, a very luxurious lifestyle.

He was also a very good rally driver.

David became a target for Newcastle supporters when he left after he made one or two disagreeable comments about the club but I know he loved his short time on Tyneside. Ginola told me that he expected to end his football career at St James' Park. Newcastle fans have Kenny Dalglish to thank for that. In the first six months of his time with us, I never saw anything better. He was amazing. Then, for some reason or other, people got on his back because he never tracked back and defended. This followed Ginola throughout his career. People thought he was lazy but that was his style of football. In most of his time with us, he never chased back either. It was only when we had a dip in form and started losing games it became an issue.

I was suspended for the first three matches of the season thanks to a sending-off in the home fixture with Tottenham. I didn't get back in the team until December when we played Chelsea away in the league. I came on for Shaka who got a thigh injury during the game. My season was turned around when we played Everton at home in the following fixture. I wouldn't care, I'd played for the reserves at Everton the week before and had a nightmare, conceding five goals in the process. Yet I arguably had the game of my life in the contest at St James' Park. We won 1-0 thanks to a Les Ferdinand strike.

We were up against it for most of the game because Bez was sent off after only half an hour for a professional foul on Andrei Kanchelskis. I had most of my friends and family over the game as well which made the match extra special. The pièce de résistance came when I changed direction in mid-flight to tip over an Anders Limpar deflected shot off Steve Howey. I was very proud to hear England goalkeeping legend Gordon Banks say it was in his top ten saves of all time. He was one of the greatest goalkeepers that ever lived, so when a man of his reputation says something like that, it must mean something.

I got a standing ovation at the end of the game. It was an emotional moment for me and my family, who were crying because of this outpour of love and affection from the supporters. This happened a few times at Newcastle and I couldn't even start to explain how this made me feel and what it meant to me. Their appreciation more than evened out all of the bad times I had suffered at the club. I didn't have much to cheer about up until that point of the season. The team were doing well but when you're not involved you feel left out. I kept myself going by getting my head down in training and working hard, which I enjoyed.

We were still fighting on three fronts for the league, League Cup and FA Cup as we entered the second week of January but within a fortnight we only had the Premier League title to focus our attention on. After a hard-fought draw at Stamford Bridge in the FA Cup third round, we travelled to Highbury to play Arsenal in the fifth round of the League Cup. We had just beaten the Gunners in the league a week before the contest and were confident of turning them over on their home patch.

Ian Wright gave the hosts a lead a minute before the break. Kevin criticised me on television for conceding the first goal after the match had finished but the ball swerved in front of me. We had a few words about it in the dressing room at half-time. If you watch the highlights, you'll hear Martin Tyler and Ron Atkinson commentating on how the ball had viciously swerved three times as it went past me. I remember Ian Wright was interviewed after the game on TV and pointed out that I had no chance because the ball had swerved. I was thankful to Wrighty but Keegan still blamed me all the same.

The referee didn't have a good game that night. Some of the tackles were X-rated and Ginola was getting kicked from pillar to post by Lee Dixon and then Nigel Winterburn. The Frenchman eventually snapped, elbowing Dixon in the face. He got a red card. The game was highly charged and spilled over into the dugouts where Arsenal boss Bruce Rioch and Terry Mac squared up with each other. It was a disappointment to lose the game because it was a trophy we felt we could win. We then crashed out of the FA Cup in the third round. We managed to draw 1-1 at Chelsea but lost the replay on penalties after it finished level, 2-2, after extra time. I think we were unlucky in both games because we were the better side but didn't get much luck. We could now concentrate on the league. Or rather that was what we felt.

There was a lot of tension and pressure on us before the visit of Man United. I think we were six points clear of them before they arrived on Tyneside. That aside, we had a great team and were still confident of beating them. Anyone who saw the game will tell you, we battered them but couldn't score. We had several chances and Peter Schmeichel made four or five outstanding saves and they scored a goal from a counterattack. The ball came from right to left and found Eric Cantona at the back post. He hit it into the ground and across me to score. It was a proper smash-and-grab result because we murdered them on the night. People say the Liverpool result was the catalyst for our destruction that season. But had we beat Man U on that occasion we would have put nine points between us. Even a draw would've been a good result. Our lead was cut to three points after that game.

I was down after the 4-3 defeat at Liverpool and found it hard to get motivated in training. I wasn't the only one. The mood in training was low and almost sombre during this mid-slump. The upbeat bouncy nature of training had changed. I didn't look forward to training around this time. It had lost its sparkle. I think it was because we didn't know how to cope. We weren't an experienced side in the same way Man United were. Only Peter Beardsley, and later David Batty, had won a title. It was as if we were looking around for guidance but there was none there. We needed a leader or a strong personality at the back who would say, 'Right, we've gone 1-0 up, now everybody gets back behind the ball and defends it.' Pedro was our captain but he played up front.

We never changed our system throughout this period. It was 100 miles an hour all of the time. That was what we were used to and encouraged to play. Saying that, we only conceded two more than Man U that season but they scored about 15 more. We beat QPR 2-1 three days after the defeat on Merseyside before losing by the odd goal in three at Blackburn. We managed to string together three 1-0 victories against Aston Villa, Southampton and Leeds United. We were still fighting for the title but the shoe was very much on the other foot now and we were chasing Manchester United. We were all on the bus waiting to travel back to Newcastle when we heard about Keegan's 'I would love it' outburst after the game at Elland Road. One of the lads, I can't remember who, said, 'Keegan has just lost it on the TV,' but no one saw until later that night when we got home or the following day. There was a TV on the bus but it wasn't on. How did the players feel about his explosion? We all thought he was right to hold Ferguson to account for comments he made about the commitment of Leeds, and later Nottingham Forest, players. We had already agreed to play in a testimonial for Forest legend Stuart Pearce, the previous term. We had to visit the County Ground to play Forest in the penultimate game of the season.

Kevin should've been more composed but emotions were running high. It was out of character and unlike him. Generally, the gaffer was calm personified but there's no getting away from the fact that Ferguson was out of order. Some were saying he was playing mind games but many others, including us, disagreed. The Man United boss was taking gamesmanship to another level. He was questioning the integrity and professionalism of Leeds United and Nottingham Forest players. He was out of order and way out of line. We drew our final two games of the season: 1-1 at Forest and 1-1 at home to Spurs. Even if we had won both of them, we would have lost the title on goal difference. The Red Devils had a better goal difference of nine goals.

To this day people are still speculating as to why or how we let slip a 12-point lead and lose the title. There wasn't one single reason why we lost the title. There are several explanations for why it slipped through our fingers. We had a slump in form which coincided with Man United having a turnaround in fortunes. Maybe we shouldn't have changed our goalkeepers as often as we did. Maybe our manager wasn't tactically as good as other bosses in the Premier League. We could ask the 36,000 supporters, who turned up to watch us, week in and week out, why we lost the title. I bet they would all say something different. Tino and David Batty were blamed. Whatever, the buck stops with the manager. If things go well, the manager gets the praise. If things go wrong, the manager gets the blame. The board could have said we've given you £60 million to spend, why haven't you delivered some silverware? Or maybe the board didn't sign the players Kevin wanted and we were still a couple of players short of winning the title. Maybe the chairman says look we've bought Ferdinand, Ginola, Barton, Hislop and then Asprilla and Batty, that should be enough. We don't know.

Maybe we had too many individual flair players whereas Man United had more of a team. So, it's all hypothetical because we didn't win the league. The media, pundits and writers had a lot to say about us that season. How we should be doing this and that, and we will never win the league if we didn't do this and that. At the beginning of the season, Kevin was told he couldn't win the league without a new goalkeeper. The next thing that happens, Shaka Hislop arrives. Then we are told we need a defensive midfielder and David Batty turns up at St James' Park. We're not scoring enough goals, and then Faustino Asprilla is signed. What happens next? We throw away the title. Batty was a hard man on the pitch. It was an unusual signing because Batty was a defensive midfield player yet Kevin still wanted us to play the same way. So, you could say he upset the rhythm of the side, through no fault of his own.

I remember going out onto the pitch on the last day of the season to salute those magnificent supporters after we drew with Spurs for the customary lap of honour. It was heartbreaking. We were all distraught. Darren Peacock was crying and there were tears in the eyes of several others. We didn't know what the future held I suppose. We were thinking was the team going to be broken up?

Every season I had been at the club, up to that point, was generally finished on a high. This was our best season ever, yet it felt the worst. Had we won the title it would have changed everyone's life for the better, forever. You get more respect around the world for being a champion. You would get better contracts and more money. We missed out on so much. They probably would have built statues of us all at St James' Park. I know this time, era, is cherished in the memory of every Newcastle United fan.

There was something special about the period; something intangible enveloping the city, yet at the same time, you could almost touch it. Music, culture and politics were changing and we were part of that zeitgeist. I am aware that we are still loved and cherished for the carefree, swashbuckling way we played our football. I know supporters were excited before a game and got an enormous amount of pleasure out of our time there. But we failed to deliver any silverware and it hurts deeply. There isn't a day that goes by without thinking about what could've been had we delivered that trophy to those loyal supporters.

Kevin Keegan quitting was a massive bombshell. The players heard the gaffer had tendered his resignation to Sir John Hall at the end of the previous season for failing to land the Premier League title. Sir John rejected the offer and persuaded Kevin to stop. We still didn't expect him to walk out but then maybe we should have seen it coming. Did Kevin think he couldn't motivate or take the team any further at this point? Maybe this was true, we were having a wretched run of form up to that moment in time and couldn't buy a win from anywhere. I remained the first choice up until that reversal at Blackburn.

The Blackburn episode turned out to be a watershed moment for the direction of the club because Kevin offered to resign after our lacklustre defeat to Rovers. Nevertheless, Keegan was still in charge for the visit of Tottenham two days later. We beat them 7-1. Within a week of this, Keegan had resigned. There was no clue or hint that Kevin was going to leave, quit or whether he got pushed. You could never really measure whether he was happy or unhappy because his demeanour or body language was always the same.

We went back for preseason in 1996 and it felt a little different. It felt like something had died. Maybe we were all emotionally and psychologically scarred from last term's exploits. You hope you can improve on the previous campaign. That was the aim every year, to get better and better but as soon as we had a couple of bad results the memories of last season came flooding back and doubt set in. It was still fresh in my memory.

There were loads of rumours and speculation about us signing Alan Shearer, just as we were about to go on tour to Thailand, Singapore and Japan but once we got on the plane to the Far East, we were largely cut off from any media frenzy. We were oblivious to the signing of our new £15 million striker. We didn't know anything about it until he turned up in Thailand for training. We were already out on the training pitch going through our warm-up and stretching exercises. We were lying on the ground and couldn't see anything. All of a sudden, we heard this crunch, crunch, crunch and thud, thud, thud noise on the grass. We looked up and couldn't see anything for what seemed like hundreds of photographers. Then all of a sudden there was a parting in a sea of snappers and out ran Alan. It was surreal. The media wasn't as fast back in those days so we were completely in the dark.

The gaffer said, 'Boys, this is Alan Shearer.' We were like, fucking hell! We couldn't believe it. We had signed one of the world's best strikers, top goalscorer from Euro 96 and the Premier League. It was totally unexpected. Everyone was excited by his signing. It not only captured the imagination of the supporters, public and media but us players as well. I had played against Alan a few times when he was at Blackburn. He was strong and tough and he caught me in the face with his studs once when I was diving. It was a 50/50 ball and it wasn't intentional. It didn't stop it from hurting. When he got his body in between the ball and the player, a rampaging rhinoceros couldn't take him out. I previously mentioned that our defensive record was as good as Man United's the previous season. The only difference was that we didn't score enough goals. With Alan signing, he had the extra 15 to 20 goals missing from the side that finished runners-up.

I know Les wasn't very happy about Alan taking the number nine shirt off him but there was never a problem between the two of them. They became great friends. Alan was the club's biggest capture, the most expensive signing in the world at the time, and would've got anything he asked for. There were a lot of dissenters saying Alan and Les were both target men and wouldn't be able to play together but they proved them wrong. They were both perfect foil for one another.

Alan was a big personality and a strong character. He was a funny guy too. There were times when he didn't say much but, when he did, his remarks would be cutting, funny and straight to the point. When he was interviewed on the television he spoke well, straight and, to paraphrase Oscar Wilde, he could talk without actually saying anything. There were never any off-the-pitch scandals with Alan, unlike many of the game's superstars. That's why he was called Mary Poppins by our chairman. I know many see that as an insult but it was a compliment when you think about it because he was without any skeletons in his cupboard. He was a great role model for kids and professionals alike. Shearer and Ginola clashed on the odd occasion. Why? Maybe David's work ethic wasn't as strong as Alan's. They were both superstars, they were both strong-willed, had strong personalities and were their own men. They were both different in their own way. I remember once in the changing room after a game where David got quite animated. He jumped up and waved his finger at Alan and screamed, 'Fuck you Shearer, who do you think you are? You fucking bastard!' I didn't hear what Alan had said but David was furious. Alan didn't react at all, he just laughed and said, 'Good one!' This wound up Ginola even more because Alan didn't bite and it didn't seem to bother him. We were all astounded when it happened because someone had sworn at Shearer. We all had great respect for him so no one spoke to him like that.

When we got back home, from our tour of the Far East, the gaffer asked if I would take part in a photo session for the newspapers and match day programme. I wasn't aware of what was planned or who was involved but I was happy to oblige. I turned up and it was Alan. The photographers wanted some pictures of our new striker shooting. Man, he hit the ball so hard that one shot brought blood to the surface on my arm! He's shouting, 'Howay man, Pav, my daughter could stop these.' I'm telling you, it hurt like hell. And he's shouting, 'Come on, Pav, can you stop this, and this, and this!' When we finished, the gaffer, who was watching the proceedings like a proud father from the sidelines, said, 'Well done lads, go and get a shower.' I went into the dressing room and I couldn't take my shirt off at first. When I did eventually peel it off, I looked in the mirror and I was red, black and blue all over. I even had the sponsor imprint off the ball tattooed on me! I thought I'm not going in the showers looking like this, Alan will take the piss! So, I did a few stretches for 15 minutes and waited until he finished before I had a shower.

Alan was extremely influential in the dressing room. He was very vociferous and encouraging towards all the lads before we went out. When he said something, you listened. He had a lot of respect in the changing room. You didn't want to let him down and you wanted to do well for him. It would have more effect if Alan was shouting and encouraging than someone else. Venners was especially good at doing this as well.

Faustino Asprilla was another great character. I'm not sure what he made of Shearer's arrival at the club but he was always asking Alan where and what time he had to be at training after every session. Shearer would tell him everything but the truth. Consequently, our Colombian striker was always late and got fined. Tino was always pretending to be ignorant of everything, yet I knew he was aware of all that was going on. There were times when I'd ask him for something and he would reply, 'I don't understand you and don't know what you want.' There were other times when I would be talking to one of the lads and he'd interrupt. He'd say, 'Pav?' I would say, 'What?' Then he would say, 'Fuck you!' in his funny cartoon voice. I'd just shake my head. He was hilarious. He had a real dry sense of humour.

There was another time when the gaffer was a bit late so Tino stepped in and made an outstanding impression of him naming the team before the kick-off. Kevin walked in behind Tino while he was in full flow and stood and watched it all. We were crying with laughter. Tino thought we were laughing at his take on Keegan but he was unaware he was standing behind him. When he realised something was up and turned to see Kevin, he humbly apologised. I never saw Tino get angry or upset with anyone. He had a fantastic sense of humour. He never said much but when he did, he would have you in hysterics.

Everybody loved Tino, although I think the residents of Darras Hall were happy to see the back of him and his partying. On the pitch he would be a genius for about an hour, performing tricks, nutmegs and running rings around defenders and then, all of a sudden, he would switch off and lose interest. That was Tino all over. When Dalglish first came in Tino got more games because he found a formula to give him a free role with Ferdinand and Shearer. The downside to that was Beardsley and Ginola were dropped.

I know I have said we go into every new season with renewed optimism but that wasn't the case until we signed Alan Shearer. It certainly gave us a boost ahead of the Charity Shield. Usually, the Premier League champions take on the FA Cup winners but since Man U won both competitions, we were invited to provide the double winners the opposition on the Premier League's traditional curtain raiser. The whole occasion was an anti-climax and we let down our fans, who were magnificent, once again, despite a 4-0 defeat. I'm thinking here we go again and where do we go from here? It was my first and only appearance at Wembley. I don't have any fond memories of England's famous showcase arena because not only did we lose the Charity Shield, in the home of English football, but I saw the Czech Republic lose to Germany in the Euro final less than two months previously.

I was on the bench for the club's opening fixture of the new campaign, a match we lost 2-0 at Everton but I was back in goal for the following game at St James' Park against Wimbledon which we won 2-0. Shearer scored a 20-yard swerving free-kick to net his first goal for the club, although our £15 million new signing had a perfectly good goal ruled out at Goodison Park the week before. It was a tremendous goal and a fitting statement of intent from our world-class striker.

I remember the first derby game at Sunderland in 1996 when none of our supporters was allowed in to watch the Premier League new boys. I had a few friends and family inside the ground because players still got complimentary tickets for every match. My friend and his wife from the Czech Republic were at the game. I never really gave it much thought but I'd kitted them out in some Newcastle United coats the week before and they decided to walk up to the game in our club colours. I saw him in the stands when I was warming up and nearly shit myself. I'm screaming at him, 'Take the jacket off! Take it off!' He just waved back. It was like a comedy sketch. I repeated, bellowing at the top of my voice, in Czech, 'Take the jacket off! Take the jacket off!' I thought someone was going to kill him. He's not going to get out of the stadium alive. He eventually cottoned on and took it off. He later told me he got all sorts of abuse from the Sunderland fans but they never beat him up. He probably got away with it because he couldn't speak English.

It might sound a strange thing to say but it was a great game and one of the last matches to be played at Roker Park. The atmosphere was quite intimidating. You could almost feel the hate and venom spilling over onto the pitch from the terraces. Shearer was getting all sorts of abuse. The Sunderland supporters were telling our £15 million striker that he wasn't very good, or words to that effect. We hadn't won many games on enemy soil at the time, although our recent form was good against them, so it was great to beat the Mackems.

Martin Scott netted from the penalty spot to give the hosts a 1-0 lead before two headers from Peter Beardsley and Les Ferdinand wrapped up the points. I remember the game well. As the clock was running down, I started dribbling in the last minute of the match. We were 2-1 up, and our players and Keegan were screaming at me to clear it. I took the player on before clearing a long ball up field. People might think I'm crazy but I got a thrill out of it. Life doesn't get much better than this. Winning 2-1 on the ground of your bitter rivals and showing the paying public I had a bit of skill was the cherry on the cake. I wasn't showboating or taking the piss. I never took the piss when

I was dribbling with the ball. I was always comfortable with the ball at my feet and enjoyed the challenge of taking on a player. I preferred doing that to kicking it out for a corner or a throw-in.

Surely, it's better to clear the ball down the other end of the pitch away from danger than give a team another chance in the last third. The supporters loved it as well and it gave me a big buzz when they cheered me on. I did this all of my career even when I played for the national team. My brother would be saying, 'Oh no he's going to get caught out and give me a heart attack,' but I never did.

The following day in training Keegan pulled me to one side and said, 'Pav, everybody has seen you do this now. It was the talking point on Sky and in the papers about your dribbling. Be careful in future because everyone will be looking out for you now.' I remember Alan Hansen talking about it on Match of the Day, saying how brave I was. It's probably the only positive thing he ever said about me.

We put quite a run together after the stuttering start of two defeats in our opening three league games; three defeats if you count the Charity Shield. We won seven league games in a row including the 5-0 triumph over Man United at St James' Park. Was it the greatest game or the best result I was ever involved in as a Newcastle player? Possibly, when you consider the quality of the opposition we faced that day. But there were other games such as Antwerp away when Rob Lee scored a hat-trick of headers in a 5-0 victory. We played Man United off the park. Darren Peacock, Ginola, Big Les and Alan scored, Philippe Albert's outrageous chip, provided the coup de gras.

The game could've been so different had the referee not been on top of his game. My international colleague Karel Porbosky dived over me to try and win a penalty but referee Steve Dunn waved it away. Man U had a bad spell after this, losing three in a row. Yes, it was a famous victory but they still went on to win the title. I'd rather we won 1-0 and claimed the league championship than win 5-0. We won the battle but not the war. The following week we went to Leicester, played poorly and lost 2-0. That is why we didn't win the title. Sometimes we couldn't raise our game for lower-league teams.

We failed to capitalise on a few games to struggling sides that term. The team had a good run in the UEFA Cup this season. We despatched Halmstads of Sweden in the first round, before overcoming Ferencvaros in the second round. The 4-0 scoreline in our home leg suggests we romped to victory in a game, where Ginola netted an absolute cracker. The Hungarians provided tough opposition, certainly in the first leg where they beat us 3-2. In the third round, we faced French opposition. I remember I dropped a cross in the away leg at Metz, which Keegan wasn't happy about after Peter Beardsley put us 1-0 up from the penalty spot. I think David Ginola got fouled.

Two late Tino goals ensured we got through to the quarter-finals against Monaco. Both were typical Asprilla strikes. One was an instinctive header after Darren Peacock put the ball back across the box. The Columbia international celebrated by hanging his shirt on the corner flag at the Gallowgate End. The second was sublime. He drew the defender, fainted one way, then went the other before delightfully chipping the oncoming goalkeeper. It was exhibition football. Unfortunately, Tino's corner flag shenanigans proved costly. He got booked for it and consequently ruled out of our quarter-final clash against Monaco at St James' Park. Both Shearer and Ferdinand were missing through injury and we were a bit toothless up front. We eventually lost 1-0 before crashing 3-0 in the south of France.

Once again, it was a tournament we felt we could win. We never seemed to get the rub of the green or that little bit of luck that would've seen us land a trophy. Although I thought it was a bit strange, former manager Ruud Gullit having a priest bless St James' Park because he thought it was cursed, I still understood it. When Keegan quit, Newcastle tried to bring in Sir Bobby Robson, who was manager at Barcelona, but he wanted to honour his contract at the Camp Nou. It was just my luck.

Had he taken the job then, maybe my career would've turned out much better. Unfortunately, it got even worse for me. Pedro let me know he feared the worst when Dalglish was linked with the job. He made it known he never got on with Kenny and knew his days were numbered at the club. He said he was a dead man walking. Kenny tried to destroy his career at Liverpool. There were a few people at the club, at the time, who voiced similar sentiments.

Supporters were still coming in to watch us train when he first became manager but he stopped them not long after he took over. By the start of his first full season in charge, no fans were allowed in at all. Pedro, Ginola and I were always in the big noses' team. That is what everyone called us. I don't know who gave us the nickname but it stuck. We always won, yet none of us could get a game on a Saturday. No one could beat us in Kenny's time. It wasn't just me who had this feeling but Pedro and Ginola, two of the best players to ever don the black and white shirt. I didn't mind Dalglish not liking or rating me as a goalkeeper. It was the lack of respect. I wasn't the only one. He was the same with Darren Peacock, Philippe Albert, John Beresford and Rob Lee. I couldn't believe it at half-time in one game when he tore into Rob. We thought he liked him. Yet there he was, tearing into one of Newcastle's best players.

Dalglish quickly lost respect in the dressing room with typical behaviour like this. It was not a surprise when Pedro and David moved on at the end of the season. Beardsley went to Bolton and Ginola went to Tottenham. I was back in the first XI for the last four matches of the season. I can't remember the reason why Dalglish put me back in. Maybe he wanted to see me in first-team action or wasn't too keen on Shaka, I don't know. I do know I kept four clean sheets and we had conceded goals in the previous five fixtures before I got back in. It helped us qualify for the Champions League. We qualified because we had a better goal difference than Liverpool and Arsenal. We all had the same points. The 5-0 home victory over Forest on the last day of the season and the results not going well for our rivals was a fitting end to a turbulent campaign. The fact that our North-East rivals, Middlesbrough and Sunderland, got relegated was the cherry on the cake for our supporters. What a change from finishing runners-up last term.

Last season it was as if we had been relegated yet this time it felt like we had won the league, such was the contrast of emotions. I was back as the club's No.1 and I thought I deserved it. The praise the team and I were getting was great and we got a good bonus for it. It was like Groundhog Day because I had been here several times in the past. The sad aspect of finishing runners-up and helping Newcastle into the Champions League for the first time in their history, I never got a game in it. I only got as far as the bench. It was another eventful season and one to reflect on what might have been.

I felt we were unlucky once again not to pick up some silverware. I seriously believe had we not been without Alan Shearer for a large part of the season we could have won, not only the UEFA Cup but the Premier League title. It was also a season where we saw Kenny Dalglish replacing Kevin Keegan in a similar way to what he did as a player at Liverpool in the 1970s. Unfortunately, things were never the same with Dalglish in charge. The club went backwards and never recovered from when he was appointed.

Chapter Seven: Tommy Wright

Tommy Wright was already a professional at the club when Kevin Keegan took over as manager. He joined the Magpies in 1988 from Linfield, a team famously linked to Newcastle United through club legend Jackie Milburn, who managed the Irish side in the late 1950s and early 1960s. Wright may have been brought to the club by another iconic figure, fellow Irishman Willie McFaul, but it was Jim Smith who gave him his first-team debut.

Smith was not impressed by Dave Beasant, an £850,000 McFaul signing from FA Cup-winning Wimbledon, and soon replaced the England international with the Northern Ireland shotstopper. Wright quickly became a key part of the team, making his debut during the 1988-89 season and helping to strengthen the defence. He played in over 70 league matches, consistently proving himself as a reliable presence between the posts as he competed for the No.1 spot with veteran John Burridge and the precocious Pavel Srnicek.

Wright's time at Newcastle coincided with a challenging period for the club, as they struggled to maintain their place in the top tier of English football. Despite these difficulties, Wright's contributions were highly regarded by both fans and teammates.

In 1993, after five years with Newcastle, Keegan broke Wright's heart by accepting a £500,000 offer from Nottingham Forest. Although injuries hampered his progress, Wright left a lasting legacy at St James' Park and is fondly remembered by Newcastle supporters for the dedication and stability he brought to the goalkeeper position during a turbulent time for the club. His double save at Bristol Rovers in the 1992-93 promotion season was reminiscent of Gordon Banks at his best and remains unforgettable for those who witnessed it.

Best Sweeper-Keeper in the World

I was Linfield's reserve goalkeeper at the time Newcastle came calling. Newcastle only had one fit goalkeeper,

Gary Kelly. The club originally invited a young Coleraine goalkeeper called David Crooks for a trial game. The game got cancelled because of fog and David wouldn't stay another week so the manager, Wille McFaul, called my manager (former Middlesbrough goalkeeper) Jim Platt and asked if he knew anyone else. He mentioned me and told Willie to call (ex-Northern Ireland manager) Billy Bingham to get a report. I flew over for a month's loan and ended up winning a full contract. I was about 24 or 25 at the time, so you could say that all the stars aligned for me to give me this great opportunity.

Gary had done well in the first half of the season I joined and I think we finished around eight in the old Division One, before the Premier League was formed. I got injured in pre-season ahead of the 1988-89 campaign and Willie brought in Dave Beasant and Andy Thorn from the Wimbledon FA Cup-winning side during the summer. Dave was the No.1 goalie with Gary Kelly as No. 2 and I was out with a knee injury. The season didn't start well for us despite winning every pre-season game. I remember we went down to Liverpool and won 2-0 after our dodgy start and Wille got sacked the Monday after the win. We were only about seven or eight games into the season.

Jim Smith came in and didn't really like Dave Beasant and I made my debut in January 1989 away to Aston Villa. We lost 3-1. Jim was a very knowledgeable manager. I remember Kevin Brock putting a towel over his clothes in the changing room. I asked him why. He told us that Jim was partial to throwing cups and teapots at players. He did have a temper on him and he could flip very quickly but I always appreciate Jim because he gave me my debut. I knew it was going to be difficult to get in the side because the club had paid nearly a million quid for Beasant, which was a lot of money at that time, but he put me in the side and had faith in me which I am grateful for.

We lost in the play-offs to Sunderland which was disappointing. After that, the pressure was on Jim. In the background, you had the takeover going on with Sir John Hall so there was a lot of unrest at the time. There was a home game against Wolves and some fans got on the pitch and one tried to attack Jim in the dugout. There was an ugly atmosphere around the place at the time. At first, it didn't bother the players but as it went on it did because of the negativity around the club. Nobody liked the uncertainty and wanted it all sorted out. Once it was sorted the only way was up.

Ossie Ardiles was already in place when the take-over was completed. Training was all relaxed and it was play, play, play under him. There wasn't much structure to anything at all. He kick-started a lot of young players' careers at the club. We played an attacking brand of football that didn't get us over the line because it wasn't a winning brand of football. There was one game against Charlton where we were 3-0 up at half-time and we ended up getting beat 4-3. He wanted to attack all of the time so we were involved in a lot of reverse 4-3 and 3-2 results but he gave all the young lads opportunities to establish themselves.

When I first joined the club, you'd hear the other players talking about the kids, saying this one was going to make the team and that one was going to make the first team. Then when they got their professional contracts and started training with the first team you could tell they were going to go on to greater things. It was amazing that there were so many of them coming through at the same time.

I didn't play for Ossie for a long period until Pavel got injured. Then I got in and enjoyed playing under him. I asked Ossie why I wasn't in the team and he told me it was because Pav was his No.1. Pav didn't start the season very well before he got injured but Ossie was very loyal to players and wouldn't drop them if they weren't playing well.

Kevin Keegan coming in was a surprise and you could see immediately what impact he made on the club. Before he arrived, our crowds were down to about 15,000-16,000 at home. In his first game against Bristol City, it was a sell-out and there were about 10,000 locked outside the game. After that, it was a bit topsy-turvy until the end of the season.

Everything was a bit more structured from Kevin but he knew what he wanted from his team. He filled us full of confidence but sometimes it was like two steps forward and three back as we were fighting relegation. I remember we beat Sunderland 1-0 on Sunday and then went to Wolves and they hammered us 6-2. The most important thing was staying up that season because you knew that Kevin would go out and buy better players and we would kick on, which we did.

The following season we won 11 games in a row and I was very proud to be part of that. That laid the foundations for promotion that season. Kevin was such an enthusiastic, bubbly character who joined in training. He didn't do a lot of coaching. Derek Fazakerley did a lot of the structure of training. Kevin was similar in a way to Ossie in the fact they had great careers as players so when they spoke, you listened. Terry Mac was another bubbly guy. He was another who had a great career so, although he didn't take a session, you listened to him when he spoke because he gave great advice.

Terry was Kevin's eyes and ears and if you had a problem you could go to him. He often spoke at half-time but they both kept it pretty simple for the players. It was never complicated. They were a really good partnership and created a positive atmosphere around the club. Even in defeat, they were positive. It was a case of 'We'll sort it out next game' and they didn't dwell too much on the past. We did talk about the opposition but it was more about us than them and what we could do rather than what they might do to us but Kevin filled us with so much confidence that we felt we could beat anyone.

I remember having an unbelievable game at Bristol

Rovers in the promotion season and Kevin said I was 'the best sweeper-keeper in the world' after the game. I remember making a double save, where I tipped a free-kick onto the crossbar and then it looped up and came down the other side of the goal and as Marcus Stewart was heading it into the goal I managed to get back across and managed to get a hand to his header.

Another game that sticks out for good and bad reasons is the 3-2 win away at Birmingham where I got injured and Kevin Brock had to go in goal. I ruptured my thigh after John Beresford left a back pass a bit short. I was out for a long time and didn't get back in the side that season. Had I been out for a couple of weeks I reckon Kevin would have put me straight back in the side but Pavel got back in and did extremely well for the rest of the season. I did enjoy that promotion season because we went up but I was disappointed I didn't get more games.

We didn't have a goalkeeping coach when I joined the club and then Kevin brought in Jimmy Montgomery for a couple of days a week and Pav especially improved enormously. Pav had problems initially because Ossie wanted him to come for everything and command his box. Pav wasn't used to that. It wasn't a part of his game so most of his early mistakes were from coming for the ball. Once he settled down, he developed into a great goalkeeper and we both got on really well. There was no animosity between the two of us. If either of us was in the team we would try and help each other.

Kevin signed some good players in our promotion season such as Rob Lee, Andy Cole, John Beresford and Barry Venison among others. I don't think Kevin got any of his signings wrong. They contributed to the promotion season. Those signings lifted the dressing room. Brian Kilcline was such a great leader on the pitch. A manager is judged on his recruitment and Kevin got it spot on.

I remember before the season started, we all went to Sir John Hall's place for a barbecue. Sir John made a speech. I can't remember it word for word but he said you'll be failures if you don't get promoted. It was quite clear he was backing Kevin and we started the season so well that it gave us a load of confidence. In the end, we won the league quite comfortably.

Not everything was smooth in the beginning, however, and it was quite bizarre when Kevin quit that time after the Swindon game. We used to have our pre-match meal at the Gosforth Park Hotel. Freddie Star was there and he did a short five-minute stand-up sketch. Kevin did say to the squad, 'Whatever happens today, this has nothing to do with you.' We wondered what it was all about. The timing was strange. He'd made his mind up that he was going after the game. There were many famous Kevin quotes and the one, 'It's not like the brochure said' was one of them. That just showed how determined he was to get the players we needed to get us promotion.

My leaving was a surprise because I'd just got back in the side. Either Pav got injured or sent off. Kevin called me and asked to meet me in a hotel on the Monday after a game. We had a cup of tea and he told me Nottingham Forest had come in with a really good offer. He told me he knew their wage structure and they would offer me a good contract. It was far better than the Newcastle contract in the end. I was disappointed and told him I didn't want to go but he said he was going to bring another goalkeeper in. When a manager tells you that you know your time is up.

I travelled to Forest the next day and got the deal done. I don't speak ill or bad mouth people usually but I think I was a better goalkeeper than Mike Hooper. So, I was slightly disappointed to be replaced by him. I picked up an injury after two or three months and the move turned into a disaster in the end. I never got out of the physio room for two and a half years.

It was a shame Newcastle didn't win the league at that time but I reckon it was because of the squad's lack of experience. Man United had it in abundance. Then there was the pressure of Newcastle not having won anything for years. Kevin didn't take defeat very well and he could be quite cutting after games. This is where Terry Mac came into his own lifting people. It still disappoints me that I had to leave but, it goes without saying, I loved my time at the club and Newcastle is always in my heart.

Chapter Eight: Kevin Scott

Kevin Scott's career at Newcastle United saw him become a stalwart as the Magpies underwent seismic changes under the leadership of Sir John Hall off the pitch and Kevin Keegan on it. Released by Middlesbrough as a teenager, Scott later joined United as a youth player after former World Cup-winning England legend Jack Charlton saw him play for Durham City in the Northern League. Scott made his first-team debut in 1984 and went on to cement his place as a reliable and steady presence at the heart of Newcastle's defence. Known for his strong tackling, aerial prowess, and composure on the ball, he became an integral part of the team's back four.

During his nine-year tenure on Tyneside, Scott captained the side, showcasing leadership and resilience. His performances earned him the respect of teammates, managers, and fans alike. The Easington-born defender's legacy at Newcastle is one of dedication and dependability, playing with heart and determination to help lay the foundations for the club's future successes.

Scott also stands as a tangible reminder of Keegan's relentless pursuit of success. 'Special K' deemed the reliable central defender surplus to requirements halfway through Newcastle's inaugural Premier League campaign. Yet, rather than harbour any bitterness, the popular defender understood his manager's position and decision, wishing his hometown club well as he embarked on a new challenge with Tottenham Hotspur. Scott remembers his ten years at the club fondly.

Captain Scott

I remember Kevin flying off in a helicopter in 1984 after the team had played Liverpool in a farewell friendly when I was a supporter. I was signed by Jack Charlton later that year. I was offered £90 a week which I turned down at first because I was getting more in the paper factory where I was working in Hetton. Jack was away fishing when I came down to sign and then United legend Joe Harvey came in and asked if there was a problem. I told him that I was getting paid more in the factory. He then gave me a free bus pass to swing the deal. No, I'm not making this up. This is where the club was at the time.

We had lots of good young players when I signed as an 18-year-old. The likes of Paul Gascoigne, Joe Allon, Ian Bogie, Paul Stephenson with Colin Suggett as the youth team coach. Colin was still running the academy a few years later when he brought through the likes of Lee Clark, Steve Watson, Steve Howey, Alan Thompson, Robbie Elliott and others. There was a lot of good northern talent coming through the books at Newcastle.

The Newcastle youth team I played in, with the likes of Gazza won the league and the FA Youth Cup so we were the top dogs in North-East at that time in terms of young talent. Joe Allon scored loads of goals while Gazza did most of the providing. We also had Gary Kelly in goal who was a fine goalkeeper.

It was certainly exciting when Kevin came to the club as a player. After he left it was a kind of transitional period where we had lots of managers that came in and then left. I thought it was a joke at first when I heard Kevin was coming back to manage the club. It came out of the blue because there was nothing in the papers and nothing on the TV. Then he came and the buzz it created with the supporters went straight through the club and the players, who were just as excited. It was something special and we knew something special was going to happen.

Under Ossie, who made me captain, he just wanted to play one way, whether we won or lost 4-3 or drew 4-4. Ossie was the first manager I played under who encouraged me to play out from the back but some of the results we were getting were crazy. Then Kevin brought in Brian Kilcline and Barry Venison and everything just tightened up. Later on, Steve Howey dropped in alongside me and it was just a bit more organised at the back than it had been previously. Derek Fazakerley as coach was a big help, being a centre-half himself. We had a great balance what with Kevin and Terry Mac messing about with the strikers, Andy Cole and Rob Lee etc and Faz sorting out the back four.

Kevin was great. All he wanted was what was best for the club. He took the captaincy off me and gave it to Killer which was fine really because it took the pressure off me and I could just concentrate on playing. The season we just survived Kevin asked me and Gavin Peacock to sign a new contract but because it was on deadline day I wouldn't sign it. I wasn't sure whether we would stay up. That was why he took the captaincy off me. I didn't hold a grudge against him but I didn't have a contract all of that summer.

Back then you would park your car at St James' Park and you'd have to walk through the supporters to get inside the stadium. Kevin's first game at home to Bristol City took me nearly 20 minutes to get inside the ground. After that, we all started coming in earlier to fight through the fans. Before that, it was sometimes uncomfortable because the fans were a bit disgruntled but Kevin changed all of that.

The game against Portsmouth was a strange one from my point of view. For one, I was suspended because I got sent off the game before and two, I made my wife go to the game in labour because Kevin told me I owed it to the club to go and support the lads. Needless to say, it was a great day all-round because David Kelly scored the winner and my first son was born. Chris Guthrie the kitman, and his wife, made sure everything went smoothly in the players' lounge when my wife went into labour.

Then we had to go to Leicester in the last game of the season and try and get something to make sure we stopped up. The pressure on that game was tremendous. Obviously, we didn't know the result didn't matter until after the game was finished. We just knew we had to try and get something to ensure we would be staying up. It was a massive relief.

The following season we had an incredible start, and it was all due to the fans, I think. Kevin got the fans involved with everything. He opened the doors at the training ground to let them in. Some days there were thousands there. I loved training more than the games to be fair. It heightened the intensity and it also gave me a chance to get forward and score goals, which Keegan was all for. He wanted to entertain the fans and would join in. It was great to see him and Terry Mac diving around in the puddles and stuff.

I expected us to be strong at home at St James' Park but not so much away but we were just as strong away from home. The atmosphere at away games made it almost like a home game. I remember getting cheered off the bus when we turned up. We had this lovely feeling that we weren't going to lose every time we went away. You rarely get those feelings in your career.

People often wonder about Kevin's team talks but they were very simple. We just made sure we played to our strengths. I'm sure he had other teams watched but when Gavin Peacock and David Kelly were in form, and later on Rob Lee and Andy Cole, there were very few, if any, teams that could stop us.

We went on that fantastic run, which ended at home to Grimsby. It was a setback but we weren't too disheartened. We just thought, 'Let's go again next week.' These were the times when the chairman Sir John Hall was travelling to away games on the train with the fans. He was buzzing just like the rest of us.

Under Ossie, I think I was the oldest at 24 at one point. Then Kevin put all these players together and it was a perfect blend and we all had a part to play. Kevin Sheedy, Barry Venison and Paul Bracewell had all played for top clubs. These guys had a massive effect on the team. We started to believe we could go places thanks to those lads.

The last game of the 1992-93 season against Leicester

was incredible. The buzz, the atmosphere, it was amazing. The celebration didn't stop after the game, it just went on and on for a few days until the open-top bus tour around the city. There was a sea of black and white wherever we looked that night, whether it was the streets or a house you looked in, everything was black and white. I even remember one of the kitmen hanging from a tree. The supporters' appreciation was very special.

Another game that was special to us and the fans was winning at Sunderland. We hadn't won there for a lot of years. In fact, I only ever lost one game as a player against Sunderland and that was the 1990 play-off semi-final under Jim Smith. That includes the youth team. Keegan made a big thing of it as well. He kept us in a hotel the night before just to make us aware that it was a big game. Those games were always about the supporters.

It was a big shock to lose Gavin Peacock and David Kelly after we'd just been promoted. I thought the team would stick together for a little bit. Kevin had already decided who was moving on. There were players on the end-of-season trip who knew they weren't going to be in the team in the Premier League.

Bringing Peter Beardsley back was very similar to when Kevin came to play for the club. He still had a good few years left in him and we knew what he would bring to the club. I remember my first day at the football club as an 18-year-old. I'd never met Peter in my life but he was waiting for me with a pair of trainers and some new boots. You need players like Peter to galvanise the older and younger players.

I remember playing against Andy Cole when he was at Bristol City a few weeks before we signed him. We'd heard he might be coming to the club in the warm up and then he hit the ground running and just didn't stop scoring. Then he had Peter alongside him who was one of the best providers in the game. Peter did the same for Gary Lineker when playing for England.

I didn't score many goals for the club but I do remember scoring against Wolves with an 18-yard header in a 1-0 win at Molyneux. That brings back fond memories. I couldn't wait to play against the top Premier League players. Even when you're playing in the lower divisions, players still watch Match of Day. It was harder to play in the top flight but after a slow start, we eventually found our feet.

My transfer to Tottenham was out of the blue and a bit cutthroat to be fair. I'd just bought a new house and hadn't even lived in it. Kevin called and asked me to come to the stadium. I thought something was up but didn't know what. I got to the stadium and he had his hand on the phone. He said he'd decided to sell me and that someone was on the phone I might want to talk to. He told me if I stayed, I'd be the fourth choice. I guessed he already had players lined up to take my place. He handed the phone to me and it was Ossie. Ossie asked if I'd fly down and meet him in a hotel and that was it. Kevin was quite cutthroat as Liam O'Brien and David Kelly discovered. He kind of knows when your time is up and lets you know. He had his eye on how he wanted to move the club forward. I never got a chance to play against Newcastle when I left. I was injured when Tottenham came back the following year. Then I was at Charlton on loan when Newcastle was playing them in the FA Cup and Spurs wouldn't let me play because it was an FA Cup game and they didn't want me cup-tied.

I think all of the negative pressure on the team played its part in not winning the title under Kevin. All of his time at the club was moving forward. Then, all of a sudden it hit a wall and it was a different kind of pressure and I think it got to the team at the time.

Chapter Nine: Liam O'Brien

"I fancy O'Brien over the wall," said Lennie Lawrence, then Middlesbrough manager, and co-commentator, at the Sunderland versus Newcastle Tyne-Wear derby at Roker Park on October 18, 1992.

Those words have since become entrenched in Geordie folklore and inspired an iconic song, set to the tune of "My Old Man's a Dustman." "Liam O'Brien, Andy O'Brien, any, any, any O'Brien, who put the ball in the Mackem's net? O'Brien, O'Brien!"

The goal elevated the former Republic of Ireland international to legendary status on Tyneside. It also ensures that the Irishman never has to buy another pint of Guinness for the rest of his life when frequenting Tyneside hostelries.

O'Brien arrived at St James Park in 1988 in a reported £275,000 deal from Old Trafford. The Irishman played 36 games and scored six goals in the promotion season playing a pivotal role in United's return to the top flight. The Dublin-born playmaker confessed the goal against fierce North-East rivals Sunderland was probably the highlight of a rollercoaster five-and-a-half years on Tyneside, admits he left the North-East with a heavy heart and hailed Toon supporters as the "best in the world."

"O'Brien, O'Brien!"

I was on a week-to-week contract at Manchester United at the time Newcastle came calling. Alex Ferguson was the manager and he offered me a two-year deal to stay at the club. I was on a week-to-week contract for financial reasons because the contract he offered me wasn't very good. It was only £100 a week. So, I stayed on a week-to-week from July 1 to the October, November of 1988 and I wouldn't sign it.

When these things happen, a manager tends to mess you around a bit. I just got my head down and played well in the reserves. He then put me back into the first team. We played Wimbledon away, Everton, and Aston Villa was my last game at Old Trafford and I got man of the match. A few days after the match I got a call from Newcastle asking if I'd be willing to talk to them. They could call me because of the week-to-week contract situation and any transfer would go to a tribunal.

They asked to meet me between Manchester and Newcastle, at a service station in Leeds. I had a good chat with Mick Martin and Colin Suggett, who were the caretaker managers at the time. They offered me a bit of security because my wife had just our first child a few weeks previously and I was getting a bit panicky. They offered me a three-year contract. I was really happy with what they said and offered. It was a fantastic deal for me and my family. I signed the week after I played in a 1-1 draw against Aston Villa. Jim Smith was waiting in the wings to come on board at the time. Newcastle was trying to work out his contract and compensation at Loftus Road. He tried to sign me for QPR when he was manager there so he knew I was coming to the club. Jim came in and it took off for a little while at first.

We used to train at Benwell back then. The facilities weren't that great. There wasn't much there. It was always windy. Didn't matter whether it was a summer's day. We'd call it the "Windy City." That was the way it was with most clubs back then though, with basic training facilities. I liked Jim Smith and enjoyed working with him. He knew all of the leagues. He was an old-school manager. He'd lose his head and his face would go bright red but he knew how to get teams promoted, which he nearly did. He signed some very good players to get us out of the league. I know we got relegated that first season he came but we nearly made it through the play-offs. Unfortunately, the team down the road beat us.

Ossie (Ardiles) came in after Jim and he was a really nice bloke, very placid, quiet and humble. I felt a bit sorry for Ossie. The players loved playing for him. We played some lovely attacking football but defensively we were poor. There's been a lot said about playing the youngsters instead of the experienced players, like Roy Aitken and Mark McGee, but I heard he had to cut the wage bill and get those players out of the club. He kind of nurtured the young homegrown players and some went on to be great players: Steve Watson, Lee Clark, Steve Howey, Robbie Elliott, and Alan Thompson. They were just inexperienced. I was really surprised the club allowed Alan Thompson to leave. He was a very, very good player. He went on and had a fantastic career, as did the others for their home clubs and others.

Ossie didn't get the backing of the board and there was a boardroom struggle at the time. He didn't get the funds he needed to bring in the players he wanted. He brought in David Kelly and one or two others but that was it. If you ask most of the players, they would tell you that they enjoyed working with him. I heard Ossie bought David Kelly with his own money, or loaned it to the club. Not sure how much of that is true. Ossie asked me about David because I knew him from the Republic of Ireland squads. I told Ossie that he works very hard and would be a great signing for us. He did very, very well for us as you all know. We were all sad when Ossie got sacked.

We heard the rumours that Kevin Keegan might replace him. A few of us thought that it wouldn't work because he had no managerial experience. We all knew he was a great player, a Ballon d'Or winner, England captain and a great player for Newcastle. As a manager, it was a big gamble. It was a gamble for Kevin as well because if it didn't work out, he would have sullied his reputation.

All of those doubts soon disappeared though. His man management was very good. He was very charismatic, had a presence about him and had a vision for the club. I remember him sitting down with us all at Benwell and saying we're all starting with a clean slate and he was going to give everyone a chance. He told us he loved the club and it gave the club and the city a whole lift when Sir John

Hall brought him in. The whole city did need a lift and he gave it to them. Keegan was very driven and wanted the club to do well. He did that, probably much quicker than he thought would happen.

We needed the lift at the time. We were really struggling. We needed the points to stay in the division. I remember the first game Kevin was manager at home to Bristol City. We won 3-0. It was a full house and people were locked out. They couldn't get into the ground. He was great with the players. He made you feel like you were on top of the world. He was one of those managers you wanted to play for.

Derek Fazakerley would take most of the training with Kevin taking one at the end of the session. He'd often join in, in a shadow game or a game amongst ourselves. There was never any mad, off-the-scale training. Kevin would be trying to boost our confidence, getting us to believe in ourselves more than anything. Most of the time he'd let Faz get on with it.

In his team talks, Kevin would tell us to express ourselves, be confident and entertain the fans. There was no pressure on the players that we had to do this or had to do that. He wasn't in your face. At most clubs you have the good cop, bad cop scenario but that wasn't the case with Kevin and Terry McDermott, who was great with the lads. He was a great player for Liverpool and Newcastle and won so many trophies, European Cups and caps for England. He would never put on a training session but he'd often come and talk to the players, such as myself, and give advice because he was a great midfielder himself. Whether it was the timing of your runs or something else. He gave you something to think about. He wasn't just the joker of the pack. He had a real interest in the players. He was a lovely guy and I've got a lot of time for him.

Kevin didn't have a lot of funds at the time, maybe because of the power struggle behind the scenes with the Magpie Group and then chairman Gordon McKeag. His first two signings were Brian Kilcline and Kevin Sheedy: two fantastic signings. Sheeds won league titles, an FA Cup and a Cup Winners' Cup with Everton and was capped by Ireland, and played in a World Cup. Killer won the FA Cup with Coventry City. Killer was a really good organiser and both players were great around the young lads. Bringing those two in was a masterstroke. It settled us down and we needed them. They were experienced and they were winners.

We went into the last game of the 1991-92 season at Leicester thinking we had to win it to stay up. As it turned out we didn't need to win it, because other results went our way, but we weren't to know that at the time. Gavin Peacock put us 1-0 up and then they equalised through their captain Steve Walsh in the last minute. Walsh then put through his own goal and it cemented our place in the league. I'll never forget that game. The fans came onto the pitch. The relief was tangible. It helped us to kick on and made us more determined to not let it happen again. It's what Kevin said to us at the end of the game.

Kevin knew he had to strengthen the squad if we were to kick on. We needed solid foundations, a good goalkeeper, and a solid back four. He brought in Barry Venison, John Beresford and Paul Bracewell, as well as converting Steve Howey into a centre half, who went on to play for England. Training even stepped up a gear as we were told to express ourselves. I can't remember much about preseason training but I was suspended for the first three games of the season after getting sent off at Derby County. Kevin Scott and Kevin Brock also got their marching orders in the 4-1 defeat, so I had to wait for my chance to get back in the team.

There was no talk about promotion, that I remember, but we knew we would do better that season because of the quality of the players we brought in. Training was brilliant and everybody loved going into training every day. We won the first ten games of the season and the 11th was at Sunderland, our big rivals. They were giving it the big one that they were gonna stop our run and, of course, we wanted bragging rights and to equal the old consecutive victories in Division One record by Tottenham.

We went 1-0 up thanks to an own goal (by Gary Owers) and then Gordon Armstrong equalised. We had a couple of chances before we got the second but we were the better team on the day. I had always taken the free-kicks around that distance, 20 to 30 yards, and I was confident of scoring as I had done so earlier. I heard a voice saying "I'm taking this," just before I stepped up, and it was John Beresford. I told him in no uncertain terms that he wasn't. I told him I was going to put it where the goalkeeper was standing. I was confident he would move from that spot. Fortunately, he did move, I got a good connection and hit it sweetly over the wall into the top corner of the net. I was thrilled to see the back of the net bulge.

First and foremost, we won the game but it was one of my pals who later said, 'You don't realise what you've done, do you?' I said, 'Yeah, I scored the winner.' He said, 'No! You won't ever be forgotten for that goal because we've beaten them on their patch for the first time in something like five decades.' It's true, the Geordies have never forgotten it and even have a song about it. I couldn't be more thrilled.

There's an iconic overhead photograph of the goal. Everyone is standing watching the flight of the ball, which hadn't hit the net, while I've wheeled away with my arm in the air in celebration. I just knew as soon as I hit it, that it was going in. It was a great feeling and what a photograph, by the way.

It was probably my favourite game for Newcastle. I know I've probably scored some better goals but the game at Roker Park was the most memorable. Was it my best goal? I don't know. I was lucky to have scored some good goals for Newcastle. I got a good one against Middlesbrough in the League Cup. I scored a sweet volley from outside of the box against Oxford in a game where we got hammered. I scored a goal against Sunderland the year before in a 1-1 draw, which technically was probably a better goal, but the one in our promotion season was very special.

I missed the last few games of the season though shin splints. Never had it before in my career. There was so much pain. Even in the last game of the season against Leicester, Kevin asked whether he could put me on for ten minutes because I'd done so well for him but I was in so much pain I couldn't. It was an injury that just needed rest. It was much appreciated that he was thinking of me though, even though I was absent through injury. All of the hard work came to fruition and we deserved promotion to the Premier League. It was a credit to all of the players, backroom staff and the management. I got myself a winner's medal. I was there for the celebration and the bus tour at the end. It was an amazing occasion.

The two most consistent players during my time at the club were Gavin Peacock and Robert Lee. Even when we were a poor side Gavin could get a goal and get us out of a hole. I don't think Gavin got the praise he deserved for what he did for us. Rob Lee was just one of the best I'd seen and he got better and better as the years went on.

I get asked in Ireland all of the time, what the supporters were like. You had to live there to understand what they were about. Football is a religion for them. They are so passionate about their club that it hurts. I know it's an old cliché to say they were like the 12th man but they really were helping the team get over the line. When they're in full voice there isn't anywhere in the world better or could equal the atmosphere at St James' Park. For me, they're the best fans I've ever come across.

We had a great team spirit and everyone got on with each other. There were no clicks at Newcastle. Tommy Wright lived near me so I suppose I went out with him more than most. It's funny, people inside the game say you help a team to promotion and you lose your job. It happened to a few of us after we got promoted. That's football. Kevin wanted to kick on and take the team forward, bring new, better players in and he was given money to spend. He let Gavin Peacock go, David Kelly, Kevin Scott, Killer, and myself of course.

Six or seven months before I signed for Tranmere Kevin made me know that they were interested and did I want to sign for them because there was a chance I wouldn't feature much. When a manager says that you think well, I better speak to them. I spoke to John King, the manager, and I was supposed to sign in the August. My wife was pregnant with our third child at the time and I didn't want to leave her to deal with all of that alone. I also wanted to play in the Premier League and see if I could still do it. I managed to get a few games for the club in that time in the Premier League.

In the January, Tranmere came back for me. John King said he was still interested and asked whether I'd come. I had just come back from injury and I wasn't getting back in the team so I decided to go. We were unlucky at Tranmere. We got into three playoffs in a row but didn't quite make it to the Premier League. We had some good players: John Aldridge, Pat Nevin and Gary Stevens.

I was surprised Newcastle didn't win anything under Kevin, given his passion and vision for the club. They were so close in 1995-96 when they were 12 points clear. It's a shame it kind of fell apart at the end. I never wanted a club to win something so much. Unfortunately, it wasn't to be but hopefully, in the future it won't be too long before they finally win something.

Chapter Ten: Gavin Peacock

Born into a Newcastle United-supporting family in South Shields, Gavin Peacock's affection for the club was predestined. As a young boy, his first replica jersey was that of Newcastle United, and as a bairn he idolised the legendary Malcolm MacDonald, proudly wearing a "Supermac" T-shirt.

Peacock joined Newcastle United in 1990 for a somewhat pricey, at the time, £350,000. He made an almost immediate impact under Jim Smith and his successor Ossie Ardiles. Yet it was under Kevin Keegan that the diminutive, tenacious striker fully flourished. Special K told him to go out, express himself and 'drop hand grenades' all over the pitch, as former Liverpool manager Bill Shankly once told KK.

His skill on the pitch, eye for a pass and goal quickly endeared him to the St. James' Park faithful. During his time at the club, he was instrumental in helping the Magpies secure a place in the top tier of English football, becoming a fans' favourite with his spirited performances and crucial goals.

Despite his strong bond with the club and its supporters, Peacock's time at Newcastle was cut short by personal circumstances. After his wife gave birth to their son, Jake, who had a disability, the family needed to be closer to their relatives for support. This profound family need forced Peacock to make the heart-wrenching decision to leave Newcastle United for Chelsea in 1993.

Leaving the club with a heavy heart, Peacock's departure was felt deeply by both the player and the fans. His love for Newcastle United never wavered, and he left a lasting legacy at the club. Gavin Peacock's story is a poignant reminder of the deep connections between players and their clubs and the personal sacrifices that often go unseen in the world of professional football.

Proud Peacock

The first football strip I had was Newcastle United. My

grandparents were from South Shields so I spent quite a lot of time in the North-East as a kid. The family would travel up in the school holidays to see them. I had a Supermac (Malcolm MacDonald) t-shirt as a kid as well. He was my hero. It's unbelievable how things turned out. Who could have predicted that I would later play for Newcastle and captain the club and help us get to the Premier League?

My granddad Tom was quite emotional when I signed for Newcastle. He gave me some simple but great advice. "If you sweat blood for the team the supporters will forgive any mistakes you make on the field. They want to know whether you will die for the team because they would do it."

Those words stayed with me and I did make mistakes and the fans did forgive me.

As a teenager, I was in the same Under-15 England squad as Ian Bogie and Tony Nesbit, a couple of talented Geordies who were great lads. My father Keith, wouldn't allow me to sign for any professional clubs at the time because he told me I was playing too much football. There were a lot of small clubs trying to sign me, cough, like Liverpool, Arsenal, Tottenham, Aston Villa, and QPR, who I eventually signed for. Terry Venables was the manager at the time and they were in the top flight. He was a bright young manager back then. They had some top players such as Tony Currie, John Gregory and Clive Allen. They also had a reputation for bringing young players through as well. I thought I'd stand a better chance of making it as a professional at Loftus Road than anywhere else.

Terry eventually left the club and Jim Smith, who went on to manage Newcastle, came in and gave me my first team debut. I eventually signed on loan for Gillingham, where my dad was the manager. He tapped me over the breakfast table while I was having my Weetabix. He then rang Jim Smith, who he knew quite well as they were friends. The loan turned into a permanent move and my

career started to develop from there. I only stayed there a year and then Harry Redknapp took me to Bournemouth. I was lucky to have my father by my side giving me advice. When Harry showed interest my dad said, “Go, he’s a bright football manager who is on the up and will make it.” It was a record transfer fee for Bournemouth at the time so, there was a lot of pressure on me to perform.
I didn’t stay long at Bournemouth because Newcastle came knocking. It was a normal day of training at Bournemouth and Harry was on the phone. He was always on the phone. You never knew whether he was doing a deal or putting a bet on the dogs or horses. Then after training Harry approached me and said Newcastle have come in for you. As soon as he said it, I thought, this is the club I’ve been waiting for. The manager was Jim Smith, who gave me my debut for QPR. He’d been keeping track of my development as a footballer.

My wife, Amanda, and I had just bought our first house and we’d just fixed it up all nice. I came home and told her Newcastle had come in for me and we had to move. She burst into tears. She asked, ‘Where’s Newcastle?’ I said, ‘It’s up north and it’s cold, but it’s a great club and we’re gonna go.’ Joking aside, we, had three of the happiest years of our lives at Newcastle.

I felt as if I was coming home. At the time, Jim Smith was under a lot of pressure. The previous year he’d lost to Sunderland in the playoffs. Newcastle had some big players at the club when I arrived: Roy Aitken, Mark McGee, Micky Quinn and John Burridge, one of football’s great characters. As I came up to St James’ Park to negotiate the deal, I bumped into Ray Ranson, who said, “Just sign, because if this takes off it will be electric!”

The day before I signed, Jim told me he’d increase my wages, give me a three-year deal and give me a nice signing-on fee. As I got to the ground, he ushered me into his office and then dropped a bombshell saying, ‘The board think I’ve offered you too much money.’ I didn’t know what to do. I was gonna sign anyway but thought I'd talk to my dad first. I couldn't get a hold of him as he was on the training field. I then called the FA, who weren't very helpful so I just said to Jim I would sign on reduced wages but only for 18 months, which was a risk, given I was newly married and could get injured. Jim agreed and a year later, because I'd done well clubs were lining up to take me. I didn't have an agent so my dad always helped me with that side of things.

I was only 22 then and felt as if I was doing well. The fans liked me and I liked them so I wasn't feeling the pressure the way the other lads were. Jim then got sacked or left and Ossie Ardiles came in. At training on the first day, he said he liked me when he was the Swindon manager. He said you're like a diamond but the edges need polishing. He then played me in the diamond formation behind the front two.

Ossie was a lovely man and brought a lot of the young players through. He allowed us to play with freedom. This guy was Diego Maradona's mentor. Ossie had a great amount of football knowledge and wanted to give the Geordie fans the type of football they loved. He indeed did deliver that but we'd end up losing games 4-3 because we weren't good defensively.

We were aware of the takeover by Sir John Hall and the Magpie Group but as young players, these things just rolled off our backs. Ossie and Clarky were very close. He was like a son to Ossie, they'd play fight and stuff like that, jabbing each other. Ossie was hard to understand at times because of that heavy Argentinian accent. Obviously, became obly, in his vocabulary. We were playing at Barnsley one time and the conditions weren't great. The pitch was uneven and rock-hard. Ossie told us that 'The pitch is obly bobbly.' The lads had hands over their mouths trying to keep the laugh in but every one of us loved him and we all grew under him as people and players.

Ossie got sacked on a Saturday, I think it was, and

there were tears around the training ground. I remember driving away thinking, 'Where do we go from here? Who are we going to sign? What is going to happen to the club?' The takeover is still in the background, we're not doing great in the league and we needed someone to turn the ship around and there was, that someone.

I heard we'd signed Kevin Keegan as our next manager on the way home as I was crossing the Tyne Bridge. It was a 'wow' moment. He was my childhood hero. Had his posters on my wall. I remember my dad telling me as a youngster, pointing at Kevin and saying he was a self-made player. He's made the best of what he can be. Look at his attitude, his physique, and he's someone you can emulate. He was one of football's first millionaires. He had everything. Immediately I was excited.

The following day we went to the training ground and he pulled all of the players and he got us together in front of him. He's only like 5ft 7 but his presence made him made him like a giant. He said, 'If any of you want to leave this football club then come and see me in my office afterwards and we'll arrange it. But if you want to stay and fight for this club, we will survive this season and then we will take off. Watch it happen.'

This is exactly what we needed. It inspired me and I get goosebumps just thinking about it. What an inspiration! What a motivator. He'd been away in Marbella for seven years playing golf with the likes of Sean Connery. He'd not seen a match in that time, maybe he watched some on the TV but not live games.

The first game was against Bristol City. I watched him go around the players having a word with them: David Kelly, Liam O'Brien, Lee Clark, and then he got to me. He says, 'You're the man today. Bill Shankly used to say to me, 'Go out there and drop hand grenades all over the place. Go and cause trouble. I was like, 'Wow!' The late great Shankly said that to Keegan and now he's saying it to me. When I ran down that tunnel, I felt 10 feet tall. I didn't score but I ran all day and made two goals. Later on, when Kevin became England manager, Paul Scholes scored a hat-trick against Poland. After the game, Scholes got interviewed where he said (Kevin) the manager was a great motivator of men. He added that he told him something Bill Shankly said to him as a player and go out there and drop hand grenades. And here's me thinking I was special. I'm joking of course.

Kevin said to us that he'd treat us all like men but if we behaved like boys, he would treat us like boys. He could be hard on you if he stepped out of line. He did so with Micky Quinn. Quinny did an article in KK's early days saying something like, 'If Kevin fell in the Tyne he'd come out with a salmon in his mouth.' He called Quinny into his office. He had the article behind him and didn't say anything. Kevin didn't play him much after that. Not sure if it was the article that did it. By the way, I loved playing with Quinny, he was a proper number 9. Kevin then shifted him out.

I think all managers have to be good motivators but there always must be a little fear there as well. Kevin had that. There was one time Kevin played me wide, which I didn't like. I was playing in front of John Beresford, who kept pulling me back and telling me to tuck in. I wanted to get forward and score and Bez is getting me to defend. Kevin shouted something, I said something back, and he said, 'If you don't pull your socks up, you'll be off in a minute.' I was the captain at the time and playing well, scoring goals for fun but he was the boss, so fair enough.

Terry Mac was a great buffer for Kevin and he too was a great motivator. Kevin was clever, he knew who could play off each other. He was trying to get me and Lee Clark to play closer together. He pulled me into his office once and said, 'Look at my team and the balance and harmony, from when the goalkeeper rolls it out to Barry Venison and then Lee Clark comes short. David Kelly goes long and Rob Lee drops in here. The blend was special and it worked well. It was difficult for him when he first came because the pool of players he had to work with wasn't great but he did what he had to do to keep us up by bringing in the likes of Brian Kilcline.

Pavel Srnicek and I signed up within a week of each other and we roomed together. Not many people knew much about him as he came from the Czech Republic. We both stayed at the New Kent Hotel in Jesmond. Pavel was a giant of a guy. He was really humble. It is a quality you can't teach people. He was a great shot-stopper but a bit erratic in the early days. Yet because of his humility, you just knew he was going to be a learner. The years that followed proved that because he went on to do very well and what a cult hero he became. I was in Canada when I heard he died. It was so sad. The fact he had a big heart and he died because of heart complications was a bit ironic. The day we got promotion and did a lap of honour and then he revealed the Pavel is a Geordie t-shirt was such an iconic moment.

I loved playing with David Kelly. Ned was fit, honest, could run the channels, was good in the air and very mobile. Not only that but he scored some very important goals for us and lots of them. Kevin was very good at moving on to the next level. He brought in Andy Cole, who was a razor-sharp player. It took him a few games to settle but after that, he just took off. Then he sold Andy Cole. Where do you go from there? There was only one, Alan Shearer, or two, with Les Ferdinand. People talk about Kevin not being a tactical manager but he sold Cole to bring in Ferdinand and then Shearer, that's a tactical move, isn't it? It showed he had wisdom and a magnetic personality to bring people to the club. Not only people with great ability but with character too.

The promotion season was very special. We won the first 11 games, the last of which was a win at Sunderland. Liam O'Brien scored a great free-kick. He's been dining out on that goal he scored against Sunderland at Roker

Park ever since. He's a great lad, and very funny too. Kevin brought in Venison, Beresford and Bracewell. Three defensive players. Some might have been surprised but he wanted to play out from the back to set the foundations for our attacking ambitions to flow. When we were winning in our promotion season, we couldn't wait for the next game. We were steamrolling teams. They couldn't live with us.

Then after a few games, Kevin brings in Robert Lee for £700,000 from Charlton, which was not only a steal, it was a masterstroke. My dad was at Charlton at the time and Rob was coming toward the end of his contract. Kevin asked me about him. I told him to get Rob Lee, he has all-round ability. He's not reached his full potential yet and my dad rates him highly. Middlesbrough were in for him as well. They were a Premier League team and we were in the old First Division. Their manager was Lennie Lawrence who was a former Charlton manager. He knew Rob very well. Rob had spoken to Boro and was now with Kevin in his office. Rob said he'd like to get home to London now and then and Kevin told him it would be easier to get to London from Newcastle. He told him Newcastle was closer to the south than Middlesbrough and he'd get home sooner. Rob said, 'Oh really? OK, I'll sign.' So, Kevin's superb persuasive nature and Rob's bad geography led him to sign for us. Just look at how he turned out. He was arguably the best pound-for-pound signing Kevin ever made. He got better every game and went on to play for England. He was another down-to-earth guy. I've heard some people say Londoners don't settle in Newcastle but Rob and I did. Rob is an adopted Geordie.

We tore up the league. Teams were afraid of us and we were full of confidence. I felt I could score a goal or make a goal in every game I played. When you got the ball at St James' Park, all of a sudden, the crowd made this roar and it gave you goosebumps. You felt like you were floating on fresh air. There were times when David Kelly or I got the headlines and what Kevin would do is come out and say, 'John Beresford was incredible and will play for England,' or something like that. He would profile the other players so they would get the credit they deserved as well as those making headlines. That helped create a deeper team spirit where we were fighting for each other. In training, the standards were so high. We policed ourselves. Kevin didn't have to say anything because we wouldn't let the standards drop.

The year we got promoted Amanda got pregnant with our first child. As the promotion went on the pregnancy grew, the early flutters and kicking of the belly right up to the last game of the season against Leicester where my unborn son Jake was kicking every ball. Two weeks after that game Amanda goes into labour and it is a very difficult labour. It was a forceps delivery, epidural and then Jake was delivered and I was relieved after 48 hours. He put his arms out and I saw that two-thirds of his right forearm was missing. It was a shock. We only got one scan in those days so we didn't know. We had all of the trauma of the pregnancy and then this. With Limb deficiency there can be other problems like brain, heart and lungs, so we were grateful everything else was alright.

Through all of this Kevin was ringing me and I was keeping him informed. I said to him we might have to move back to London because that's where both our families were and we'd need their help with Jake. Kevin showed great compassion to me and Amanda. He said he didn't want me to leave. He told me he was bringing in Peter Beardsley and spoke about how I would fit in with him and Andy Cole. He said he would understand if I wanted to go back home and added that he wouldn't price me out of the market. Within a month Glenn Hoddle, who was interested in me when he was Swindon's manager, called me as the Chelsea manager. His first phone call was to Newcastle and the fee was £1.25 million, which was a big fee then. Shearer had just recently gone to Blackburn for something like £2.75 million. I said yes to Glenn. He was a good football manager and I believed I would grow under him. Kevin said to me that I would learn more from Glenn Hoddle in training because he is a genius.

It was a bittersweet move because me and Amanda loved it so much in Newcastle. I remember seeing a goals round-up on YouTube not long after that and it shows me in my first game as captain against West Ham. The camera zooms in on me, I take a deep breath as I'm coming out of the tunnel and then the roar of the crowd hits me. I thought, 'It doesn't get much better than this. I'm captain of Newcastle.'

The season before where I scored in a 2-1 win at Leicester to stay up. My grandfather Tom had the first of several strokes so he couldn't go to the game. He was in hospital so I went to see him and gave him my number eight shirt. He couldn't say much but there was a tear in his eye as I gave it to him. When he eventually died a few years later my dad gave me back the shirt. He left a note saying he never washed the shirt because he told my father I had sweated blood for the team. That sums up the family connection that I had in Newcastle and the way I could translate that into my game, and the relationship I had with the fans. Although it wasn't the way I wanted things to end it was a great way to close a chapter on my career.

It was a masterstroke by Glenn Hoddle to get Ruud Gullit to play at Chelsea. He was a fantastic player. He could take two players out and everything he did on the pitch was class but when he became a manager he changed. He'd put the team sheet up in the dressing room and there were times when you'd played the week before but the week after you weren't even on the bench. I was captain at Chelsea and played most of the time under Glenn Hoddle the previous three years. I thought I'd better go and see Ruud and see what was going on. I was in the last year of my contract and at the end of the season I was available on a free transfer. I said I'm happy to be a squad player and fight for my place but if I'm not in your plans we should talk about it. He never spoke to me again after that. I trained with the kids with David Rocastle and John Spenser. We were treated appallingly. It was so bad that Dennis Wise drove to his house and told him that he should try and communicate with the players better.

The difference between the man management of Keegan and Gullit was tangible. They couldn't be further apart. So, it wasn't a surprise when Rob Lee was ostracised. Then he decided to take on Shearer, which is a different kettle of fish. It was a fight I knew he wouldn't win. Would I shake Ruud's hand if I met him now? Yes, I would but it was a difficult time back then but time moves on.

My dream scenario? To come back to Newcastle as the club chaplain with a bit of coaching for the midfield players.

Chapter Eleven: David Kelly

You would be hard-pushed to find another player in the history of Newcastle United who has made a bigger impact than David Kelly. In less than 18 months the Birmingham-born striker netted 35 goals in 70 games as he helped the Magpies stave off relegation before helping fire the Tynesiders to promotion and the Promised Land of the Premier League.

Kelly arrived at St James' Park in December 1991, for a modest £250,000. It has been rumoured Newcastle couldn't afford the fee and manager Ossie Ardiles allegedly loaned United the money. The former West Ham striker arrived at a critical juncture for the Magpies, who were languishing near the bottom of the Second Division and facing the grim prospect of relegation to the third tier for the first time in their history.

Kelly's impact was immediate. His work ethic, determination, and knack of scoring crucial goals quickly endeared him to the St James' Park faithful. The 1991-92 season, as fans remember, was particularly turbulent for Newcastle. With the team teetering on the brink of relegation, the charismatic Kevin Keegan came in to take the reins, infusing the club with new energy and hope. Kelly's contributions during this period cannot be underestimated. His goals and leadership on the pitch were instrumental in stabilising the club during a perilous time. This foundation allowed Keegan to implement his vision, which eventually led to Newcastle's ascent to the Premier League.

Scoring the winner against fierce rivals Sunderland may have ensured legendary status at St James' Park but that goal wasn't as important as the one he netted at home to Portsmouth in the penultimate game of the season 27 days later, on April 25, 1992. Kelly flicked on a long ball by Ray Ranson to Micky Quinn who returned it first time into his path. The Republic of Ireland international struck it first time on the half-volley just inside the 18-yard box, the fans stood open-mouthed in disbelief as time seemed to stop still for a moment just as the net bulged - que bedlam! The noise would've woken the dead in every cemetery on the West Road and a 20-mile radius around the stadium! Had it not been for Kelly's heroics, the club might have faced the ignominy of third-tier football, a scenario that could have dramatically altered the trajectory of the club's history.

Kelly's time on Tyneside culminated with a hat-trick on the last day of the 1992-93 season at St James' Park in a 7-1 win over his former club Leicester. He would be forgiven if he left the pitch whispering, 'My work here is done.'

Kelly's Heroes

Brian Little who was manager of Leicester City at the time left me out of the team. Then, the guy who replaced me scored a hat-trick for City on the Saturday. I went in to see Brian after the weekend and asked why I wasn't playing. He said, 'You haven't scored for seven or eight games so I changed the team around.' I told him if I wasn't playing, I would be leaving because I didn't want to play reserve team football. He said, 'You've only been out of the team for a week, Ned.' I told him that's not the point and wanted to play in the first team.

A week later he phoned to tell me he was going to sell me and three clubs were interested: Sunderland, Wolves and Newcastle. I told my uncle straight after I got the call and he said, 'You've got to go to Newcastle because if you do well there in the No.9 shirt, you'll never be forgotten.' I took my uncle's advice but the irony of the situation was that I ended up playing for all of those clubs. Ossie Ardiles was the manager and Tony Galvin was his right-hand man. I knew Tony from the Republic of Ireland team.

I remember going to the old training ground at Benwell and thinking, 'It's fucking freezing here!' Proper Baltic and bleak! The bizarre thing was that we had a decent team. All the youngsters were coming through and we had the likes of Micky Quinn, Kevin Brock, Gavin Peacock and

Kevin Scott but we couldn't get the results under Ossie. They brought me in to score a few goals to hopefully make sure we avoided relegation.

I got on really well with Ossie. He wanted to play the beautiful game really but we didn't have the lads to implement what he wanted. He was one of the best players in the world in his playing days. He won just about everything as a player. We had all of these wonderful players coming through. You could see Clarky was gonna be special. Alan Thompson was a good player, as was Watto and Steve Howey. They all went on to do something really special for the club but weren't ready at the time for Ossie.

Talk of Kevin Keegan coming in was weird at the time. Sir John Hall was in around the club at the time and he was trying to make things happen. When we heard the rumours of Kevin coming in, we were thinking, 'Why? What has he been doing over the past several years? What club has been at? Where has he been coaching?' A lot of it was disbelief and that wasn't just the players, it was from the fans and some of my close friends at the time. Hats off to him though. He managed to turn things around.

Training under Kevin was brilliant! It was small-sided games and finishing. It was as if we just needed to score more goals than the opposition and I was thinking, 'This is right up my street.' Kevin used to join in and was still pretty decent despite being on a golf course for several years. Derek Fazackerley was a very important member of the group. He did all of the coaching, set plays and defensive work. Faz knew all of the intricacies of football. Kevin on the other hand made sure everybody was happy and promoted the fun and feel-good factor around the club. He made sure we were confident enough to beat whoever we were playing.

All players have habits or superstitions if you like, whether it is putting your left boot on before your right boot. I used to get to the ground really early. I'm a bugger for not being late. I hate it. I remember coming in early for

Kevin's first game at home to Bristol City and there were thousands of fans swarming around the ground. Normally you wouldn't see anybody that early. I thought none of the lads would be able to get parked. I kind of realised then that things were going to change and this was different. The expectation levels automatically changed after the Bristol City game from doom to hope after we beat them comfortably, 3-0. The expectation had changed, despite us being in a relegation battle. It was as if a magician had turned up to change our fortunes

A derby game is the best game to play as a player, regardless of which club you play for because it means so much to the supporters. I'm a West Brom fan yet I do commentaries for Wolves and the Wolves versus West Brom games were great, as are the Blues versus Aston Villa, Liverpool versus Everton and Newcastle, Sunderland. These are proper derbies as are the others all over the country.

I was lucky enough to score in a 1-0 win over Sunderland at St James' Park. Liam O'Brien's goal at Roker Park is one of the best goals I've been involved in football. It was an unbelievable moment. The feeling at the time was euphoric. If anyone says, 'It's just another goal' is talking a load of bollocks. They are extra special, especially when you win. Saying that, my favourite Newcastle goal is the one I scored against Portsmouth which more or less ensured we would stay up. It was a special goal.

It's weird because for years I thought I'd smashed it into the top corner from outside the box. I never scored many outside the box. Most of my goals were inside the box between six and 10 yards. Then I saw a video of the goal a couple of years back and realised I was five yards inside the 18-yard box.

Kevin's team talks were very simple. It was a case of, 'We have better players than they have.' He would add, 'We're going to close the ball down very quickly. He'd tell me and Gavin Peacock not to track back, which was unusual for me because I was always full of running. I'd like to harry people and force them into mistakes.

Gav and I were both goalscorers and we'd often have words with each other if one of us didn't pass to the other. So, yes, we did fall out with each other at times but it was only because we wanted the team to do well. There were loads of times when we could have passed to each other because we were in better positions but we were both selfish strikers. I absolutely love him. He is a lovely human being, a great lad. In the first year, Gavin Peacock was the best player at the club. He was a really intelligent player. In the second year, it was Clarky, he was so reliable. I think it was us two that played the most games that season.

In the promotion season, just before the end of that campaign just look at the quality of players Kevin brought in, the likes of Andy Cole and Scott Sellars. Before that, he brought in Kevin Sheedy and Brian Kilcline to help keep us in the league. Then he got Rob Lee, and what a player he was by the way. The pre-season after we stayed up was very important. Kevin brought in Bez, Paul Bracewell and Barry Venison. He brought in quite a few new faces who were quality signings. We still had the gang of young players but he brought in seasoned professionals. The expectations rose because of that and we knew we were going to be challenging for promotion.

We won our first 11 games of the new season. Who does that? Nobody. That was simply because of the business Kevin had done in the summer. We were a much stronger, balanced team all over the pitch after the summer. Kevin then added Andy Cole around March time. I remember his first training session. He scored something like five goals in one of the games. Straight away I thought, 'This kid is the real deal.' And he was. He was a magnificent goalscorer.

We crowned the championship title at home to Leicester City, my former club, with a 7-1 win and I scored a hat-trick. I've still got the match ball in my garage. I had a really good time at Leicester and kind of rebuilt my career. Before that, I was at West Ham and didn't have the best of times there. It was always a difficult game for me because I knew most of the staff and a lot of their players. Kind of ironic how it turned out that the last game of the promotion season was against Leicester and the last game of the relegation fight was against Leicester.

We won promotion weeks before the season ended and we partied for weeks too. I remember clinching promotion at Grimsby. On the way back Kevin stopped the team bus at a pub but it was closed. But being handed the trophy on the last day of the season in front of our supporters was really special. There are hundreds of pictures of the day and when you look at the quality of that team to the one the season before was vast. There were quality players in the team that were going to do well in the Premier League.

My leaving the club was bittersweet. I didn't want to leave because I loved it at Newcastle but it was kind of funny at the same time. I was driving home to Birmingham with my wife, Claire and my son Zac, after we won the league. They were in the back and my hat-trick ball was in the front with me. Then I got a call from Kevin out of the blue.

'Alright Ned?'

'Yes, fine, gaffer.'

'Where are you going?'

'I'm going home for a couple of weeks.'

'Come in and see me.'

'I'm not turning the car around and driving another hour and a half. What's happening? Are you selling me?'

I just had this feeling he was going to sell me at the moment. I don't know why.

'Pull off the motorway, I need to have a proper chat with you.'

I pulled over and I'm thinking, 'He's fucking selling me. My language is terrible at the best of times and I'm effing and jeffing while I'm trying to pull off the motorway. Kevin then called me back.

'Look, we've had a brilliant season but em, well, I've had a couple of bids for you. I know you will be a bloody nightmare if you're a substitute for me. I know you won't play reserve team football. You only want to play in the first team.'

'Who is in for me?'

'Can't tell you yet.'

'Who are you signing?'

'Can't tell you that.'

'Well, I'm not going then.'

'What do you mean, you're not going?'

'I'm not going. I'm not going until you tell me who you're signing.'

'I can't, it's not been sorted out yet.'

'OK, then I'm not going.'

So, we had a bit of an argument and we put the phone down on each other. He phoned back a few hours later and told me to calm down a bit and said Forest and Wolves were interested. I told him I'd go and speak to them but added I wasn't going to sign for anyone unless he gave me my signing-on fee and all my money. He said he wasn't going to do that so I slammed the phone down on him again, telling him I wasn't going until he told me who he was signing. He kept on saying he couldn't tell me and I told him I wouldn't tell anyone.

'I'm signing Peter Beardsley.'

'Fuck me, gaffer, I'd sign Peter Beardsley instead of David Kelly.'

He burst out laughing and said, 'Are you gonna speak to them?'

'Yeah, I've got 12 months left on my contract and I've got a few bits and bobs to work out with my money. Fair play, you're only getting better players in.'

I even turned to my ball and said, 'Peter Beardsley! How

good is he?'
The ball didn't say anything. And that was it. He was trying to get better players in and Peter Beardsley was a better player than me.

I still kept an eye on the scores when I left and went to a couple of games. I was as gutted as the fans when Newcastle missed out on winning the Premier League title. Man United won it because they had a better group. It doesn't matter what people say, whether it was, 'We should have done this, we should have done that, we were unlucky,' etc. During the build-up, you're making decisions all for the right reason but the best group always wins the league. It's like when we won the Championship in 93, we were the best group by a country mile. Man United were the best group that year just as Man City have had a few years where they've had the best group.

The be-all and end-all of any club is the supporters. They are the only constant. Owners and players come and go and managers come and go. The supporters, the faithful, are always there, supporting. Like I said, I didn't want to leave because I loved it at Newcastle but understood what Kevin was trying to do.

Chapter Twelve: Micky Quinn

The iconic No. 9 jersey has often been a burden for many wearers in the past, as they struggled to shoulder the weight of expectation and history. This cannot be said of Gallowgate favourite Micky Quinn, a £680,000 Jim Smith buy from Portsmouth on the eve of the 1989-90 campaign. Quinn embraced the famous shirt and proved himself a worthy wearer, announcing his arrival in true swashbuckling style by netting four goals on his home debut in a 5-2 win against fellow promotion favourites Leeds United. It permanently endeared him to the St James' Park faithful and immediately cemented his place among Newcastle's iconic No.9 wearers.

The Liverpool-born sharp-shooter plundered 34 league goals during his debut season as the Magpies narrowly missed out on promotion following a play-off semi-final defeat to fierce rivals Sunderland. Injury then robbed Newcastle of his services for the large part of his second season, during which manager Smith was replaced by Ossie Ardiles. Without Quinn's goals, United slid toward the third tier. By the time he regained full fitness Newcastle legend Kevin Keegan was in the manager's hot seat. Unfortunately, the pair didn't see eye-to-eye after a newspaper article appeared to criticise Keegan and Quinn was largely ostracised from the side.

Quinn still played a part of the club's blistering start to the 1992-93 season weighing in with several important goals before the popular striker was moved on by Keegan after 59 goals in 115 appearances. The fans' favourite confessed he didn't want to leave the club and despite his treatment, still looks back fondly on his time on Tyneside.

The Mighty Quinn

I knew the kids coming through were special and Ossie knew that as well. That is why he introduced them to the first team and first-team football. He wanted me to lead them so he made me club captain. Ossie was told to get rid of all the experienced players, such as Mark McGee and Roy Aitken. In the end, there weren't many of the more experienced pros left. It was probably me and Benny Kristensen. Ossie told me to take them under my wing and look after them so I introduced them to the Big Market and Quayside. It didn't do them any harm, did it?

Lee Clark was my apprentice so I got to know him before he came and trained with us. It was only a matter of time before they made their first team appearances. I played in Watto's debut when he did that summersault throw-in. He got such a bollocking off Ossie for that after the game. I think it was just a shame we didn't have more experienced players around to help the kids. I got injured and there was no one really to help. I remember Clarky going down the left, crossing it and I scored but I collided with a post and did my cruciate ligament and that was that. It was the start of the slide. We just couldn't defend.

Defending wasn't in Ossie's makeup. We lost on penalties in one game to Tranmere in the Zenith Data Cup after it finished 6-6. Me and John Aldridge got a hat-trick each. Ossie didn't last long after that and Kevin Keegan came in. I knew Kevin through Mick Channon and Alan Ball, my old boss at Portsmouth, and the horses. Kevin was also my hero as a kid growing up in Liverpool. I'd met him three or four times. I also knew Terry Mac from his Liverpool days.

I felt gutted for Ossie because three months or so isn't enough time to build a team. I think it was Douglas Hall who pressed the panic button but the writing was on the wall. I didn't know what Kevin was doing after he retired at that time. He came into a big fanfare. He was a hero at the club and it was like the Second Coming. I was injured when he arrived. He told me he wanted me back as quickly as I could but with a cruciate injury, it takes time not only to get over the injury but to get your sharpness back. Kevin put me in straight away but I wasn't ready. I was like a ghost. I wasn't there. I was a bit better in the next game against Swindon and got the winner. That was when Kevin actually buggered off after the game.

Kevin was super clever. He made sure he won before he fucked off down the road to his home in Southampton. He was lured back after a few reassurances from Sir John Hall. He dropped me and then I got on against Portsmouth and managed to flick the ball on for Ned Kelly to score and we won 1-0. That was the game that kept us up, although we thought we still had to go to Leicester and win, we managed to stay up that season.

I did an interview with the press, and I've always been honest in interviews, and I've said that Kevin was still finding his feet as a manager and finding out about the division which he knew little about. How could he? He was playing golf for seven years in Spain. He was on a learning curve. Kevin took what I said personally. What I said made big headlines in the tabloid press. Kevin accused me of taking money for the interview, which I didn't and I told him that. He then dropped me.

The following season he called me into his office and we made up, although I hadn't fallen out with him. He told me that I was popular with the fans and they loved me. He also said he was going to sign some good players and get promotion, which he did. I couldn't hold down a place in the team in the following season, even though I'd score every time I played or got back in the side. I'd score then get dropped the next game. I'd score again and then get dropped again. I played against Portsmouth at home and I scored two goals and it should have been three, one goal got disallowed. It was the best I'd ever played in my life, that is nearly 600 games as a professional. My link-up play, my touch and the team played some brilliant football. Then I was dropped for the next game. It was then that I knew that he still had a bug about the interview I did. I kind of knew my time was up. He then sold me to Coventry.

We started the season like a house on fire winning the first 11 games and playing some fantastic football. We had a sticky patch where we didn't score a goal for a couple of games and I went to see him before we played Charlton. I asked if I was in the team and he said no. I then asked if I was going to be a sub and he said no. I said you might as well let me play for the reserves so I can keep sharp and ready if anyone gets injured or suspended. He then turned it around and asked whether I was refusing to travel with the Newcastle United squad. I said no, that's not the case. He then repeated the line so I repeated my line about trying to stay sharp. In the end, I told him to fuck off because I knew I couldn't win the argument. I did get back in the squad but then Coventry came in for me. I didn't really want to go but it happened that quickly and he couldn't wait to get rid of me.

It's a big regret I didn't get to say goodbye to the fans or the players as he literally sent me to Coventry, on and off the pitch. I did keep my eye on what was going on at St James' Park because I knew we'd get promoted. We played some beautiful football that season. I went to Coventry and I saw Kevin's face on every ball I smashed into the back of the net. As a professional, you want to prove people wrong and I wanted him to know he'd made a mistake letting me go.

Kevin later told me that every time he'd switch on the TV, he'd see my name and that I'd scored another goal in the Premier League. Apparently, he stopped answering the phone to Sir John because he kept asking why he'd got rid of me. Sir John didn't want me to go. He sent me a lovely letter after I left saying he appreciated everything I did for the club. He disagreed with what Kevin had done but he had to stand by his manager. He didn't have to do that but it was a lovely touch from a lovely man.

With the likes of Clarky, Watto, Howey and Robbie Elliot I knew they had the makings of a fantastic team. It was no surprise Newcastle got promoted. Kevin had the financial backing and he just kept adding fantastic players to the squad, such as Andy Cole. Kevin was never afraid of dropping players as well. When Coley came, he dropped

Ned and then Gavin Peacock was moved on and they signed Peter Beardsley for £1.5 million, which was cheap as chips. You can't argue about the quality of Beardsley. Newcastle played free-flowing football, which the fans loved and they went from strength to strength. I'd pay good money, as in going through the turnstiles, to watch good football. I'd pay to see a Pep Guardiola team, a Jurgen Klopp team, and I'd pay to watch Kevin Keegan's Entertainers. I especially loved Newcastle spanking Man United 5-0, being a Liverpool fan. That Newcastle side had style and grace and it was such a shame they didn't win the league.

Why didn't Newcastle in the league? There were a number of factors. Tino Asprilla, although he was a top-class player, I think he upset the balance of the team. Tino was a maverick and scored some unbelievable goals but I don't think he was a team player. Another reason was David Batty coming in to replace Lee Clark. Clarky was at the top of his game for me and a very underrated player in my book. Clarky could create. He could score. He was a bundle of energy and I thought he brought more to the table than Batty. The balance of the side wasn't quite right when he took over from Clarky for the last 10, 11 games. Clarky should have played, for me. Maybe Faz going as well played a part as he was the one who did all the defensive side of the game for the team.

The 4-3 game epitomises everything about Newcastle and Kevin at that time. They'd score and take the lead but they couldn't sit on it. The attitude was, 'Let's get another goal and another goal.' It was an astonishing game.

Ironically, Ossie's training was light years ahead of Kevin's training. Kevin was all simple five-a-sides which was the Liverpool way. It certainly worked for them over the years. I loved Ossie's training and looked forward to going in every day. A lot of people think Kevin is a lovely fella, and rightly so, but he did have a steely side to him. He would give a bollocking and he wore his heart on his sleeve. The first three- or four-months Kevin was learning on his feet and he'd make a lot of changes to find a way to keep us up. After that, the following season, he didn't have a lot to moan about because we won most of our games and we were top of the league. I would love to have been part of it but it wasn't to be but I still look back on my time at Newcastle with great affection.

Sir John Hall announces Kevin Keegan's arrival

Pavel Srnicek on Tynemouth Longsands

Lee Clark beats Nigel Clough to the ball

David Kelly and Lee Clark celebrate promotion

Main image:
Mick Quinn ready to pounce

Paul Ferris and Derek Wright
in the treatment room

Rob Lee
midfield maestro

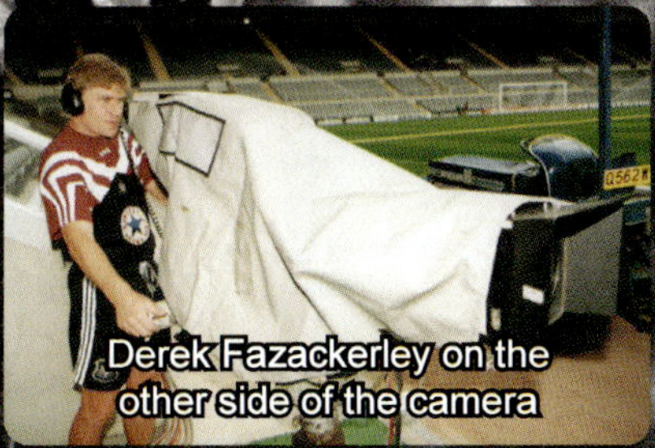

Derek Fazackerley on the
other side of the camera

Barry Venison and Paul Bracewell rooming together

Darren Peacock in typical action

Main image:
Andy Cole and Scott Sellars celebrate

Marc Hottiger clears the ball

Ruel Fox blows out the candles on his birthday cake

Main image:
John Beresford beating his man again

Keith Gillespie celebrating another goal

Warren Barton in the Centre Parcs shirt that was only worn once by the team

Les Ferdinand training with a medicine ball

Tino Asprilla enjoying some down time

John Beresford, Les Ferdinand and Rob Lee on international duty

Ruel Fox, John Beresford, Rob Lee, Lee Clark, Scott Sellars and Warren Barton admire Shaka Hislop's new car

Philippe Albert looking for another goal

Main image:
Post match reflection with David Ginola

Main image:
Another goal for Alan Shearer

Rob Lee, Lee Clark, Robbie Elliot, Steve Watson, Keith Gillespie, and Peter Beardsley in a new kit photoshoot

Chapter Thirteen: Derek Wright

Derek Wright's tenure as a physio at Newcastle United is the stuff of legend. Recruited by former boss Jack Charlton over dinner, the meeting was far from ordinary. Big Jack regaled Wright with several fishing stories more enthralling than the Jaws franchise and, by the end of the meal, Wright was hooked and thus began a journey over choppy waters that would span four decades.

Wright joined Newcastle in 1984 and quickly became an indispensable part of the backroom team, known for his dedication and expertise. His 'magic, healing hands' worked wonders on countless players, helping them recover swiftly and effectively from injuries. Over the years, he saw the club through its highs and lows, the most memorable, of course, were the rollercoaster days of The Entertainers under Kevin Keegan.

His commitment to the club and its players went beyond just physical treatment. Wright was a calming presence in the dressing room, offering support and encouragement during challenging times. Players trusted him implicitly, knowing they were in the best possible hands.

Despite his professional prowess, Wright had his lighter moments too. Infamously, his magic failed him off the pitch when, dressed as a pink fairy on a Magpies squad Christmas night out, he tried to flag down a taxi with his wand but found himself powerless. This amusing anecdote highlights the human side of a man who dedicated his career to keeping Newcastle United's players in peak condition. Wright's humble legacy at the club is one of unwavering commitment, expertise, and with a touch of humour.

The Wright Stuff

I was an apprentice at Arsenal when I was 16, when Malcolm 'Supermac' MacDonald was the star player but unfortunately didn't make it as a professional. I was quite interested in medicine at school and the Arsenal physio at the time was Fred Street, who was also the England physio. I used to badger him all the time, asking questions about medicine and he thought that I should study it as I seemed to have a flair for it. Once I knew I wasn't going to make it as a professional I decided to concentrate on sports science and physio work.

My first job was at Fulham when Malcolm MacDonald was manager. I knew Malcolm from my Arsenal days. Fred Street gave Malcolm a call when I passed my physio exams and asked him to take a chance on me. I was about 23 at that time and Fulham was in the old Third Division.

I arrived at Newcastle in 1984 but I do remember a few games Fulham had with Newcastle when I was there. The old grey away strip sticks out in my memory. Kevin and Terry Mac played in one game at Craven Cottage. I think it was a 2-2 draw but Fulham beat Newcastle at St James' Park, 4-1 that season. It was amazing because the Newcastle fans applauded Fulham off the pitch after the game. I'd never seen anything like it. It was amazing. There are not many home crowds who would do that.

I remember all of the young lads coming through under Ossie Ardiles: Lee Clark, Steve Watson, Steve Howey, Robbie Elliot and Alan Thompson. You don't realise at the time how good they were and how important they were to the club and what they went on to achieve. They were then bled into the team and when they got there, I thought, 'Hey, these lads are decent and they were all Geordies.' Being a local lad myself, it was great to see.

All of the lads were good in their own right and had their individual personalities but Lee Clark seemed to have something more about him. I remember seeing him as an 11-year-old at Benwell and he stood out from the rest. He was also a bit of a cheeky Charlie. He hated getting beat or losing, something that resonated with me. Later on, when he was an apprentice, I gave him a job to do and he ripped up my treatment room floor. He had one job, buffer the floor and he forgot to put the pad on the machine and ripped the floor up. He kept repeating, 'I'm sorry Mr Wright, I'm sorry Mr Wright.' Apart from that, he was a good lad. I kind of knew he would do well in the future.

It was disbelief when I heard the news Kevin was coming in as manager. I was thinking, 'Surely not. But at the same time, I thought, 'Brilliant, if it's true.' The excitement of what could happen over the next few weeks was brilliant, never mind the next few years. The feeling was unique because it rarely happens in football, that feeling of positivity and that we're going to do it. We're going to get out of this relegation scrap. Kevin created that belief. Then it snowballed and once it started no one could stop it. My biggest worry was that Kevin was going to get us out of trouble and not be there the following season to carry on.

Kevin came to me just before we signed Paul Bracewell and told me he was going to sign him. I asked whether he wanted me to do a medical. He said he knew his ankles were shot but there was no need because he'd played 40 games the previous season. So, if he did that the previous season then he's pretty much gonna do it again. Whereas if another player has played three or four games then it will most likely be the same again. We knew Paul was gonna be alright but we would still have to look after him. We would bag him full of ice and then roll him out for another game and he was generally fantastic for us and never let us down.

I remember training at Maiden Castle very well. I told my kids that between 3,000 and 5,000 people used to turn up and watch us train. They'd go, 'Yeah, right, dad.' They don't believe me. The burger and ice cream vans used to turn up and the fans were entertained. It was a fantastic time. Going into training was great. Kevin and Terry would be there early challenging everybody to a game of head tennis and squash football, would you believe? I remember playing squash football against Kevin, and getting absolutely battered by him. Everything was so enjoyable.

Everything was going well and when things were going well there were rarely any injuries. I remember Kevin, jokingly, saying he was gonna have to make me redundant because I didn't have anyone to treat. Faz was involved a lot in training and we'd both prepare for pre-season training. Faz would often come and ask my advice, which was much appreciated. We rarely got any injuries in training.

There's a myriad of reasons why players get injured. I know boots have changed and got lighter as the years have gone on but I don't think they play a part in injuries in the modern game. Under Kevin, we had a bunch of robust players who enjoyed training and playing and hated being injured and being in the treatment room. It was a joy to be around those players during that period. They weren't hiding or trying to hide. They wanted to be on the training pitch and the field. We had injuries of course but they were rarely serious under Kevin and they were relatively short-term. Peter Beardsley suffered a depressed fractured cheekbone after a challenge by Neil Ruddock in a friendly but he was another who was rarely injured. He had a small knee operation one time but he was playing a couple of weeks later.

Not winning the Premier League is one of the biggest disappointments of the club's modern history. I can't answer why we failed to win the league that year. As I get older, I've often thought, 'If only we did that,' or 'did this.' It was devastating. It took me a long time to get over it never mind the players. I remember Man United just kept on going, nicking games, Schmeichel was unbelievable and Cantona would be popping up all of the time scoring goals. We had a couple of bad results and the snowball slowed down, and for whatever reason we just didn't carry it on. Although we missed out, I was convinced we would win it within the next couple of years. Unfortunately, that didn't happen.

I was shocked, like everyone, when Kevin left but I also knew that if things weren't right for him, he'd leave. It was an incredible five years with him. I remember Arthur Cox telling me to remember these times because this only comes once in a lifetime. I looked at him at the time and didn't understand what he was on about. Obviously, with the benefit of hindsight and the years that have passed since, I understand what he meant. Kevin was great to me. He did a lot for me as a person. He wasn't just a great manager, he was a man's man and so honest. He lifted everyone with his bubbly personality and his leaving was sad, more than anything else.

Of all the games played during the Entertainers' era, I reckon the 7-1 home win over Leicester City at home in the promotion season stands out. The game away at Bolton stands out as well. We won 3-1 in the season we missed out on the title. Also, the home game against Portsmouth where David Kelly scored in a 1-0 win ultimately kept us in the second tier. Then there are games when I felt really bad, the 4-3 away defeat to Liverpool. It was horrific. Then on the other side of the coin is the 5-0 home win over Man United. They beat us 4-0 in the Charity Shield and to be honest, I was shattered from the trip to Thailand and Japan and I'm sure the players were tired as well because they were flat on the day. Once we recharged, we picked up again resulting in that 5-0 hammering. I had a feeling that we would win every game at that time and I've never had that feeling since. Goals were flying in from everywhere. Yes, we conceded a few but we generally scored more than the other teams and won.

Kevin was very hands-on, interested in what you were doing and let you get on with it. He didn't interfere with your decisions e.g., if you went to him and said, 'Gaffer, this player isn't ready, we should give him a few more days.' He never once questioned my decisions. For a long time, I was working on my own and he asked if I needed any help and that's when we brought in Ferra (Paul Ferris). He would ask you about your personal life and take a real interest. The banter was unbelievable. That was a massive part of the everyday and Terry Mac played a big part in that. He would always rib me about my weight and we'd have bets about me losing weight. It was all good fun, no malice.

He'd write me letters fining me for something and address it to the Billy Bunter Physiotherapy Society. The banter was flying when everyone was around but one-on-one he was very supportive towards me. He rang me when I retired and said I should be proud of what I achieved and I got quite emotional about the call. It meant so much to me to be appreciated. I saw him recently and he hasn't changed. Just the same.

Terry Mac was really important to Kevin. It was like a marriage. He'd often pop in and see me. He called me Del-Boy and he would ask if there was any injury news so he could report back to Kevin. Terry was probably the biggest Mickey-takers at the club, regularly ripping you to pieces. Then Kevin would chip in, 'Terry, you can't say that.' Then he'd be backing him up. They were like a double act, Morecambe and Wise.

I was aware of the fans cheering me on whenever a player went down. There was one time when the opposition physio was going to see to one of his players and the crowd were cheering me on. I was fully aware of it and thought there was no way I was gonna let the other guy beat me. Then it became a kind of cult thing. The lads then got involved and started blocking the other physio to ensure I'd win the race. I thought to myself that I needed to stop being selfish but once it started, I couldn't stop.

There wasn't one player I loved more than others because I loved them all but without evading the question I'd say that the whole group under Kevin's time, were my favourite players. The thing for me is that when Newcastle have been successful, there's been a good team spirit. They've gone out together as a group and had meals, a few drinks and they used to bring me, Ferra and Tommo (Ray Thompson) and Faz with them. That team spirit was really important and not to be underestimated.

Chapter Fourteen: Brian Kilcline

Hailed as "the most important signing" Kevin Keegan ever made for the club, Brian Kilcline quickly endeared himself to Newcastle United supporters for his never-say-die attitude and full-blooded commitment to stopping the Magpies from sliding into the third tier of English football for the first time in the Tyneside club's history.

The £250,000 signing from Oldham Athletic describes his two years at Newcastle as the "best of his career." That's some statement considering Killer lifted the FA Cup with Coventry City in 1987 and wasn't a regular in Keegan's side as the Magpies plotted a way back to the Promised Land of the Premier League.

The uncompromising centre-half is far from your typical footballer. Resembling more of a Viking warrior, or a Lord of the Rings character, than an FA Cup-winning captain, Killer showcased his warrior spirit while weaving spells on opposing strikers shouting, 'Thou shalt not pass!' as he magically steered the Newcastle ship to safety.

Killer relished his time on Tyneside. The former Sky Blues captain admits he still gets butterflies and goose-bumps every time he approaches Washington services and gets a glimpse of the Angel of the North, the Tyne Bridge and the cathedral on the hill. You know which one.

Killer firmly believes Newcastle should have won the Premier League in the club's first return to the top flight in 1993, admits he left St James' Park with tears in his eyes, and reveals the true story behind ponytailgate.

The Life of Brian

We should have won the Premier League in our first season after promotion. We were that good. The team had that element of surprise, as in, nobody knew us. It happens a lot with new clubs that go up. They do well in the first half of the season before being found out in the second half of the season because teams, coaches and managers are more familiar with the way they play and can combat it. The better teams can carry it through until the end of the season that is why I believe we should have won the league. We could have done it and nearly did it a couple of years later.

I was at the crossroads at Oldham, in a state of existential crisis and not sure what to do. Then I received a call from Kevin asking whether I'd like to come to Newcastle for talks and help keep us in, what was, the old Second Division. I didn't go to (Oldham boss) Joe Royle or (coach) Willie Donachie and ask to leave. I'm guessing Kevin phoned the club because how else would he have got my number?

The call from Keegan was memorable because I could hear Terry McDermott chirping away in the background. There was such a jollity surrounding the conversation. It was like listening to a couple of enthusiastic school kids. Keegan said, 'Come up and have a game.' It was like you'd got a call from one of your mates and he'd said, 'Fancy a kick around down the Rec?' They were so bubbly and positive. It radiated down the phone. At the time I wasn't playing in the first team at Oldham so it was nice. I thought, 'I'll have some of this.'

I didn't even look to see where Newcastle was in the league. Kevin Keegan had phoned me up and asked if I wanted to play. That was enough for me. I didn't get a signing-on fee and I signed for less money than I got at Oldham to come to the club but there were a lot of bonuses included such as keeping the team up, promotion etc.

I phoned Lynn, my girlfriend at the time who later became my wife, jumped straight in the car and as we were approaching Washington Services I thought, 'What's going on here?' I started to get goosebumps, and butterflies and the adrenaline started to pump the nearer we got to Newcastle. As soon as we arrived at the ground it hit me like a tonne of bricks. The nerves were all tingling, my stomach was churning and I couldn't wait to pull on the black and white shirt and get out there. I'm like this before every game and I won't settle down until I've either headed it, kicked it or twatted someone.

I trained on the day I signed, which was a Friday, to blow the cobwebs away because we played Barnsley the following day. I trained with the kids and I was happy as a pig in shit. I was playing football and there were all these good players surrounding me. I didn't get a sense of doom and gloom around the place or that the players were feeling sorry for themselves. The young lads were all full of beans. You'd never guess we were in the mire.

After training Kevin asked how I felt. I said, 'Great. The youth team aren't bad, are they?" Keegan replied, 'That's not the youth team. That's the first team.' I said, "You're joking!" There didn't seem to be any of the seniors there, like Micky Quinn or David Kelly.

Initially, I came because of Kevin Keegan but then, when I got to the ground and pulled up at the big gates, it hit me. The ground is immense. I got it immediately. I was used to playing at Notts County which was a small ground with old wooden terracing. At Coventry, they had a compact ground but it wasn't in your face the way St James' Park is. Then Keegan and McDermott come bounding down the steps like a couple of kids in the playground to greet me. You can't help but be impressed by how welcome I was.

I can't remember what the conversation was but I initially signed on a month's loan. This eventually caused a row between Keegan and the board. He wanted to sign me permanently. It caused Kevin to walk out after the Swindon match because there was no money to sign me. It prompted the manager to say, 'It wasn't like the brochure.' I remember it all kicking off before the Swindon game because I was stopping in the Gosforth Park Hotel, with Keegan and McDermott. Lynn had gone down to get a pot of tea and the staff had told her Kevin wasn't happy with things. I'm not sure if Sir John Hall was there or not but the gaffer and his assistant checked out of the hotel on Friday night and decided they weren't coming back. It was all resolved within a day or so after the match. The board were playing politics with each other at the time, so I'm led to believe, and Sir John Hall didn't have full control of the club at the time.

Ironically, I never had much to do with Sir John Hall, despite the fact his Mrs lent him the money to buy me from Oldham, so the story goes. We went to his house a couple of times for a Christmas party or an end-of-season do but that was it. Although I did bump into him not long ago and he came straight over to me and shook my hand, which was a nice thing to do. I've never mixed with any of the directors or chairman of any club I've played for. Never wanted to be part of the politics, wanted to play football and have some craic with the lads.

Keegan was very determined and set in his ways about how things should be done correctly. He had the place fumigated the week before I arrived and had showers put in. Although Benwell was fine, it wasn't good enough for what he wanted so it was no surprise we moved to Maiden Castle and Chester-le-Street.

Keegan wasn't too enamoured with the open-top bus tour of Newcastle after we'd won the league. He thought it was ridiculous because we hadn't won anything of note. That was the measure of the man's high standards and the success he craved. He was also big on families and that the wives and girlfriends were all looked after. Aside from the serious stuff, which to be fair, they were few and far between, both Kevin and Terry were very funny guys and Keegan could tell a great tale.

As a matter of fact, there was a funny tale that came out just as we were about to play Grimsby. Kevin and Terry had been down to watch the Mariners before our game. Just before the match, they stopped off for a curry and, while they were watching our next opponents, Terry couldn't stop farting. The Lady Mayor was sitting alongside them in the stands. Keegan and McDermott were telling me this story when they got back much to my amusement. Lynn thought this was hilarious and decided to write a letter from the Lady Mayor to Kevin Keegan and left it for him in the Gosforth Park Hotel.

The letter more or less said, 'How nice it was to see Mr Keegan and Mr McDermott at the game but pointed out that one of us needed to visit a doctor to resolve our problem with flatulence.' Terry would always pick up the mail before breakfast and his face was a picture when he opened the letter. He nudged Kevin and they were whispering and giggling at the same time. Lynn kept it a secret for a week or so before she let the cat out of the bag.

There was such a lovely feeling at the club. It was like I was at home. Being back at home for me is being in the house I was brought up in with my parents, brothers and sisters. I don't know why but it is a lovely feeling when all of the family is gathered. I get the same feeling every time I go back to Newcastle. It was meant to be for me to move to Newcastle. It was like sitting in a comfy chair. Everyone from the receptionist, and tea lady to all the staff, they were all lovely people. There was no moaning about how bad things were, and the club at the time was in bad shape. They could have whinged on but they didn't. It was all positive.

I remember Keegan very well from my playing days. We (Notts County) had just been promoted to Division One and were due to play Southampton. The coach, Howard Wilkinson, pulled me to one side before the game and said, 'Keegan has just come back from Germany. Show him what he's been missing and kick fuck out of him.'

'No worries,' I replied. I went out onto the pitch and when the final whistle blew at the Dell, we'd lost 3-1 and Keegan had scored two.

Wilkinson asked, 'What happened?'

I said 'I couldn't get near him.' Every time I pulled my leg back to kick him, he'd gone! Everything was one touch with him. I got murdered that day. Keegan also got the goal in the return game at Meadow Lane in a 1-1 draw.

They were top of the league at the time.

Keegan didn't do any of the coaching. That was down to Derek Fazackerley. Kevin was more like a motivator. Faz would do the warm-ups and set pieces. More often than not it was a glorified five-a-side game. The games were brutal, incredibly competitive and intense. If you dallied on the ball, you'd get snapped in two. And because the players we had were so good we could do it. The intensity wasn't as high at the weekend so when we came to play on a Saturday it was a lot easier.

Kevin liked to see how the players could handle playing at such a high standard. In the past, there were some shocking trainers. I wasn't the best in training unless there was a ball. Some players held back during the week and let it all out on a Saturday. Then other players were brilliant in training but shit on a Saturday.

Kevin and Terry Mac were great at watching players and if they weren't training well or underperforming, they'd know there was something up and they'd pull the player into the office for a chat. Brian Clough was another manager who was great at this. Cloughy's sides were always filled with young kids who didn't worry about the world. He'd have a couple of old heads around them like an Archie Gemmill, John O'Hare or John McGovern. This would allow the kids to just go out and play and the older pros would look after them. Sometimes you can overthink football and that's when it becomes complicated.

Keegan had a tough job at Newcastle but Terry Mac was the perfect foil for him. People have questioned Terry's role because he wasn't a coach but he was someone Kevin could bounce ideas off. He was also another set of eyes for the manager. Sometimes Terry would see things the gaffer had missed. He'd have his back.

Kevin made me club captain which was a tremendous honour. Despite that he never really consulted me over team matters, and why would he? He had Terry Mac to do that. The only time I gave some input was one time when KK, Terry and Faz were pondering who to play up front because we were short of strikers because of injury. I turned to Kevin and said, 'Do you not remember that tale you told me about how Bill Shankly told you to 'go and drop hand grenades all over the pitch?' Well, Clarky can do the same. He'll run all day and cause chaos.' Clarky was probably the best finisher in the club at the time. The boss did that and Clarky scored in a 2-0 win I think it was.

Keegan and McDermott played in one of the greatest sides in the English game at Liverpool. They were both England internationals and played with top-class players. Both of them know what certain players should and shouldn't be doing. People forget that Terry Mac was an awesome player in his day. Keegan could have brought anyone he wanted in to help him. He chose his former Liverpool teammate. Terry Mac was also a fun guy with a great sense of humour. He put a smile on the faces of not only Kevin but the players as well.

When I first went to Newcastle the club were in danger of dropping into the third tier of football for the first time in the club's history. Confidence was low in the camp. I remember saying to a couple of players before kick-off, 'Fancy going to warm up?' They were like, 'Fuck that. I got abused the last time I did that.' These were the days when the players parked their cars outside the Milburn Stand. Many a time a player would go back to find a wing mirror off or the car scratched. The supporters intimidated a lot of players they felt weren't doing their best.

The kids we had at the club were excellent. I played alongside Kevin Scott who was a good player. Steve Watson and Alan Thompson were the fullbacks and they were two cracking footballers. Then there was Steve Howey. I'm not so sure if I was looking after them or if they were looking after me. Their youth and exuberance knew no bounds. All I did was talk them through the game. They were typical Geordies. They wanted to get the ball down, get forward and score a goal. I was never that way inclined. So, I'd let them bomb on but I made sure they came back and tucked in. I'd say, 'Hey, I'm an old bastard here and I need looking after.' It planted a seed in their heads and reminded them of their responsibilities and they did it superbly. I looked after them differently. If someone was being naughty with them, I'd sort them out.

Barry Venison and Paul Bracewell were the same age as me. We played for England Under-21s together. These experienced lads came in later and helped settle the younger players as well. These were all good trainers as well. They were setting good examples. Brace had a multitude of injury problems. He'd had ankle and knee problems but he still trained hard. I'd heard Billy Whitehurst did him in a tackle at Newcastle when Brace was playing for Everton.

Billy knocked out two of my teeth when I was at Coventry and he was playing for Oxford. I went to head a ball and he kicked me in the face. It wasn't a diving header either. I nodded a ball out at the back post and whack! I was knocked clean out. He was a typical big strong forward I liked playing against. There was never any verbal that I can remember. I'd never get involved with that side of the game anyway. I never celebrated scoring a goal too wildly as well. It could always come back to bite you on the arse. It would be OK to do it in the last minute or in extra time but that was about it.

I get asked about the year we escaped relegation to the old Third Division quite a lot. It did look bleak and was there a time when I thought we wouldn't get out of it. Kevin and Terry created such positivity around the place we were swept away by it. You can't think like that or rather you didn't think like that. I'd never been relegated as a player at that time. I have to say, I've not seen anyone go so grey as quickly as they both did in all my life from February 1992 to May of the same year. They were as grey as badgers. At breakfast, Grecian 2000 was often the topic of conversation but there was never any outward show of tension or worry despite the fragility of our situation. He was calmness personified.

We went to Port Vale and beat them 1-0 where Steve Watson scored. I played against my old muckers Keith Houchen and Peter Swan. Only three or four months earlier we'd faced each other in the reserves while I was at Oldham and I had a shocker. I was buggered if I was going to face the wrath of my wife's tongue again so I spent the game kicking lumps out of them. Houchy said after the game, 'That was more like the old you" and "You've landed on your feet here, they're not a bad side, are they?'

Keegan looked after me very well when I was at Newcastle. A lot of the time he'd let me go home to West Yorkshire after training on the Friday and told me to meet up before the game at the ground. This was the same at Leicester for our last game of the season. I'd got down to Filbert Street early because I hated being late. It was the same for training at Benwell or Maiden Castle. I'd get there around the same time as Ronnie who made the tea, coffee and soups. I found somewhere which hadn't been cordoned off and parked up. Ronnie was a fat old man, broad Geordie and a smashing fella. He reminded me of old Albert when I was a youngster at Notts County. Albert used to make the tea out of stockings. Twenty years later I see Ronnie, this incredible character. Not so much Sid the Sexist but Ronnie the Tea Man.

We put a bit of a run together after a stuttering start under Kevin. We went to Cambridge and won 2-0. I was up against Dion Dublin, with Steve Claridge running off him. They were in the promotion places if I remember rightly. The game suited me perfectly facing the big man up front. Then we beat Glenn Hoddle's Swindon at St James' Park, 3-1. The manager was there for the game but I can't remember if he came into the changing rooms after. We'd won and the players were high on the result. We'd jump in the shower or bath, get sorted and we'd all go our separate ways. I went back to West Yorkshire and when I came back in on Tuesday everything was sorted. If anything had been wrong Ronnie would have told me the minute he'd handed me a cup of tea as I got to training.

To be honest, every game in the run-in towards the end of the season was like a derby in terms of intensity and pressure. Yet every game should be played as if your life depended on it. The following season, when we got promoted, we played with the same intensity but it was a lot more enjoyable because there wasn't the pressure of relegation hanging over us.

We had good players who tried to play football, even when we were struggling when I first joined. Take Micky Quinn for example. I played against Kenny Dalglish a dozen times and I couldn't get anywhere near him for his big arse. Quinny was the same, except his backside was even bigger, so players couldn't get near him. He was a great finisher and what a great lad. Liam O'Brien, brilliant, Brocky, superb, Mark Simpson was the same. Then there were the young lads who all had their strong personalities. They were learning from the older pros as well. This was all down to Keegan and McDermott. He kept bringing in lads with good habits. The humour and camaraderie were good.

There were some very funny lads at Newcastle. It must've been good because Gavin Peacock became a priest. Joking aside. Gavin was a nice lad, a good player and a goalscorer. If he had a bit more pace, he would've been a great player. Ned Kelly was a funny fella. He was near the knuckle at times but his humour was taken the right way. A fit lad and he could catch shadows. Scored some great and important goals for us to keep us up and then fire us into the Premier League.

I got injured in the Wolves game and then missed the home game to Tranmere and the trip to Ipswich which we both lost 3-2. I returned for the Millwall game which we lost 1-0 and then got thumped 4-1 at Derby where we got three players sent off. Our recent good run had been turned on its head and we were back in trouble with five consecutive defeats.

At Leicester, in the last game of the season, their supporters got on the pitch and tried to get at the Newcastle fans. It would've been unnerving for some. Ned was a former City player. I know he got some stick and jumped in with the away supporters for safety. I've been lucky in my life that I've escaped loads of precarious situations. No one approached or threatened me in that game. It would've been bizarre if they did because I would've had a go back. The biggest memory of that day at Filbert Street for me was the look of anxiety, panic or terror on the faces of the directors in the hotel before the match. I remember saying to them, 'It's just a game.' I could block out the importance or whatever the consequences were. I'd done it my entire career.

I never remember Keegan dishing out any bollockings. He used a lot of motivational quotes and had them written above our pegs in the dressing room and around the ground. Kevin was an inspirational man but most of the time the lads didn't need it because they knew what they were going to do. For most of our promotion season, I spent a lot of time geeing the players up because I was out of the side. I started the promotion season but then got injured and only featured sporadically after that. Steve Howey took off as a centre-half around then. He turned into being a hell of a player.

There was no mention of promotion when we got back for pre-season training. We just carried on from where we left off at the end of the previous campaign. Newcastle, St James' Park and the training ground just had an aura about it. We'd moved from Benwell to Maiden Castle for the start of the 1992-93 season. At first, there weren't any supporters there but then they must have got wind of it because they started to turn up in their thousands and in all kinds of weather. There was one day where it lashed down and we were playing in one of our small-sided games. I slid to tackle one of the lads, and because it was wet and raining, I took out about ten supporters watching from the sidelines. It was like watching dominoes fall. They loved it! I heard one say, 'This is brilliant! I've just been tackled by Killer!'

I only had two problems in all my time when I was at Newcastle. The first was that I had to leave because I wasn't getting a game and the second was when my hair was cut on the end-of-season trip to Cyprus. Bez's wife Katherine tipped Lynn off that the lads were going to cut my hair. The pair of them had a short holiday while we were away in Ayia Napa. The fact that it was premeditated makes it worse for me. Lynn dismissed it at the time as nothing but banter but because she was away, she couldn't have tipped me off anyway. It was bad enough the instigators cutting it while I was asleep. They wouldn't have done it while I was awake, I can tell you that for nothing. Some people might think, maybe, I'm being a bit precious or sensitive about the incident but I wouldn't mess with people's clothes or personal belongings.

I've always been one for a bit of craic, verbal, piss take and drinking games but never cutting clothes up or anything like that. I wouldn't even cut someone's socks up. I had to grow up very quickly and at 17 I was playing in a man's world in a drinking culture. I missed out on the whole playing games side of things. Lynn has often sewed up some trousers when I've been away and when I've come to put my foot in the leg, I've fallen over. Yes, it is funny but no harm had come to my clothes.

I'd been drinking with a few of the lads around the hotel pool and fell asleep. When I woke up, the first thing I saw was my hair in a wine glass and I was raging! There was no one around so I was out on the hunt. I can't remember who, but I got tipped off that Faz and Venners were involved. I went looking for them and the first person I saw was Faz, so I smacked him. He just took it and didn't say anything. Faz knew he'd done wrong.

In hindsight, I'm sorry I hit Faz because that is a sign of weakness. I'd have been a better man not to have done it. I wasn't a better man back then. I was an angry man hell-bent on revenge. Then I went to get Venners. When I finally caught up with him my anger had subsided somewhat. 'You're not even worth the effort,' were my words to him. I didn't find out about Brace's involvement until later. The three of them were involved in the holding, cutting and disposal of my hair.

I've read that my ponytail had been cut off but I didn't have my hair in a ponytail at the time. They'd managed to cut one side of it off so it was lopsided. Then Ned Kelly cut the other side to try and level it off and made a right arse of it. To be fair to Ned, Tommy Wright and Liam O'Brien, they calmed me down because I was on the warpath looking for blood. I was a bit of a lunatic back in those days and probably necked a bottle of whiskey that day.

The drink has always had repercussions on me in life. I've lost money, a captaincy, a wife and a daughter because of the drink. The irony of having a southern Irishman on one side and a northern Irishman on the other attempting to keep the peace was not lost on me. It was hilarious. At the time nearly a century of sectarianism had been fought on two sides of the divide. Yet these two, and Ned who, like me had Irish blood, took the sting out of the episode.

Lynn went crazy when she walked in and saw the state of my hair when I got back. She wanted to kill him. You don't want to upset her. She would've taken a knife to him if she could have got anywhere near him. When my lovely partner calmed down, she reckoned it was only because Venners was jealous of my hair and wanted the best mane of hair in the club and to paraphrase the shampoo advert and her words, 'He's not worth it.'

I was one of the senior professionals and in my eyes, I felt as if I'd lost the respect of the dressing room after that had happened but when we went back for pre-season training it was time to draw a line underneath it. I pulled Barry Venison to one side before training and said, 'As a human being I fucking detest you, stay away from me. As a footballer, I admire you but as a person, I have no time for you.'

Venners had his problems just like everybody else. Although he was one of the senior players, he was still a daft young lad like the rest of us but he'd crossed the line and there was no going back from that. You shouldn't do things to people that you wouldn't like done to yourself. Word got back to the manager and Kevin and I had a chat about whether the incident was done and dusted or would there be any repercussions. I expressed my disappointment and regret about it and also told him a little bit of something special had died. I was still fully committed to the cause and getting us back in the Premier League. We were like a jumbo jet on the runway, ready to take off, and by God we did.

In life, the bad things stick in your mind more than the good things. It is tough to try and pin down all the good times at Newcastle because there were so many happy memories. We'd escaped relegation to the third tier of football, been promoted to the top flight and took the Premier League by storm, all in less than two years. It was so smooth, like velvet. It was a great time to be at Newcastle. It was a fantastic time to play football there and a privilege to be part of it all.

Leaving Newcastle was the hardest decision I've had to make in my football career. I wasn't ready to become a coach. I wasn't even sure I wanted to do it anyway. I only wanted to play football. I was still young enough and it was tough because Newcastle was such a nice place to be. I've been lucky enough to have had so many good times in my career but without a doubt the two years at St James' Park were the happiest of my career. If you stood still, you'd be left behind. Things were changing or happening so quickly. The squad, the stadium and the standard of players were phenomenal. I never went banging on Keegan's door demanding to play. How could I? The two lads playing in front of me were class and I knew what I was.

Lynn and I were both in tears as we drove away from St James' Park to go to Swindon. The realisation I wouldn't be coming back hurt. I used to love that drive up the A1, seeing Ronnie (the tea man) at training, the games on a Saturday, the afternoons I'd have out with Kevin Sheedy and Ned and where I lived at Tynemouth. I've always kept an eye out on my old clubs and I was as gutted as everyone when they didn't win the Premier League title in 1996.

Kevin said I didn't need to leave Newcastle. I could stop if I wanted to. Did he have me in mind for a coaching role? I don't know. In the last 18 months at the club, I wasn't playing in the first team very much. I was in the reserves but I was helping out on match days with the lads, giving them encouragement and support when I could. As much as I loved doing that I wanted to play. Keegan made me feel part of what was happening but at the same time, I didn't feel part of it. It was a Catch-22. The club was growing rapidly around me and I felt as if I was being left behind. I'm not feeling bitter here, on the contrary, I understood. I was in my early 30s at the time and coming to the end of my time. I was past it in a lot of sense and when I got injured and saw Steve Howey pair up with Kevin Scott, I knew it would be a struggle. They were two good players. I wasn't going to kid myself I would play before them but I did a job when called upon. More often than not Keegan stuck me up front. I think the gaffer was just doing it to entertain himself and have a laugh.

I went to KK and told him I wanted to play and knew it couldn't have been at Newcastle. I would have gone anywhere to do that. The manager couldn't give any games because the squad had improved beyond recognition in my two years and the standard of player in my position was phenomenal. I felt as if I still had plenty to offer and when a move to Swindon came up, I jumped at it. Little did I know what was going to be unveiled at the County Ground. I would've stopped at St James' Park if I had that so-called mythical crystal ball.

Keegan and Terry Mac helped me so much. They helped me out the door in a nice way. Newcastle was probably the only club I didn't get chased out of. Leaving the club was the hardest thing I've ever had to do in my football career. I loved it. I could see what was going to happen and how it would evolve. It gave me great pleasure seeing the club getting better and better and better, watching from afar. I can't speak highly enough of Kevin Keegan, Terry McDermott and the Newcastle experience.

Chapter Fifteen: Derek Fazackerley

Derek Fazackerley joined the Newcastle United coaching staff in 1990 under Jim Smith. The former Blackburn centre-back, known in the football kingdom as Faz, joined the Bald Eagle's coaching staff just after the team narrowly missed out on promotion to the top flight. Following Smith's departure, Faz had little involvement in new boss Ossie Ardiles's plans but played his part in coaching the reserves and nurturing the precocious youngsters who eventually broke into the first team under the Argentine.

Faz, however, played a bigger part with Ardiles' replacement, Kevin Keegan, who was no less swashbuckling in his approach as Newcastle faced the threat of relegation to the Third Division. But Faz's pragmatic approach helped balance Newcastle's attacking style with defensive solidity. United managed to avoid relegation in the 1991-92 season before a reversal in the team's fortunes saw the Magpies romp to promotion as champions of the First Division.

Faz's tenure at United is remembered for his ability to provide defensive stability and tactical discipline, complementing Keegan's attacking ethos and playing a vital role in the club's successful promotion campaign and rise as Premier League champion wannabes. There a several theories as to why Newcastle didn't win that elusive Premier League title in 1996 and one of them points to the fact that Faz left United to return to his hometown club Blackburn. If only he had stayed…

Coach

I hadn't long been finished playing and was player-coach of Kumu in Finland when I got a call off Jim Smith, around the October of 1990, saying there was a job at Newcastle looking after the reserves. I knew Bobby Saxton, Jim's coach, from my playing days at Blackburn. Jim told me it was a difficult period at the club and all about the takeover by Sir John Hall and the Magpie Group and how volatile it was around the club.

I went down and had an interview, well, it was more of a chat with Jim and Bobby, had a look around the place and then I stayed for a night game they had against Bournemouth. I went into the stand and watched the players come out and warm up and as the teams were being announced some of the players were getting booed. It was a real eye-opener to see all of this discontent. Regardless, I accepted the job anyway and it all kicked on from there. Jim got the sack in March of 1991, Ossie Ardiles came in, which lasted about 12 months and then Kevin came in.

I was still the reserves team manager and contemplating my future when Kevin joined. He had no managerial experience and no backroom staff to bring in if you like, so he asked me and Colin (Suggett), the youth team coach, to stay on and help him until the end of the season and that's what we did. Kevin coming in lifted the spirits of the supporters. They obviously remembered him from his playing days and he had such charisma he lifted the whole place, which wasn't there beforehand.

The game today has changed massively and it seems to be micro-managed by coaches almost. Yes, we played a lot of games, five-a-side as such but the players were coached. Kevin knew the players he wanted so he could play a certain way but they were told how to react if a move broke down and were aware of their starting positions. It is true we didn't spend a lot of time drilling tactics into players but they were coached on how to defend and keep their shape. Most of the time we were encouraging players to express themselves, create and score goals, but the players were aware of their defensive responsibilities and some days it worked better than others.

The club was in danger of going down to the old Third Division for the first time in its history but we had the belief we would stay up. We were also aware it could happen. Big clubs have slipped into the third tier before and it could happen again. We managed to stave off relegation, buy a few players in the summer and set off like a house on fire the following season.

The recruitment that summer was good. We signed players who had played at the top level like Paul Bracewell and Barry Venison and players with the potential to play at the top level like John Beresford. These players were hugely influential in turning the fortunes of the club around.

Brian Kilcline was a huge signing, initially, to get the club going in the right direction. I can't remember all of the signings we made but those three were hugely influential. We did concede a lot of goals when Kevin first came in and I told him at the time that it was down to the way the players were being asked to play. Ossie was very much the same. He wanted his team to play open attractive football. The centre-backs were being exposed because the full-backs were spending more time in the opposition's half than our own. We had to bring a bit of reality to the play and defend a bit more intelligently. Bringing Killer in was key to that. He had a dominant personality both on and off the pitch.

Sometimes Kevin and Terry Mac would consult me about players they were going to sign. They asked me about Rob Lee, which of course I knew from my playing days. I told Kevin he was a good wide player, had pace, good feet and scored the odd goal. I asked why they wanted to know. Kevin said he's just turned down a move to Middlesbrough. Apparently, Middlesbrough was too far north for him. Kevin said he was talking to him the following day, and persuaded him Newcastle was closer to London than Middlesbrough and the rest, as we say, is history.

Pavel Srnicek was another good professional, with a fantastic personality, a dedicated goalkeeper and a tremendous athlete. Some of the things he used to do were incredible. When he first came to the club, he was our reserve team keeper. I remember his first game for the reserves away at Blackburn. He played really well that night and you could tell by his athleticism and stature that he had the makings of a very good goalkeeper. He then fought his way into the first team and made the goalkeeper shirt his own.

Kevin pulled off a masterstroke getting Sir John Hall to buy into his vision for the club. He told him if he invested in new players, he would get tremendous support and he did. There was a season ticket waiting list and the stadium got redeveloped which was not cheap but had to be funded hand-in-hand. We signed some really good players. If you look at the Premier League now, the investment to just stay in the league is huge.

If you look at our first game back in the Premier League, we lost 1-0 at home to Tottenham, ironically managed by Ossie Ardiles. Then we lost away at Coventry and our first point was away at Man United. Had anyone said we would qualify for Europe at that point no one would have believed you. But we brought in some fantastic signings and we kicked on and everyone was talking about us. We must have played more on Sky Sports television than any other team, including the two teams who finished above us, Man United and Blackburn.

It was disappointing to get knocked out of Europe so early after we started so well against Antwerp. Individual errors cost us against Athletic Bilbao, where we let two late goals in the home leg. They beat us 1-0 away and went through on away goals. It was a shame it didn't last long because it was a fantastic experience.

Opening up training to the supporters wasn't new to me because when I played at Blackburn Rovers, we didn't have a training pitch and had to train in a public park so, we were used to people wandering up and watching us. Although it has to be said there weren't two and three thousand like at Maiden Castle. One Easter time we had thousands there and unfortunately Philippe Albert ruptured his cruciate ligament, which was not nice for anyone to see. We had to organise an ambulance to ferry him off to hospital. On the other hand, the players knew they had to conduct themselves properly and perform at the highest standards. The management didn't need to drive the training standards, the players did that for themselves.

It's difficult to pick out one player who stood out because we had so many good ones at the club. Peter Beardsley obviously springs to mind. He could score goals and create them. Peter could get the crowd going, if there was a lull in the game, just by sprinting over to take a quick corner. Then you have David Ginola who for about six months was the best player in the Premier League. What about Andy Cole and the goals he scored? Peter provided many of his goals. It is very difficult to pick out one player given the quality we had at the time. Rob Lee was outstanding. Kevin Sheedy was really important to us when he first came as was Scott Sellars. You can't dismiss how good these players were but if I was pushed, I'd say Peter Beardsley was the best of the bunch, but then were most of the players Kevin brought in.

The supporters were incredible. When they saw, what Kevin was trying to do everyone got behind him. I think the fact Newcastle was a one-club city also helped so everyone in the city was cheering for them to do well. It created a fantastic atmosphere inside and outside St James' Park. The whole city was buzzing. We'd had a few years of struggle before that and then we had a ride. Kevin called it a ride. He asked, 'Whether I'd like to come along for the ride,' and I said I did. It was a fantastic ride. Everyone bought into it and everyone was on board and it was such an enjoyable time to be there. We appeared to be everybody's second favourite team.

I got an offer to go back to my hometown club, Blackburn, halfway through the 1995-96 season. It was a difficult decision to make, given the position we were in the league at that time. On the other hand, Blackburn was in the Champions League so that was a big draw. Newcastle later came to play us and we beat them 2-1 with Geordie lad Graham Fenton scoring both goals. That game pretty much killed Newcastle's Premier League ambitions. I obviously have mixed feelings about that given the tug of my hometown club and the club that adopted me but I'd been away from home for about seven years and I was missing watching my kids grow up.

Chapter Sixteen: Paul Bracewell

Kevin Keegan showed he was not afraid to make tough, controversial decisions in pursuit of success when he swooped to secure the signature of Sunderland captain Paul Bracewell after he refused to sign a new one-year deal, only weeks after skippering the Wearsiders to a 2-0 defeat to Liverpool in the 1992 FA Cup final.

Newcastle's fierce rivals demanded £700,000 for the highly decorated top-flight midfielder's services but a tribunal set the fee at £250,000, a steal for such an accomplished top-flight player. The former Everton favourite won two league titles and a European Cup Winners' Cup winners medal during his time at Goodison Park and brought some much-needed maturity, experience and knowledge alongside Special K's inexperienced young guns.

Nicknamed "The Iceman," on account of having his ankles encased in ice after every game, the all-action, combative midfielder didn't take long to win over any Geordies sceptical about his allegiance, when he smashed a 25-yard left-foot rocket past a helpless Southend goalkeeper, only ten minutes into his debut.

The Iceman

How it used to work back in my day, in the 1980s and 1990s, on the third Saturday in May you were offered a new contract. If you didn't accept it your name was automatically put on the PFA (Professional Footballers Association) list of available players. I'd just played for Sunderland in the 1992 FA Cup final and was offered a new one-year contract, which I declined. Subsequently, I was put on the PFA list.

A friend of mine from Liverpool rang me and said Terry Mac had been asking whether it was true that I was a free agent. I said 'Yes, it's true.' Terry Mac then rang me and said Kevin (Keegan) would like to meet me at the Gosforth Park Hotel. I told my wife to turn on the telephone answering machine and don't answer any calls until I came back. I met Terry Mac in the reception of the hotel on the Sunday. He took me up to Kevin's room. He met me and said, 'As Sunderland captain this will be a massive move if you come here. If you want to turn around now and leave the room I will understand.' I was happy with what he said and what he offered and I turned up at the club on Monday morning for a medical and the rest is history, as they say. It was a massive gamble. I knew what came with pulling on the black and white shirt and how I was in for a rough ride if it didn't go well but I signed a three-year contract and the move went really well.

Kevin was like a breath of fresh air. What he told me he was going to do, as in the new signings, he followed through on. He wanted me to try and hold it all together with my experience while he brought in all of these new players. I was one of Kevin's first signings and Newcastle continued to build on that.

We trained at Maiden Castle. There were two, three, 4,000 fans there watching us. Kevin was all for getting the fans involved with what was going on. Most of them couldn't get game tickets for the home games because they had sold out. This was Kevin's way of keeping everyone involved. There was always a great atmosphere at training, it was always very competitive and most importantly it set us up to win games.

Kevin put a good group of players together. We all bonded, there were no clicks and we all got on. As you can see every time there is a reunion for The Entertainers, we all go back and meet up. To keep going back after 25-30 years, tells you what type of team we had, as individuals and collectively as a team. We had a very close-knit squad and they all became some of my best mates: Barry Venison, John Beresford, Lee Clark, Robbie Elliott, Steve Howey, and Steve Watson.

My debut was memorable, at home to Southend. I scored a goal from 25 yards and that was the start of something special. It was probably my best goal for the club. Coming from Sunderland, the game against Southend was always going to be important for me and I needed to get off to a good start, which I did. We then went on to win 11 games on the trot.

Going back to Sunderland was tough. It was a derby game and they're massive games anyway. There was added pressure, after all of the years I was at Sunderland. I didn't come from the North-East but I understood what the derby was all about: have a right good go, work hard and get the tackles in, which is what I do. The people from the North-East like good football played.

In the dressing room before games, it was never about the opposition. It was about what we were gonna do. It was very positive individually and collectively. The way the game has evolved these days there is lots of analysis about this, that and the other. Kevin's attitude was, 'I've got good players, go out and do what you're good at.' That was the common theme.

Terry Mac was a good sounding board for Kevin, as was Arthur Cox as well. Terry was an amazing player in his day. He won titles and European Cups as well. He had a lot of experience. He would go around the players and speak to them, giving them the benefit of his experience. He was a fun guy around the place too. Always had a smile on his face and tried to get the best out of the players. There was a really good team behind the team as well, including Arthur Cox and Derek Wright the physio. There were lots of funny stories at the time, none more so than the one where Brian Kilcline got his hair cut on a trip away after we won promotion. I don't think Brian found it funny at the time but, after a few drinks were flowing, a pair of scissors appeared and someone cut his hair.

It's hard to pick out the best player at the time because we had a few: Peter Beardsley, Rob Lee, and Andy Cole had an unbelievable spell at the club. Despite having all of those unbelievable players, we had a good team. It was all about the team and not the individuals. Yes, the individuals got the glory but it was all about the team at

Newcastle.

After promotion to the Premier League, it was the start of an incredible journey. I know the club has had their ups and downs since then but people still remember The Entertainers era. I think the biggest compliment about that time is that Newcastle was everybody's second team, which I think is brilliant. Newcastle was the team that everybody wanted to see and watch. There were always full houses whether it was home or away.

The Newcastle fans are incredible. I recently visited the stadium with a Tottenham coach. He was blown away by the stadium. I said you should come when it's full and understand what the atmosphere is like here. Every player looks forward to playing at St James' Park for the atmosphere. People talk about the supporters being the 12th man, and they were. The atmosphere they create is unbelievable and it's nice to see them in full voice again.

The local lads were very important to the team. Sir John Hall was a big advocate of 'let's get the local lads pushed through into the first team.' The local lads bring an important ingredient to the table. The fans love to see one or two of their own playing for the team. It's like the fans are living their dreams through them. They can relate to the local lads and the fans did the same with Pavel. He was a really nice guy. He worked hard at his game to be a better goalkeeper but my abiding memory of him was that he was a top, top guy. He was kind, would do anything for you and wanted to be the best he could in his profession. He is sadly missed, a lovely man.

I have all of these great memories from my three years at the club. It was a special time and I feel blessed to have been part of it. Yes, it was a shame we didn't win any silverware but what a time we had trying.

Chapter Seventeen: Barry Venison

Barry Venison arrived at St James' Park in the summer of 1992, bringing a wealth of experience and a cabinet full of silverware after several trophy-laden seasons on Merseyside. The Consett-born defender-cum-midfielder's arrival certainly raised a few eyebrows on Tyneside when he joined the club from Liverpool in a £250,000 transfer. It was another bold yet shrewd signing by Kevin Keegan, given that some supporters were unsure due to his past as captain of Sunderland, Newcastle's fierce rivals. Nonetheless, any apprehension regarding his former allegiances quickly evaporated following a fully committed display on his home debut against Southend.

Venison's leadership qualities were evident from the outset as he shared captain duties with Brian Kilcline. The former Liverpool defender played a crucial role in Newcastle's promotion to the Premier League in the 1992-1993 campaign and in cementing the club's place among the top tier's elite, while finishing third in the 1993-1994 season.

Venison's contributions in the early days of The Entertainers should not be underestimated. His ability to read the game, combined with his work ethic and professionalism, made him a key figure during a transformative period for the club. Additionally, his solid defensive skills and versatility earned him two England caps in midfield.

Venison's time at Newcastle ended in 1995 when he moved to Galatasaray but his legacy at Newcastle is remembered fondly. He was part of a squad that laid the foundation for the club's subsequent successes and growth.

Why United didn't win the Premier League in 1996 is a popular debate among Newcastle supporters and Pavel Srníček has his theory. The big Czech Republic shotstopper reckons the Magpies would have lifted the trophy had Venison remained on Tyneside given his leadership skills and will to win.

Crossing the Great Divide

I've heard a few people say 'eyebrows were raised' when I, a former Sunderland player, signed for Newcastle. Think it was more likely pick axes were raised rather than eyebrows. I could hear fans in my imaginary mind saying, 'Get that Mackem bar steward out of here!' Not many people know this but I was rejected by Newcastle as a youngster. I used to train with them but they wouldn't sign me as a schoolboy and that is how I ended up at Sunderland

I met Kevin halfway down the motorway, we had a good chat. You know what Kevin's like, he could sell second-hand shoes to you if he wanted to. I'd been at Liverpool for six years. I knew my worth, what I could bring to a team, what I could bring to a club, and what I could give to a manager because I had confidence in my ability. Straight away I bought into his vision for the club and where he wanted to take it. He told me about the players he was going to bring in and I never had any second thoughts about joining.

The fact that I had played for Sunderland in the early part of my career didn't even cross my mind. I think the fans could see I was fully committed to the club through those early games where we won 11 games in a row. I've given my all for every club I've played for, I've had to because I wasn't talented enough so, I had to work hard. I was all about energy, passion, organisation and helping those around me. I certainly enjoyed my time at Newcastle, that's for sure.

The whippersnappers were phenomenal for us in our promotion season. The likes of Clarky, Steve Watson, Robbie Elliot, and Steve Howey had quite a bit of experience for youngsters. They'd played a lot of games for Ossie Ardiles before Kevin came in. They had a lot of passion, energy, and commitment and were like a pack of hyenas at times but they were a great bunch of lads. They'd always listen, they were very coachable and absorbed everything. They wanted to learn and they trained hard every day. At times they led the way for others, new players especially could see that the way they trained and played was a minimum. They played a big part in the success of the team at that time.

Then there was Pavel. What an athlete first of all. There wasn't an ounce of fat on him. He could've been a gymnast because he was very flexible. He was a great professional and a pleasure to be around. He was fairly quiet in the dressing room but on the pitch, he was fairly vocal. It might surprise a few people but he was also a leader. We had several of those in our dressing room and he was one of them. He trained his socks off every single day. Worked like a trojan. A gifted, talented gentleman.

I never thought we would turn out to be "The Entertainers" and everybody's second favourite team. Kevin had a plan and wanted to push the boundaries and bring in big signings. We didn't know where it was going to take us but every day in training and on match days it was such an enjoyable environment to be in. The atmosphere was unbelievable, thanks to the fans. I often used to say to the younger lads, 'This isn't normal.' I told them to enjoy it as much as possible because this would never happen again in their careers.

The North-East is a great social environment. The community would come and watch us train and we would go into the community and help do things for them too, like presentations and opening things. Kevin encouraged us to do that. He wanted us to create a bond with the fans in the community. I never thought what can we go on to do but I genuinely believed we could win every game we played. It was a great place mentally, to sit in the dressing room and believe we would win, home or away. The players we had and the way Kevin had us set up we knew we could score, two, three, four goals or more every game. We also knew the vulnerabilities because of the attacking attitude. It was great to watch.

I was one of the workman-like players in the team and responsible for trying to fill in the gaps and it was a role I thoroughly enjoyed. The day-to-day was phenomenal. Kevin would come into training every day full of enthusiasm. Everything was changing. Everything was done at a fast tempo and everything was a fast tempo in training and it was really good.

Terry Mac was brilliant ... at moving the goalposts in training, getting the fish and chips in at the Wetherby Whaler and the sandwiches, taking the bets and doing a bit of retail shopping. All joking aside, Terry was the eyes and ears of Kevin. They had a close relationship. He didn't do any coaching but he got on with all of the lads. You can't underestimate his vast experience. He knew what the younger lads were going through and was on hand to help them. He was a big help to all of the lads.

We were set up very much in the way Liverpool set up. We never worked on formations, the back four, attacking plans or set pieces and the great Liverpool teams never did any of that too. We would work on having the tempo as high as we could, energy, intensity, closing down, hunger, and aggression for 90 minutes. We never had coaching on any of that. The players didn't need any coaching on that. We knew it.

I knew within two weeks of Philippe Albert being at Newcastle what a threat he was in the opposition box and what a passer of the ball he was and not just from set pieces. He could carry the ball forward and we thought, 'Let him go, release him, and I'll fill in for him.' Everybody worked off each other. It's called football intelligence. The training ground was the incubator for that.

New signings that came to the club would struggle with the tempo in training. We were playing eight-a-side in small spaces. It was bang, bang, tackle, tackle. The tempo was high. Goals were flying in left, right, and centre. The link-up play and running off the ball was fast and, I wouldn't say it was all instinctive because that would sound flippant but all the players understood what Kevin wanted and bought into it. It was all about hurting the other team with fast running and pressure. It's exactly what those great Liverpool sides did.

I'm not a great one for remembering certain games but I do remember the last game of the promotion season in the 7-1 win over Leicester City. Think it was because we wore our new sponsored kit and Kevin played me in the centre of midfield and it went well. He must have thought I could do a job for him in there. It was a great way to end the season. We clinched the title at Grimsby away, possibly the most glamorous place to win the league, not.

We had a great night. The fans had a great night and we earned the right to play in the Premier League. To end the season in front of our home fans with a shower of goals was a great way to finish the season. It's difficult to explain to people who weren't there what fun we had, exuberance and putting smiles on the faces of supporters. Even when things went against us, we knew we could bounce back.

Was I surprised by the welcome, support and the thousands on the street who came out to celebrate our open-top bus tour around the city? No, I wasn't. That sums up the supporters' fanaticism. When we got back to the Civic Centre, seeing Kevin address the supporters on the balcony was like watching royalty, a king, addressing his subjects. It was an amazing feeling and an amazing night.

We had no idea how well we would do in the Premier League. We thought we'd do OK but I think we surprised ourselves. We set ourselves up against well-established top-flight clubs, with seasoned internationals. Others may have thought we'd blow hot and cold. Sometimes we were but I don't think those clubs expected us to be so consistent over our debut season in the Premier League. I recently watched some clips of those games and was astounded at the speed and high quality of our play, the quickness of our interaction, the power of our movement forward, the individual goals, and the team goals. Nobody expected that every week but we delivered.

Kevin played his part by stoking the fire, bringing in bigger and better players. He didn't bring in six players at once, he did it, player-by-player and gradually transformed the team. Kevin was the catalyst, giving us belief. Telling us how good we were as individuals and as a team. Spurring us on, telling us how far we can go as a team. He kept telling us he was going to bring in better players and we needed to get better along the way. Kevin knew we were capable of doing good things in the Premier League.

My most memorable game has to be against Aston Villa because it was my only goal, in a 3-1 win. Keith Gillespie pulled it back and I lashed it from about 30 yards. About 99 times out of 100 those shots generally end up in the stand. The fans were great after that because every time I got around 30 yards out, they were screaming for me to shoot. I could hear Keegan shouting, 'No! No! No! Pass it!' He knew the goal was a one-off. Joking aside, there were tons of games I remember and what made them memorable was because of the relationship with the fans. I had a great relationship with the Liverpool fans but they won league after league after league. The bond I had with the Newcastle fans made it the most enjoyable three years of my professional career and I was lucky enough to enjoy some good times.

I was never asked my best position and I was a makeshift centre half. I couldn't head a bus queue never mind heading a ball out of a goalkeeper's hands from 60 yards. I loved the midfield role because it suited me being a defender. I could organise things more easily from in there. I had a big mouth which was helpful to push and order people around. My contribution to the team at right-back was more limited. I wasn't a Trent Alexander-Arnold type of player getting up and down the line all game. I just felt I could make more of a contribution from the centre of the field.

Andy Cole, would I have kept him? I think the question is why he was sold? He wasn't the best trainer and some people aren't. He was a nightmare if he was in your five-a-side team because you were a man down. I don't know what happened to be honest but maybe his head was turned, maybe someone was tapping him up. I don't know that of course but his performances and commitment to the club, players and team dropped a little bit and I think that's why Kevin was happy to sell him. Kevin couldn't stand for anything like that. It was fantastic business for the club and Coley. He went on to prove he could score goals on the biggest stage. At the time, I was thinking, 'What is he (Keegan) doing?' But at the same time, I had inside knowledge knowing Cole's standards were starting to drop. So, overall, a fantastic move by the manager.

Paul Bracewell was switched on as a midfielder and could read the game and situations well. By the way, I used to room with Brace, the most boring man alive. I was in bed at 9pm before an away game. Robbie Elliott was probably the best defender we had in my time at the club. John Beresford almost played like a left winger at times but Robbie was focused defensively and he had a nasty streak too. Brian Kilcline was a good defender. That's what he was brought into the team for, to defend. In terms of instinct and working things out, it had to be Robbie. Mind you, Steve Watson was a really good defender too.

Who cut Killer's hair? Well, I was there and I know 100 percent who did it but I'd be interested to know if anyone breaks ranks and spills the beans on who did it. I immediately got the blame for it. Kevin would often come up to me and say 'What have you been doing with the young lads?' I took a lot of blame to protect the others and if someone wants to accuse me of doing it, I'll take the blame.

It never bothered me whether people said I was overrated or underrated. For a player, it is a boost to be respected and admired by your fellow teammates. It doesn't matter what those outside the game might think of you, like the press. The most important is being rated by fellow players. That is why everyone wants to win the Players' Player of the Year trophy.

My family were all Sunderland supporters but I was a Leeds United fan growing up. I loved Billy Bremner, Paul Madeley, Paul Reaney and Norman Hunter. I loved the tie-ups with the numbers on the side. They looked great. Had Kevin asked me to play in goal I would have played in goal. I would have played anywhere for him but he put me in midfield, for the benefit of the team. As a kid, I played in midfield for years and years and I started as a midfielder for Sunderland. I don't think it was a huge revelation that I could play there but fair play to Kevin, he kind of knew I could play there. I did well for him there and I got rewarded with some England caps by Terry Venables. Kevin understands the game, understands players and how to get the best out of them.

I always had a good relationship with Kevin. It was always about mutual trust and respect. It didn't end well but sometimes that happens. It was time for me to leave when I did. Kevin and I had a major falling out which we don't need to go into detail about. Was I disappointed to leave? Yes, I felt there was some unfinished business and I believed I could still give a lot to the club.

I hope someday Newcastle supporters can witness what we had in the 1990s, fast, free-flowing, exciting, heart-in-your-mouth, breathtaking football, because it was at times, what they fully deserve. They are a phenomenal set of fans. Home and away players loved playing in front of those supporters because the atmosphere was very difficult to play in. It is hard to explain to those who weren't there or didn't experience it.

Chapter Eighteen: John Beresford

John Beresford's football career, in many ways, resembles a Charles Dickens novel. "It was the best of times, it was the worst of times, it was the age of wisdom, it was the age of foolishness, it was the epoch of belief, it was the epoch of incredulity, it was the season of light, it was the season of darkness, it was the spring of hope, it was the winter of despair, we had everything before us, we had nothing before us." The passage, from A Tale of Two Cities, could be applied to Bez and The Entertainers' period. There were thrills and spills, tears and tantrums and lots of drama and subplots on and off the pitch.

United's £650,000 signing from Portsmouth experienced a gamut of emotions in a rollercoaster six years at St James' Park. The failed medical at Liverpool turned out to be a blessing in disguise for the popular, fleet-footed full-back as he wooed United's fanatical fans with his attacking prowess and overlapping runs. Beresford's dynamic playing style perfectly complemented Newcastle's entertaining, high-octane approach under Kevin Keegan. His partnership with David Ginola on the left flank became legendary, providing numerous assists, creating chances as well as helping himself to the odd goal that thrilled the St James' Park faithful.

Bez's commitment, consistency and love for Newcastle endeared him to the fans, earning him a place as a beloved figure in the club's history. His contributions on and off the pitch helped define an era of optimism and ambition for Newcastle United, leaving an indelible mark on the club and its supporters.

Mersey Misery to Fine Tyne

I was supposed to sign for Liverpool originally and I was floating on air for a couple of weeks thinking I was going to sign for one of the biggest clubs on the planet. I didn't have an agent so I went to Anfield with my dad. I did the medical and had a sixth sense that something just wasn't quite right. Then the physio came up to me and said, 'We've got a problem with one of your ankles. Have you fractured one of them in the past?' I said I had. He then said, 'Well, it hasn't set properly.'

It happened when I played for Barnsley. As you can guess, we didn't have a specialist and I was sent to the Barnsley General Hospital for them to look at it but they didn't line it up properly. I was distraught. I'm thinking, 'This can't be happening.' I pleaded with the Liverpool manager at the time, Graeme Souness, to make it work but he said the board wouldn't let him sign anyone unless they were 100 percent. 'The deal's off,' he said.

I phoned my boss at Portsmouth, Jim Smith, and told him. He's kicking off by saying, 'It's a joke.' He then said, 'Don't worry, someone else wants you. Kevin Keegan at Newcastle wants to sign you.' Now Keegan had just taken over and I'd played against Newcastle the previous season and they weren't great. They weren't a good team but Kevin was a boyhood hero of mine. Anyway, Jim told me to give him a call.

Kevin was enthusiastic on the phone when I called and told me to get myself up to Newcastle and sign. I said, 'Hold on, I've just failed a medical at Liverpool.' He told me not to worry as he'd just signed Paul Bracewell and I 'Should piss the medical.' I met him and Terry Mac at the Gosforth Park Hotel and he just blew me away. He was like, 'We're going to get promoted this year and then next year we're going to get into Europe. I'll get you in the England squad,' etc, etc. I thought he was bullshitting me at first but within those two seasons that is exactly what happened. People were saying there's no way you can play that way in the Premier League but we finished third, playing that way. I also got in the England squad.

You look now, teams that are promoted from the Championship generally fight for their lives in the Premier League. We got in the Premier League and we went for its throat. We weren't just coming to stay in the league, we were there to compete against Man United, Liverpool and

Arsenal. Keegan was a genius. He only had one way of playing and it wasn't bad.

Saying that, against Aston Villa at home, the season we were going for the title he asked me to play a different way. He asked me to tuck in and help Philippe Albert because they played with three up front, with Tommy Johnson, Dwight York and Savo Milosevic, and they were very quick. I said no problem but as he was walking away, I said to him, 'You know we have another problem, don't you?' He said, 'What?' I said, 'Gary Charles, Villa's right-wing back won't be marking Ginola, he'll be bombing on.' Gaffer told me not to worry and said he'd ask David to come back a bit. I laughed, and said, 'That's not going to happen.' He then said, 'Do as you're told.' When Kevin says that, you know that's it, you do it.

Almost immediately, a ball is clipped over my head, Gary Charles is onto it and he's clipped a ball into the box. David is standing on the halfway line, hands on hips, handsome as ever, looking great. It was weird because it was live on Sky Sports and tensions were running high. Kevin comes to the edge of the technical area and starts having a go at me. I just lost it and screamed at him, 'I fucking told you!' Everyone knows you cannot swear at Kevin. He's the gaffer for a start. For a nanosecond, I'm thinking, 'There's 36,000 in here, he won't have heard me.' I glance over at the bench and I see Derek Wright, the physio, rummaging around among the squad numbers. I'm thinking, 'Shit, he's looking for my number.' Then I see Robbie Elliott warming up and I know he's heard me. At the same time, there's only about 15 minutes gone so he won't sub me in front of the supporters and the Sky audience. That would be embarrassing. I then see the No. 3 go up and I've lost it. I'm raging. I shook Robbie's hand and looked at the gaffer and he wasn't even looking at me. He's looking at the pitch and as I go by, I say, 'Shit decision.' Then it dawned on me, that was me finished! Normally when you get subbed or go to the bench, they'll give you eye contact and say, 'Well done.' The lads all blanked me. They weren't getting involved. It was as if their silence was saying, 'You're on your own pal, we don't want any part of this.'

As the game has gone on, I've calmed down and I'm thinking what should I do? I turned to Kevin's mentor, Arthur Cox, and asked, 'What should I do?' He said, 'You want to hope and pray we win, son.' We won 1-0, Big Les scored. I went to Arthur again and he said, 'Go and apologise, if need be, beg, but make sure you sort it out now.' I went to see the gaffer, knocked on his door and told him I'd come to apologise and beg if necessary. He told me, 'Don't' be stupid and he'd been in the position himself as a player many times.' I'm thinking, 'What a manager!' Then, he didn't play me again for the rest of that season and never spoke to me for a month after it. Now, when I see him, he always reminds me of it and tells me to watch my language. I understand why he hooked me. You can't have players mouthing off otherwise it would be a free-for-all. But I was lucky because if you cross him, you're gone. He doesn't suffer fools gladly.

I think this is what happened to Coley. Andy Cole was a bit of a moody, edgy guy. He kept himself to himself. With Kevin, if he sees someone better or can improve the team he will go and get them. He did this with David Kelly who was fantastic for us in the promotion season. He replaced Ned with Peter Beardsley. We'd heard on the grapevine that we were going to sell Coley. I was thinking, 'He must have a replacement.' We didn't know about Les Ferdinand at the time. The Evening Chronicle's Alan Oliver approached me and asked what I thought. He said, 'Kevin is going to sell Andy Cole.' The first thing I thought was, 'If he's going to sell Coley he'll have no second thoughts about selling me. So, for me, it was a kick up the arse. That was how ruthless Kevin was to move the club forward: He'd sell one of his best players.

I thought it was brilliant when he went to talk to the

supporters on the steps outside St James' Park. It was so simplistic. He didn't have to do that. A modern-day manager would never do that. He told the fans, 'Believe in me.' Signing Les Ferdinand wasn't a bad replacement for Coley, was he?

There is no one reason why we didn't win the league or lose it, which is every way you look at it. It was a combination of so many things. Derek Fazakerley leaving was arguably one reason. Not having enough experience in the team was another. That includes the manager, the staff and the players. As a player, you like routine. You know what you're gonna do every day of the week in preparation for a game. You know what day off you're gonna have off, what type of session you're gonna have, right up to a 3pm kick-off on a Saturday. We had the same routine almost right up until the end of January. But everybody wanted to see Newcastle play. We were The Entertainers and Sky decided they wanted us for either a Sunday televised game or a Monday game. This put even more pressure on us because we were the team to beat. I've noticed this over the past 20 years or so. Whoever is leading the Premier League, Sky starts messing with that team's fixture list. It cocks you up. People may think it's easy to adjust to playing on a Sunday but it messes with your routine.

I was devasted we didn't win the title that year but that's not my biggest regret or bugbear, it was Kevin falling out with the board. He should have stayed for another two or three years and the club would have gone onto another level. The fallout he had with the club still does not sit right with me. He had a group of players that were ridiculously good and they would do anything for him. That's what hurts more than losing the title. Don't get me wrong, Man United weren't bad.

One of the most memorable games of my time at Newcastle was the last game of the season at home to Leicester. They were a decent team at the time. The gaffer had said, 'I know we're already promoted but I want us to win and go out in style. I want you to go out there and express yourself.' He then came to me in the dressing room before we went out and said, 'I told you this was going to happen. Now, go out and enjoy yourself.' At half-time when we were 6-0 up it dawned on me: We had something ridiculously good! At half-time, Keegan is laughing. You'd think it was a Sunday morning football team. He said, 'Come on boys, I've got to put a sub on but you're all playing well, does anyone want to give someone else a chance?' I put my hand up and volunteered to give Mark Robinson a runout. The reason I took myself off was to sit and take it all in. Lindisfarne had played before the game and the fans were bouncing. At home, I've got an artist's impression of the game. It's Lowry-esque. Every time I go past it, I'll stop, pause and take it in and think, 'I made the right decision to come here.'

It will stay with me for the rest of my life.

Chapter Nineteen: Robert Lee

Labelled Kevin Keegan's best pound-for-pound signing during The Entertainers' era, Robert Lee shrugged off earlier negative stereotypical thoughts about moving "oop north" to "the grim, cold, wet and gloomy North-East," where people eat coal from breakfast, lunch, dinner and tea, to take his place at the top table of Newcastle legends after ten years of sterling service.

The £750,000 signing from Charlton arrived at St James' Park in 1992 where Keegan transformed him "from a decent right winger at Charlton to an England international midfield player," after turning down Middlesbrough because it was too far north. Keegan's story of how Newcastle was closer to Lee's hometown of London has become part of Magpies' folklore. The popular Londoner, readily admitted that Keegan's pull was irresistible. If KK said Newcastle was closer, that was good enough for him.

The modern-day box-to-box midfielder, who started his career on the right of midfield, enjoyed greater success when he moved to the centre as United pushed Manchester United hard for the Premier League title. The former Addicks midfielder says he was devastated when Keegan sensationally quit United, as he was convinced Newcastle would win a trophy that season had he stayed as the team was fighting on four fronts for silverware. Despite the disappointment, the former St James' Park favourite relished his ten years on Tyneside.

Not Too Grim Oop North

I was brought up as a West Ham supporter as a kid. My favourite players were Billy Bonds and Trevor Brooking but my all-time football hero was Kevin Keegan in the 1970s when he was part of that great Liverpool team. I had pictures of Keegan and Terry McDermott on my bedroom wall. There was nothing sexual about it, honest. I even had the curly perm at one stage. It was dreadful. He was a superstar; the David Beckham or Gazza of his day and I always idolised him.

It's funny because I always did well when I came up to play in the North-East, whether it was against Newcastle, Sunderland or Middlesbrough. I scored two in one game against John Burridge. Not sure that counts, though, does it? I never dreamed I'd end up playing up here. I had just turned 25 and in the last year of my latest contract at Charlton and I went to the manager Alan Curbishley and said I wanted to play in the Premier League. My old manager at Charlton, Lennie Lawrence, was the Middlesbrough boss and he wanted to sign me. Boro were a Premier League club then. Charlton needed £700,000 so they could go back to the Valley.

I'm thinking, 'Fucking hell! Middlesbrough!' I didn't fancy it but I got on a flight from London. I got off at Teesside Airport. It was horrible, grey and raining, really miserable. They showed me around Ayresome Park and it was falling apart. That was horrible too. I met Lennie and the chairman Steve Gibson and they showed me around Ingleby Barwick. That was awful as well. Then I went home. I thought, 'I'm not going there or up north.' Curbs rang me and I told him I wasn't going up north. I knew West Ham and Billy Bonds were interested. They'd only offered £500,000 so I had to wait. Curbs then told me Kevin Keegan had come in for me.

I had to ask, 'Where is he?' I genuinely thought he was still in Marbella playing golf. I told Curbs I wasn't going to Newcastle or up north. He told me Terry Mac was going to ring me in five minutes. I told Terry Mac the same, 'I ain't coming.' He said, 'Kevin wants to talk to you.' I said he could but the answer was still the same, 'I'm not coming.' Kevin came on the phone and told me he'd booked me a flight to go to Newcastle the following morning.

I arrived at Newcastle Airport, it was cold and raining. I then got to St James' Park and I thought it was depressing. (Chief Operating Officer) Russel Cushing met me and took me to his office for a cup of tea. I took my wife with me and I leaned over and said to her, 'Thirty minutes and we'll be out of here.' I went in to meet Kevin and then came out of the meeting half an hour later and told my wife to pack a bag because I'd signed a three-and-a-half-year contract. To be honest, I would have gone anywhere to play for Kevin Keegan. The pull of Kevin was too strong.

People say, 'Don't meet your heroes because they'll let you down.' He didn't. Kevin was everything and more, I was in total awe of him. He was fun to be around. When he walked into a room everything stopped. He could speak to anyone: Kids, old people, royalty. I took a few bollockings off him but he turned me from a decent right winger at Charlton to an England international midfield player. He told me I was a good player and when Kevin Keegan tells you that, you must be.

Did he really say Newcastle was closer to London than Middlesbrough? He did but the story has grown legs from both of us to be honest. He said Newcastle was a bigger city and there were more direct trains and planes to London from Newcastle than Middlesbrough. We have a giggle about it still. To be honest, I didn't know whether it was true, they were both north of Watford Gap. That's all I knew.

When I first got to the club I was walking through the gym and Kevin and Terry Mac were playing head tennis. Kevin shouts for me to get a partner to play. I didn't know anyone and then I saw Franz Carr. They absolutely battered us. Kevin's nudging Terry Mac, 'How much did I pay for him?' They continued to batter us until I found a new partner in Bez. It took us three months before we beat them.

At Charlton on Fridays, the manager Alan Curbishley was very meticulous. He had a five-page dossier on who we were playing, their strengths and weaknesses, and who we'd be marking from corners and free kicks. It went on for hours and I hated it. At Newcastle on Fridays, we'd play five-a-side for about 35 minutes, with no goalies,

Kevin and Terry Mac played. It was like five-a-side with your mates. I asked Kevin who was taking the free-kicks and corners. He said, 'Well, if you're playing well, take one.' We never did any set plays. He told me he was going to sign better players all of the time and said it is up to you to keep up. Well, I got better with better players. He'd sign those players and let them play. It wasn't rocket science, they didn't need coaching, did they? Good players know how to play.

I remember Mark Lawrenson came in as our defensive coach. Kevin said Mark's gonna take the defenders this morning and we went and did some shooting practice. After five minutes Kevin is getting impatient. He shouts over, 'How long are you gonna be Lawro?' Lawro's said he won't be long while we're doing this shooting drill from Liverpool in the 1970s. Another five minutes and he's shouting again. Lawro's saying he'll not be long but Kevin's had enough. He's shouted, 'OK, you can bring them back over now.' Then we went and had another game of eight-a-side. I'm not kidding, that was the only time Lawro did any work on the defence in all the time he was at the club. He was there 18 months and that was it. Most days he'd just be wandering around chatting to people.

We had some great young players coming through. You wouldn't want them in your quiz team but they all went on to have very good careers and some of them were internationals. Mad as hatters. I'd never witnessed anything like them in all my time at Charlton. When you went out with them it was chaos, madness. They were a bit thick and that's not insulting them by the way. Anyway, I'm one to talk, Kevin told me Newcastle was closer to London than Middlesbrough and I believed him. I remember driving up on my first day and passing a sign for Middlesbrough. I thought, 'Hang on.'

Kevin built the team around Andy Cole and look how much he blossomed when Peter Beardsley was brought in. Andy Cole was all about goals. You see strikers today working the channels and closing down fullbacks. Coley never did any of that. Kevin told him, 'You stay in the box, they will do all the chasing and get the ball to you.' And that's what we did and he scored a lot of goals. I think one of the reasons he was moved on was because teams had cottoned on to how he played and so he left.

I think Kevin looked at the games before that. He'd had a row with Keegan at Wimbledon and he went home. We didn't see him for three or four days. I think he'd been tapped up by Man United. He hadn't been playing well for us and Keegan is the type of guy if you don't want to be here, he'll get rid of you. He was always like that. He only wanted players who wanted to play for Newcastle. He told me when I signed, that he was going to keep buying better players. It's up to you if you want to keep up. If you can you'll remain here if you can't you'll go.

You just need to look at Steve Guppy. He went on to play for England. He cried in training one day. He said, 'I've been here a month and I still haven't touched the ball yet.' Warren Barton said the same thing when he came. The way we trained was exactly how we played. It was 100 miles per hour whether it was five-a-side or eight-a-side.

Then we signed Les Ferdinand to replace Cole and it was a case of 'Andy who?' I was desperately trying to get Les to sign for us when I was with England. I was always tapping him. I honestly badgered him. It's a surprise I was never up in front of the FA for poaching. I saw how good he was and every time he played against us for QPR we couldn't handle him. He had everything. He could leap really high, he was strong, fast and could score goals. When he came in, with Ginola on one wing and Gillespie on the other, alongside Peter Beardsley, he was perfect for us.

When we signed David Ginola, we were getting changed for training at Maiden Castle. As most people knew, apart from David, we were sharing with the university. David is getting changed next to this big fat student. He looked at him and said, 'You English footballers don't know how to look after yourselves.' Me and Bez were creased up.

Pavel was another great guy in a squad of great guys. He was so quiet. A real family man and rarely came out with us. If he did come out, he'd drive and wouldn't drink. The last time saw him was Steve Harper's testimonial. I was chatting to him at the bar with a glass of red wine in his hand. I said, 'Alright Pav, what's going on here?' He told me he'd split up with his Mrs and found drink. It's a shame he didn't find red wine before he left.

Brian Kilcline is a larger-than-life character. He used to scare the shit out of me when I played but when I actually met him, he was like a gentle giant and softly spoken. He was a great guy to have around. Then you had the likes of Barry Venison who was a great guy when he wasn't pissed but when he is pissed, he's the devil. I've never seen anything like him. He drinks champagne when he's out. He was a great captain and a former Liverpool legend.

We were always playing tricks on each other and I heard about the end-of-season trip to Cyprus. I didn't go, I went back to London with the family. Killer was paralytic and fell asleep on a table, according to Bez, and some of the lads cut half of his hair and half of his tache. He loved his hair and his tache and while we can laugh about it now, it wasn't funny. Killer tried to find out who did it and he went to see Faz who said he was there. He didn't get to say anything else because the next thing was SMASH! Killer had smacked Faz, who said he didn't do it. Bez is hanging around his neck trying to stop him without any success. No one has admitted to doing it. Rumours say that it was Barry Venison, and I believe those rumours. It was a shame really because Killer thought the lads had lost respect for him which couldn't be further from the truth because he was loved by everyone. It was a joke that went badly, badly wrong.

David Kelly and Gavin Peacock dovetailed well together during their time at the club. They scored a lot of goals for us, not just in keeping us up, but in the promotions season, as did Andy Cole when he later joined. I think David Kelly was underrated. He was a good footballer and a very funny guy. He probably played the best football of his career at Newcastle. He scored something like 28 goals in our promotion season.

He tells a good story about when Kevin was getting rid of him. He got a call from Kevin when he was driving and Ned is thinking, 'I'm gonna be offered a new contract.' And Kevin said, 'I'm going to sell you. Ned said, 'But I scored 28 goals.' Kevin said, 'Yeah, but we're in the Premier League next season and I'm gonna replace you.' He said, 'I scored 28 goals, who you gonna get to score you 28 goals?' Kevin said, 'I'm gonna sign Peter Beardsley.' Ned said, 'Good shout, I'll drive down to Wolves.'

Peter Beardsley was ridiculous. How he trained and how he played. One of the reasons I scored so many goals was because Peter would drop in a cover for me when I was going forward. He would find you with a pass even when you thought he couldn't see you.

We had some ridiculous talent at the club. I've never seen a centre half like Philippe Albert before. I've never seen a centre-half chip a goalie until he did it and he did it regularly in training to Pav. He was such a good footballer and he was quick just before he did his ACL. I've not seen anyone drink like him either. Lee Clark and Steve Watson often took him out and he loved Newcastle. He got the culture of the city. Philippe was a great signing for the club as was Marc Hottiger, I'd watched them both in the World Cup in 1994. They were really good signings for us.

Tino was another great lad. I talk to him now and then and all he says is, Bastardo! Sheet (shit)! He didn't learn any English while he was here. He'd always play well in the big games, like Barcelona, but sometimes he just didn't fancy it if we were playing against teams like

Norwich or Coventry. It was as if these teams were below him. There was one game at half-time Kevin is screaming obscenities at him. Tino doesn't understand a word he's saying. We've got an interpreter and Kevin's telling him to tell Tino if he doesn't improve in the first 15 minutes he's coming off. Tino took his boots off, shin pads and kit and went in the shower. He'd often come out with us and we'd get him hammered. We'd also get his interpreter hammered, a young lad from university. I remember one night at Julies (nightclub) the interpreter was lying on the floor because he was so drunk. I've no idea how he passed his degree.

When we missed out on the Premier League title, we just thought we'd go again. I thought we were the best team in the league. Don't get me wrong, Man United were good too. They had world class players. They had the best goalkeeper in the world and that's no disrespect to our goalkeepers. Cantona was scoring goals for fun. They had Roy Keane and all of these good kids coming through: Scholes, Beckham, Giggs, the Nevilles. They were a bloody good team. People talk about losing the Liverpool game at Anfield but it wasn't the game that lost it for us. It was probably the Man U game at home. We battered them and it should have been 5-0 like it was the year later. The 1-0 win gave them the belief that they could catch us. We went out to Anfield to win the game. Not once in the five years under him did he say let's set up camp for a draw. He wanted to win every game.

We were good enough to win it with the squad we had but then we bought Alan Shearer for a world record fee. We were on our way to the Far East for a three-and-a-half-week tour. This was down to Sir John Hall who was ahead of his time in marketing the club. We were all sitting on the plane ready for take-off when Kevin, all of a sudden, got off. We heard rumours he was going to sign Shearer but we weren't certain.

The bizarre thing was that we couldn't fly with Alan

because of the cost of his insurance, and the team on top of that, wouldn't allow us, or rather, we couldn't fly with him. I'm not joking. Shearer had to fly on his own for the first three months after he signed for us. Shearer asked Kevin how we were going to play with him in the side. Kevin said, 'You're gonna play alongside Les, Tino and Peter Beardsley and Keith Gillespie and David Ginola on the wings with Rob Lee.' Shearer's gone, 'That's seven forwards!' Keegan said, 'Yeah, we're really gonna go for it this year.'

It was crazy because we didn't start well after we signed Alan. We'd flown back from the Far East and had to fit a game in against Lincoln because that was part of Darren Huckerby's signing. Then we went to play in the Charity Shield where we lost 4-0 to Man United and then lost to Everton 2-0 on the opening day of the new football season. We then beat Wimbledon at home and went on a good run to turn things around.

I get asked all of the time why we didn't win the title that year. When you look at Man United, they had some unbelievable young players coming through that went on to be world-class players. I think they won something like 17 out of 18 games at the back end of the season. We were the leaders and we were always playing on different days. People say that shouldn't matter but it did. They were chasing us and we felt it. With Schmeichel in goal and Cantona coming back from his kung fu kick ban, they kept winning 1-0. We'd be losing 4-3 or drawing 3-3. We'd ask how Man U did, it was 1-0, Cantona had scored and Schmeichel played a blinder. Even at St James' Park, it was the same. We beat them 5-0 the year after we lost 1-0 but it could've easily been 7-1. Schmeichel saved about three one-on-ones from Les and Tino and Cantona scored. I think that was the fatal blow.

I'm sure had Kevin not quit that year we would have won something, without a shadow of a doubt. We were such a good team. Kevin's quitting took us years and years to recover from. It was a shock to me, David Ginola and especially Alan, whom Kevin had persuaded to sign for £15 million. He had the choice of the Italian clubs and Man United. Same with Ginola. Barcelona was in for him and he told David to give it another season because he would win something.

He left after an FA Cup game at Charlton. We didn't see it coming and he didn't leave for football reasons, which is normally the case. We were still in Europe, in the FA Cup and fighting for the league, fourth with games in hand. It was my biggest disappointment in football. It was upsetting. I was devastated. I scored the last goal for him in the 1-1 draw at the Valley. I think he's the only manager to leave while the team were doing well.

It was the stuff off the pitch which he didn't like with the club turning into a PLC. Today it wouldn't happen because the manager isn't involved in those sorts of things but Kevin was involved with everything from contracts to where we stayed. Had he stopped we would have won something that season and gone on to be as big as Man United.

Kenny came and I loved him, as did the players, but the fans, not so much. I think he saw it was Kevin's team and wanted to change it. If he'd only thought, 'I've got a good team here and it only needs tweaking.' But he didn't. He got rid of Bez and replaced him with Alexander Pistone which was a terrible decision. He got rid of some really good players and bought some bad players. He swapped Les for Jon Dahl Tomasson who went on to have a very good career but he was dreadful for us.

Des Hamilton also signed for us. He was a lovely guy but not the brightest. We were always playing tricks on each other. This day Alan came to training in a new Gucci top. It looked like an England top. It probably cost a couple of hundred quid. I was injured at the time and Des came in and I grabbed Alan's Gucci top and asked Des if he could sign this England top for the lads. He signed it and I put it back on Alan's peg. Alan came in, got changed, had a shower and was putting his clothes on when he screamed, 'Who the fucking hell has done this?' I said, 'Look, it's got Des's name on it.' Alan then got a pair of scissors and went through all of Des's clothes. It was his first or second day at the club. I remember him leaving training, he looked like Robinson Crusoe. I still feel bad about that.

The only fond memory I have of Ruud Gullit was Stuart Pearce putting him ten feet in the air in training one time. On a Friday he'd have an eight-versus-eight game, English players and foreign players. It was a horrible day, pissing down and cold. There was me, Steve Harper, Duncan Ferguson, David Batty, John Barnes, Alan and Stewart Pearce, Warren Barton and they had Franc Dumas, Goma, Domi etc. They're beating us 2-0 and Ruud is giving it the big one, 'You can't win anything with British players. Pearcy walks towards me, pulls his shorts up to reveal those massive thighs of his. He says, 'Rob, when you get the ball put it between me and that big cunt.' I'm like, 'OK,' I'm not arguing with you. I managed to get the ball, and it was probably 60-40, possibly 70-30 in Gullit's favour to get there first but Pearcey hit him so hard that he went flying over. The British and foreign lads are pissing themselves. Ruud jumps up and says, 'Who the fuc... alright Pearcey. Good tackle, lovely boy, good tackle.'

It was great when he left and Sir Bobby came in. He was like a breath of fresh air. It was like playing for your granddad. He'd come to training in this tracksuit and Gola boots from the 1960s. It was like that scene from the movie Kes. I went to see him just before I moved to Derby. I was 36 and asked him for another year. We were doing well, I was still in the team and we were fourth in the league. He said, 'Freddie Shepherd does the contracts.' I'd been here ten years at the time. I went to see Freddy and he said, 'Bobby does the contracts.' I went back to the ground the following day and said, 'Gaffa, the chairman said you do all of the contracts.' 'Yes, that's right,' he said. 'I do all of the contracts.' I asked him for another year. He gave a sharp intake of breath and said, 'I can't give you another contract, your legs have gone.' I said no problem, 'Will you let me go?' I knew Glenn Roeder wanted me at West Ham. He gave another sharp intake of breath and said, 'I can't let you go, son, you're my best player.' Shearer was waiting for me in the car as I got there and I was laughing. He asked what I was laughing at so I told him, 'My legs have gone so I can't have a new contract but the club won't let me go because I'm the best player at the club.' Alan just pissed himself all the way home. Anyone else I would have had a row but I couldn't get angry at him.

I still see the local lads, Lee Clark, Steve Howey, Steve Watson, and John Beresford. There's not a day that goes by when I look back at my time at Newcastle and what could have been but we have a great time every time I come up to Newcastle.

Keegan always said the first trophy was the hardest. He was certainly right.

Chapter Twenty: Scott Sellars

Scott Sellars joined Newcastle United in March 1993, from Leeds United for £850,000. His move was sparked after Newcastle manager Kevin Keegan heard Leeds needed to raise some cash to buy a defender, having unsuccessfully pursued Sellars the previous summer. Sellars was impressed by Keegan's vision and ambition for the club, which went beyond just winning the Championship and aimed at long-term success.

Initially, Sellars struggled to adapt to the high-intensity training and all-football focus at Newcastle, different from what he'd previously encountered in his early career. However, Keegan's trust in Sellars paid off as he began to settle in, contributing significantly with assists and goals. His most memorable moment came in a crucial match against fierce rivals Sunderland. Despite a waterlogged pitch, Sellars scored the decisive goal in a 1-0 victory, instantly endearing himself to the Newcastle faithful and instantly becoming a local hero. This win was pivotal as it virtually secured Newcastle's promotion.

Sellars found Newcastle's training environment at Maiden Castle unique, with thousands of fans attending sessions, creating a lively and motivating atmosphere. The camaraderie among players, bolstered by experienced pros and young talents, contributed to a strong team spirit. Sellars played a vital role in the final stretch of the 1992-93 promotion season, helping Newcastle secure their place in the Premier League.

Despite suffering a severe injury early in the 1994-95 season and witnessing the arrival of David Ginola in his position, Sellars cherished his time at Newcastle. His tenure is remembered fondly, highlighted by his significant match-winning goal against Sunderland and his integral role in the team's promotion campaign. Another over-the-wall goal that certainly deserved a song.

Salty Sellars

I'd just gone to Leeds from Blackburn in the summer

but they needed a right back but didn't have any money. Newcastle, who enquired about me the previous summer, heard I was available and came back in for me with an £850,000 offer. It worked out quite well for all of us because Leeds sold me and bought David Kerslake and I got a move to Newcastle.

I met Kevin Keegan in a hotel at Scotch Corner. Newcastle had won something like 11 games in a row before I signed. It was the middle of March when I signed. I spoke to Kevin about what style of football we would play and where I would fit in. I'd seen bits and bobs of Newcastle's games, even though I was in the Premier League with Leeds. It was an easy decision to make once I knew they were interested. I wanted to talk to Kevin Keegan.

Taking a step down to take a step back to go up wasn't a problem. For players of my generation, Kevin Keegan was a footballing god. He was a player that was really respected and liked. He was a fellow Yorkshireman as well. When I met him, he was so easy to get along with and I enjoyed his company. What really struck me was how ambitious he was. It wasn't just a case of winning the Championship and getting into the Premier League. He wanted to go further and achieve more. Kevin was very enthusiastic and inspiring about the challenge ahead.

The facilities at Maiden Castle were great. The pitches were excellent to be fair. We couldn't get anything to eat, mind you, except a cuppa soup, which is funny when you think how important nutrition has become in the modern game now. Thousands of supporters used to come and watch us train which I found a bit strange at first but then you got used to it and it became quite interesting. Having the supporters there gave training an atmosphere which was ramped up, especially on Fridays in our five-a-side matches which were pretty intense anyway. Having the supporters there helped raise our game.

I knew John Beresford from our Sheffield boys' days. I also knew Derek Fazackerley because I played with him at Blackburn. I got to know the older pros the best like Barry Venison and Paul Bracewell. I found it difficult when I first joined. The training was tough, in terms of the intensity. It was quite well organised at Leeds with lots of focus on set pieces. At Newcastle, it was just football, football, football, played at such a high intensity. I played the final 12-13 games of the 1992-93 promotion season but in the first four games, I didn't feel as if I performed well at all. To be fair to Kevin, he stood by me and I eventually began to settle in. I then started to have some good games and got some assists and goals.

The game against local rivals Sunderland at St James' Park shouldn't have been played. The pitch was waterlogged, there were puddles everywhere. If it hadn't been for the game going out live on the TV it would have been postponed. We were looking forward to the game. The lads were telling me about the game at Roker Park and how well they'd played down there. We wanted to get promotion done as quickly as possible and I think we needed only one more point to get promoted after we beat them 1-0.

I used to take the corners anyway, so when we got the free-kick outside the box I said I'd take it and I chipped it over the wall and sent their goalkeeper the wrong way. The goal helped me to become very popular very quickly among Newcastle supporters and my teammates. It was probably my favourite goal for the club. It was really important for us and the supporters.

Kevin Keegan was a manager who put a lot of trust in his players. Kevin doesn't get a lot of credit for his tactics but he knew players, what their strengths were and how they would react with other players. He was like a chemist. He got the chemistry right in the team and how the players interacted with each other and worked well together with their strengths all complimenting others. He also knew when to bring new players in and move players on. He did that very well.

He was a massive motivator. Some days he'd come in with the opposition team sheet, crumple it up, throw it on the floor and say, 'If you can't beat these we might as well pack in.' He gave us a lot of belief, trust and confidence. That's what you want as a player. Someone who really believes in you. He'd often give you a pep talk before a game but what a motivator, such an inspiring character.

Terry Mac was important to Kevin. He trusted him, he had the gaffer's back, and he knew the game. Terry was a great player in his own right. Terry was good at picking you up when you were a bit down and always gave good advice when you were struggling. They were a great pair as was Derek Fazackerley, who was a major part of the coaching staff. One of Kevin's biggest strengths was that he knew what he was good at and what he wasn't and he would get people in to do the jobs he wasn't good at.

The last game of the Championship season at home to Leicester was a great day. There was a band on before the game. We were already promoted but we wanted to go out in style and the reigns were off to go out and enjoy ourselves. Kevin didn't say much about that game. It was a case off you go. We were very relaxed. After winning the league we felt as if we were unstoppable, unbeatable. Leicester came up that year through the playoffs. They were a decent side.

Pavel Srnicek got a t-shirt that day from Lee Clark, with Pavel is a Geordie on it. He was a lovely, sweet, caring guy. He was an integral part of the squad. An unbelievable athlete, as a specimen. He was a machine and ripped, flexible, good with his feet. He was very much the modern goalkeeper before his time, in terms of how good he was with his feet. A great character and always had a smile on his face. I always enjoyed his company.

Several games stick out from my time in Geordieland, including the 1-0 victory over Sunderland. The 3-0 win over Liverpool was special. I got two assists and was also involved in the first goal in Andy Cole's hat-trick. We were

3-0 up at half-time. We also went to Anfield that season and won 2-0 there. There were so many enjoyable games. I enjoyed our style of play. It was great football to play and be a part of. You couldn't wait to get to training, play games and be a part of a great team.

Kevin often talked about us being in the entertainment business and playing in a certain style. He recruited players who could do that. He brought in players who could dominate possession and the ball, and be creative. He even brought in defenders who could play football. Even Venners, who dropped back into the centre-back position. He could play. He even moved forward into midfield, where he got capped for England.

We had a great balance. Everyone had the basics. Then there were creative players, players who could score goals in Peter Beardsley and Andy Cole. Those two together were unbelievable. There would be games where we would be struggling and then one of them would pop up with a goal. I thought we would do OK in the Premier League once we got promoted but I honestly didn't think we'd finish top three. Think we surprised ourselves a bit. I thought we'd get results. I wasn't worried about that. I thought it would be tougher to implement our style of play in the Premier League for some reason but it wasn't, it was easier if anything.

Not sure I can repeat any of the funny stories of my time in Newcastle but there were lots of jokers at the club. The young Geordie lads were mad: Clarky, Watto and Robbie Elliott were daft, as was Steve Howey, the Mackem. We often told the kids that what we had at the club wasn't normal. They realised this only when Kevin left and another manager or regime came in.

We had some great experienced players like Killer and Tommy Wright, Liam O'Brien, Venners, Brace. We had a great balance and the squad got on well. We'd often go out as a group, especially during the international weeks because at the time, we'd just got promotion and there weren't many of us playing for our country. We'd meet for a meal on a Friday afternoon and then have a good night. It was a great, close-knit group.

I got a bad injury which kept me out for about nine months in the early part of the 1994-95 season. I was fit for pre-season training and played a few games, then Kevin brought in David Ginola, who played in my position. He was outstanding. To be honest, I spent most of my time clapping him in training. He was great to watch. He was doing things I'd not seen before. Ginola gave us a bit of a boost again after the disappointment of finishing sixth the season before.

My last game was a 1-1 draw away to Spurs. I didn't know it was going to be my last game. Like a lot of lads at that time, I was old school and wanted to play. I recognised I wouldn't be playing again after nine months out through injury and I was desperate to play games again. I was playing in the reserves but it wasn't the same. When I look back and ask whether I made the right decision to leave, I still don't know. I was watching the games in admiration and I loved being around the lads but it doesn't beat playing yourself on a Saturday afternoon.

Kevin came and told me that Bolton had made an offer but he didn't want me to leave. He said he would give me a new contract and that I could go out on loan somewhere for a month to get some games. I told him that I wanted to play more games and I couldn't see myself playing. We were 12 points clear at the time and going for the title. He said there was a chance I'd win a league medal. I was quite stubborn to be fair.

I still can't believe Newcastle didn't win the league that year. I can't honestly say why we didn't win it. Maybe because the group hadn't been there before and didn't know how to cope with the pressure whereas Man United had been there before. I drove up to watch the game against Man United at St James' Park. I also went to watch the game at Leeds as well. Keith Gillespie scored in a 1-0 win. Man United towards the end of that season did exceptionally well.

Peter Beardsley was probably the best player at the club and he came when he was about 32, 33, 34. There was no way he was slowing down when he arrived. He was super fit, trained hard, had two great feet and an abundance of tricks. Some of them were so simple but he'd drag players all over the place. He was exceptional, as were the fans.

There is nothing better at a football club when there is a connection between the players and the fans. The momentum and energy you get from that made us unstoppable at times. Sir John Hall played a big part in that connection, as well as Kevin. I'd often stand in the tunnel and look across at the opposition players and think, 'We've won this game already.' They were terrified of the atmosphere. They were the best fans I played in front of, unquestionably.

Chapter Twenty one: Andy Cole

Like a number of transfers during The Entertainers' era, the arrival of the unknown Andy Cole took Newcastle United fans by surprise. Cole joined Newcastle in 1993 for £1.75 million from Bristol City, a move that also surprised him. However, the Nottingham-born striker quickly integrated into the team, making his debut in a 2-1 loss at Swindon, followed by a full debut in a convincing 4-0 victory over Notts County.

Under Kevin Keegan's management, Cole flourished and became a prolific striker. In the 1993-94 season, he scored 41 goals in all competitions, breaking legend Hughie Gallagher's long-standing goalscoring record. His partnership with Peter Beardsley was particularly influential, with Beardsley's football intelligence and skill significantly aiding Cole's development into an international striker.

One of Cole's most memorable moments came during the last game of the 1992-93 season, where he bagged a hat-trick in a 7-1 win against Leicester City in a carnival atmosphere as the team celebrated promotion to the Premier League. The following season, wearing the iconic No. 9 shirt, he continued his impressive form.

Yet despite his success, Cole's time at Newcastle ended abruptly in January 1995 when he was transferred to Manchester United for £6 million plus Keith Gillespie. The move astounded fans and Cole himself, who had no prior indication of the transfer. This decision by Keegan was controversial and speculated to be influenced by their past disagreements.

Cole's departure left a significant impact but his contributions to Newcastle were unforgettable. He is fondly remembered by supporters for his passion and outstanding goal-scoring record. His goals at Newcastle United cemented his status as a club legend.

Taking Coles to Newcastle

The move to Newcastle came out of the blue. Russell

Osman, the Bristol City manager at the time, called and said he had accepted a bid from Newcastle for me and that they wanted to speak to me that night. A week before Denis Smith was the manager and he told me Nottingham Forest had put a bid in for me. They only offered £500,000 so Dennis said he couldn't let me go because City had paid £500,000 for me. In that same week, Denis got sacked. It seemed so random that he got sacked and then Newcastle came in for me.

It was quite easy to come and fit in at Newcastle because all of the hard work had already been done by the team. I made my debut away in a 2-1 loss at Swindon. I came on as a sub and then made my full debut the following week in a 4-0 home win against Notts County. I was surprised Kevin put me straight in the team because they were doing so well.

Kevin and Terry Mac were polar opposites. Terry was a special man. He was the life and soul of the party, very bubbly, and kept you laughing. You could never take him seriously. He was that type of character. He was very good in the dressing room and very good as an individual. Kevin was very different. He was very up and down. When things are going well, he's unbelievable but when they're not he's so-so. I think he quit about several times while I was there and then he'd come back a few days later. He was a very emotional manager or rather an emotional person.

The last game of the season against Leicester was a proper fun day out. We had already been promoted. Scoring three goals in a 7-1 win made it even more special. In the early days of the Premier League, we got a coach everywhere. I'd played virtually every game that season and we were away at Southampton and lost 2-1. We had a League Cup game against Wimbledon in midweek so after the Southampton game we made our way to London and stayed for the game. We went in for a warm-down on the Monday. Kevin asked if I was OK. I said, 'To be honest boss, I'm tired.' He said, 'Oh, if you're tired and don't fancy training you can fuck off.' I said, 'OK, if that's the way you feel, I'll do just that.' So, I went and had a shower, packed my bags and left. I took a few days off and then the media got hold of the story. Then a meeting was called where I sat down with Freddy Shepherd, Kevin and Terry and we spoke about it. I was offered a new contract and then everything was sorted out and I was back in the squad.

Peter Beardsley was and is a legend to me. I've said this many times. Peter had such a big impact on my career as a young player. What I learned from him was phenomenal at Newcastle. His football intelligence and the way he got hold of the ball was amazing. When people nowadays get excited about half turns and half spins and all of this kind of nonsense, Peter was doing all of this in the 1980s and early 1990s. Peter was a very special player.

Lee Clark was my best mate at Newcastle. He is a top, top, top man. We used to play for England when we were kids. He would say, 'Coley, come to Newcastle' and I would say, 'It's too far.' He'd say, 'The fans would love you.' I'd say, 'Slim,' my nickname for him, 'you know how far it is?' Obviously, we used to laugh about it. Then, when Kevin came in for me, I called Clarky. He had a big influence on me joining Newcastle. I knew if I went, he'd look after me and he did just that.

It was nice to break Hughie Gallagher's goalscoring record and records are there to be broken I guess but I was never driven by those things. I was very proud to have broken the record and it was very special for the Newcastle fans and to put a smile on their faces. To be spoken about in the same breath as Hughie Gallagher was special but I quickly moved on after it to the next game.

My best goal for the club? That's a tough one. Maybe the left foot volley into the top corner at home in a 4-2 win over Chelsea in 1994. In the summer after we got promotion Kevin told me he was bringing in Peter Beardsley. I was like, 'Cool.' I was buzzing to hear that news. Then he said he wanted me to wear the No.9. I told him I was happy to wear the No.8, as David Kelly wore the No.9 the previous season. He said, 'No! The No.9 is the main shirt at Newcastle and I'm going to give the No.8 to Peter. It didn't make much of a difference to me, to be honest. I know it means a lot up in Newcastle but it was just another shirt for me. So, I said, 'OK, I'll wear the No.9.' I didn't feel any weight of expectancy on my shoulders and I didn't think it would make me play any better.

Kevin was trying to make me understand the importance of the No.9 and what it was about, telling me about all of the previous greats who wore it like Hughie Gallagher and Malcolm MacDonald. I then got what he was talking about and what it meant to the people of Newcastle. To be fair I went on to score a few goals wearing it but at the time it was just a number to me.

My move to Manchester United came out of the blue. We'd played Blackburn in the FA Cup at the weekend. We were in on the Monday for the warm-down. Kevin and Barnet were in. Barnet is the nickname I gave to Terry Mac because of his curly hair. They never said anything to me at the time. I went home after training. I then sat down to watch Sheffield United against Man United on the Monday night and I got a call from my representative at the time to tell me the move to Man United was on. He said a deal had been sorted and he would pick me up in a couple of hours and take me to Manchester. I couldn't believe it was happening to be honest.

I get asked about it all of the time and people think I forced the move. I didn't. People keep saying this. I still don't know how the move came about so how do they? I know the gaffer and his assistant didn't say a word to me on the day the move happened. Kevin instigated the move. Once a manager has decided he no longer wants you it is best you move on. Was it in the back of Kevin's mind to sell me further down the line after we fell out the year before? Maybe. Kevin held grudges. He'd always have a tear-up with Venners. They were always at each other's throats.

Venners was a little bit different and he's very funny. I used to ask why they were always clashing. I was just a young pro at the time. Venners was at Liverpool and won a lot of things in his career. Kevin's mood after we lost a game was very sombre. Venners would say to him, 'If you're gonna be like this you shouldn't be around the lads.' I was like, 'Bloody hell.' Being around Kevin was like an emotional rollercoaster. You never knew what mood you'd catch him in.

There were several reasons why Newcastle didn't win the league that season, not one. When I went to Manchester United, regardless of what happened, the manager took the pressure off the players. Whatever he said in the dressing room and what he said to the media after a game was the total opposite. It was chalk and cheese. We'd get a total dressing down after a game if we lost or didn't play well but he'd tell the media we were unlucky or maybe if we'd took an earlier chance the outcome would have been different. It was always very galvanising.

When we got ourselves into that position, and Kevin lost it after Newcastle played Leeds, we thought, 'Yeah, we've got them.' For us, we believed the manager was too emotional and that will translate to the players. We thought that if the pressure was beginning to take its toll on Kevin, what was it doing to the players? Then the run Newcastle went on wasn't the best after that.

I wouldn't blame David Batty or Tino. Ultimately, the team had to go out there and win games. The manager picks the team and he knows what he wants from you. They go out there and play the way he wants you to play. So, it appeared that Kevin was nervous and it galvanised us. From there Newcastle's form was indifferent from the way they played earlier in the season. It was crazy. We even said, 'If we win the game at St James' Park, we will win the league. And we did. Peter Schmeichel was unbelievable that day. Without Peter who knows what the score would have been. But after we won, we knew we had a great chance of winning the league.

I wasn't surprised when Kevin quit and left the following season. Kevin is an emotional rollercoaster. He had a few falling outs with Sir John Hall, regarding transfers. There was always talk of him resigning. So, when he did leave it didn't surprise me.

I've always spoken very fondly of Newcastle fans. I thoroughly enjoyed my time at the club but the adulation was tough for me at the time. I just wasn't ready for it because I am just a private guy. I didn't think I was any different to the 9am-5pm fans. My job was just different to theirs. I ran around chasing a bag of leather. It just didn't seem real. I can appreciate it now I'm older and retired. The passion and love these guys had for their football club. All they wanted was for you to run around, put a shift in and try and win a game. When I was at Newcastle I did just that. I put a shift in and scored some goals and played with my heart and with passion, like I did for every club I played for.

I was never one of those guys who wouldn't celebrate if they'd scored a goal against a former club. It's why you play football, to celebrate. It's why you train Monday to Friday to try and score a goal on a Saturday. Football is supposed to be played with passion and desire. I have a lot of admiration for Newcastle fans. They are unbelievable supporters. When it comes to playing football at St James' Park, bloody hell! It was like someone had turned on a wind machine and the noise at five minutes to three from the crowd was crazy, absolutely crazy. I had a great time playing in front of them.

Chapter Twenty two: Paul Ferris

Paul Ferris is far from a conventional former footballer. He is arguably the most interesting character to play for Newcastle United since the multi-talented Colin Veitch in the club's Edwardian golden age era. In addition to being a qualified barrister with a Master's degree in the history of ideas, he also served as a physiotherapist for United during the club's renaissance in the mid-1990s. Ferris's talents are limitless; the highly intelligent ex-footballer is also an award-winning, best-selling novelist and writer.

The precocious Lisburn-born Northern Irishman joined Newcastle as a 15-year-old in 1981 and, like many youngsters who left the Emerald Isle for the cold shores of Blighty, he was dubbed the new George Best. Unfortunately, a medial ligament injury to his knee robbed the talented left-winger of a promising career at St James' Park.

At just 21, the Irishman found himself on the scrap heap. Many would have crumbled under the uncertainty of their future and used their misfortune as an excuse to turn to alcohol, drugs or crime. But for Ferris, it turned out to be an epiphany as he retrained as a physiotherapist and returned to the club in the medical department, dedicated to keeping United's superstars fit during the rollercoaster Kevin Keegan era.

The Boy on the Shed

It was 1993 and I was in the rehab room at the Freeman Hospital working with an elderly lady who'd had a stroke when a colleague peered around the door.

'There's a Derek Wright on the phone for you. He says you'll know what it's about?' I nearly dropped my patient. Derek Wright? Why was Newcastle United's physio calling me at work? When I returned the call, he said he just called to give me a heads-up because Newcastle was looking for another physio and they were interviewing potential candidates. He asked whether I was interested and I said, 'Absolutely.'

About a week later I had an interview with Dr Keith Beverage and Derek Wright at the County Hotel in Durham and they offered me a job for less wages than I was on at the hospital but I took it because it was Newcastle United and too big an opportunity to turn down.

I didn't drive at the time and got the train to the training ground in Durham. I got lost on my first day and I didn't want to be late. How could I get lost? A sweaty man at the station had said to me, 'Just follow the river. Follow the river and you can't miss it. You better hurry though. It's a fair old hike.' I'd been following the river but felt like I was going round in circles. I came to a clearing. Some builders were on the roof of an old derelict cottage they were bringing back to life. I asked the closest one to me if he knew the way. He most certainly did. He had a strong Durham accent.

'Just follow the smell of the shite, son. You can't miss it.'

I just assumed everyone in Durham was a Newcastle fan but it was clear this guy was a Sunderland supporter.

When I finally got to the changing room, Kevin was there.

I can remember it like it was yesterday. He said, "Ferra. Great to have you back. You couldn't have come at a better time. We're picking up a few injuries. Derek is desperate for the help. Welcome to the team. Let me introduce you to the rest of the backroom staff?'

It was a lovely moment because you think it was gone forever or rather, I thought my life in football was gone forever. I didn't know what I'd walked into, which was going to be an incredible time. Kevin Keegan had been my idol at school and then I got to play with him as a young professional. Now I was back at the club I loved working alongside the man I used to worship as a child. If only football was like Newcastle in the 1990s I'd settle for that every day. In fact, that period of 1993 to about 1998 when Ruud Gullit arrived was the best time I'd ever had in football and that includes my playing career.

In the early months, I relied heavily on Derek Wright who proved to be the gentleman I believed he was during my time as a young player at the club. He was generous with his time, patient with my incessant questioning and took great care in making sure I was accepted back into the closed world of professional football. I trusted him implicitly. We very quickly became a team with an unbreakable bond professionally and personally.

The treatment room was very much the heartbeat of the training ground. Players would congregate there before training and the laughter and noise would bring Kevin out of his room to inquire if anyone fancied doing any work today. The atmosphere in the treatment room was no different to every other part of the club Kevin had built in his short time as a manager.

Newcastle United in 1993 was an incredible place to be. It was a warm and friendly club. Players and staff worked together and socialised together. There was a perfect mix of young local players making their way in the game for whom playing for their local club meant more than just football. Others like Robert Lee and John Beresford who although they had no previous affiliation with Newcastle United or the city just seemed to 'get it'. It didn't surprise me that these players from other parts of the country would be describing Newcastle as the best place they'd played or the best city they'd lived in. The club, the city, and its people weave their way into your affections and once they get in, they become a part of who you are.

Kevin Keegan created something special when he was a player. He'd lifted the club on his broad shoulders and carried it from the doldrums of the old Second Division to the bright lights of the old First Division. He retired before enjoying the fruits of his labours. Here he was as a manager creating something bigger and better than anyone could have imagined. His charisma and philosophy rubbed off on all those who came into contact with him. He was charming and affable but fiercely competitive. That belief system was instilled in all those who played for him or worked for him. His Newcastle United was the club of the people. The training ground was open to the public and they came in their hundreds and sometimes thousands every day to catch a glimpse or get an autograph from one of their heroes.

Kevin was an impressive speaker and I looked forward to listening to his team talks before big games. Sometimes they were motivational, other times emotional, always inspirational. Some were longer than others but some of his shorter ones were his best. On one occasion he walked into the changing room five minutes before the kick-off of a crucial game with the opposition team sheet in his hand. He strolled into the middle of the dressing room and stood still until the chatter and clatter settled into respectful silence.

'I've read this several times boys and I want to tell you this. There's not one name on here that I would swap for anyone in this room. Now go out and prove me right.'

The pink slip was falling to the floor as he turned and his players rose as one, ready for battle knowing that their general had complete faith in their ability to win at all costs. He signed great players and let lesser ones go. Foreign players with big reputations and big egos replaced the English old guard.

Football was changing and he was leading the way. Philippe Albert, David Ginola, and Tino Asprilla- world-class international footballers who came into the club and embraced the culture of the manager and the city. Philippe ruptured his cruciate ligaments and gave me my first opportunity to really contribute something worthwhile in my new role. We worked with him diligently until he returned to the team as good as new. I was happy in my new job. I never felt envious of what might have been. I enjoyed being invisible but getting satisfaction from a job well done.

David Ginola was most distressed to discover we had no gym. Judging by his impressive physique he was used to better. In the absence of a decent gym, he developed a habit of coming into the treatment room after training and exercising with dumbbells while he chatted with me and Derek. He was a very likeable relaxed man who'd been brought up in the South of France and his upbringing was evident in how he conducted himself with us at all times.

David was all flowing locks and Gallic charm and had a very positive outlook on everything in life. I enjoyed his visits to our room where we'd throw friendly insults back and forward and discuss the events of the day while he did his weights and perfected his English. He was intelligent and well-read with interests that ranged far and wide. I enjoyed all aspects of his visits apart from one, his torso. David was 29 and the same age as me. He liked to take his shirt off while doing his weights. Every day I was forced to look at his washboard abs, impeccable pecs and bulging biceps. He was an impressive and demoralising sight. I found myself sucking my stomach in every time he was in the room. After many different approaches, I finally got him to stop tormenting me with his physique.

'Teach me some English my friend? Tell me some of your English Jokes?'

He was in his usual spot, shirt off, dumbbells pumping, teeth glistening. I lifted my head from the latest leg I was dealing with. I sucked my stomach in.

'I'm Irish. I only do Irish Jokes, David.'

He was working his pecs now.

'Oh yes. I forgot. Forgive me, Paul. You Irish are supposed to be funny? Tell me something funny my Irish friend?'

He was onto his sit-ups now. Sweat trickling, muscles rippling.

'I know one David.'

He stopped mid-sit-up.

'Tell me, my friend?'

'Did you know I spoke a bit of French?'

His eyes narrowed. He was suddenly serious.

'No, I didn't know that. That's fantastic. What French do

you speak?'
I had him.
'It's just a little. Nothing to get too excited about.'
He was up now and working his biceps again.
'A little is better than none my friend? Tell me some French?'
I walked over behind him. Picked up his training top from the floor and lobbed it in the air. It landed on his perfectly formed shoulder.
'Fuck off out of here, would you? And put your shirt on. You're killing me. I can hardly fucking breathe from holding my breath in till you're finished your exercises every day.'
The smile on his face as he pulled on his top told me he was adapting to English Football culture and he'd be here for a long time. He stopped at the door.
'You speak very good French my friend. I like it. '

I could hear him laughing as he strutted up the hall. Those early years were filled with big players with big reputations. One by one they came into the club and one by one they proved themselves to be great people as well as excellent footballers. Les Ferdinand arrived with a reputation for being injury-prone and left the club as a warrior who barely missed a game and became a legend on the pitch. Off it, he was just a thoroughly decent man who had a permanent smile on his face and was a pleasure to be around. I don't recall ever seeing him without an infectious grin from ear to ear. He developed a bond with the club and fans alike that maybe even surprised him. It was that type of individual: Les, Rob Lee, David Ginola, and the rest that came so tantalisingly close to glory in 1996. Great players with an unrivalled team spirit who bought into the philosophy of an outstanding manager in Kevin Keegan. It was intoxicating and a privilege to be a part of Newcastle United in those lofty days.

I couldn't see anything other than Newcastle winning the Premier League title as the 1995-96 season dawned.

It was only after we lost 1-0 at home to Man United that I had doubts, even though we'd battered them that night. After the game, Les Ferdinand and Warren Barton were in the treatment room. Warren was a very good professional and we were just chatting and he suggested that we should have an alcohol ban for the rest of the season. He got shot down by the others because of it but I understood why he said it. He, like the rest of us, just wanted to get it over the line.

There were times when I thought we'd thrown it away but Man United had an incredible run-in. It seemed that every time we checked their score it was 1-0, Cantona. There were times when I used to go into my local pub and there'd be the odd one after we drew somewhere, saying, 'We're bloody rubbish. Keegan needs to go.' I felt like saying, 'This is as good as football gets. You'll never have anything like this ever again.'

I was a former football player and I'd stand and watch the small five-a-side games in training in awe. It was like watching a ping-pong game. The ability of that team was incredible. David Ginola was amazing, certainly in the first six months. Kevin then brought Alan Shearer home and Alan was the missing piece of the jigsaw. I was there the day we signed him.

I got a call from Russell Cushing saying we're going to Manchester to sign a player but I can't tell you who it is. We were supposed to be driving incognito to Manchester but the car had NUFC plates. We got to the hotel and someone said, 'Your player is in there.' The door opens and there stands Alan Shearer. I was like, 'Christ, it's Alan Shearer!' He'd just dominated the European Championships. He is one of the best players in the world at that point. Then we're having a cup of tea and some biscuits and having a chat after the medical.

You could tell from the way he talked he was a massive Newcastle fan. Newcastle United mattered to him. Newcastle as a city was home for him, being a proud Geordie

defined him. He was asking me about games he'd watched the season before and incidents that had happened. I thought never mind him being a footballer, he's going to be a friend of mine because he's a really nice bloke. He was the missing piece but unfortunately, it didn't work out that way because Kevin was gone six months later.
The disappointment of Kevin Keegan leaving felt more like a bereavement than a manager resigning.

Chapter Twenty three: Peter Beardsley

Peter Beardsley's second spell at Newcastle was not without controversy. Chairman Sir John Hall was initially reluctant to sanction the £1.5 million transfer from Everton, believing the twinkle-toed striker was past his best and there would be no sell-on fee. Fortunately, Magpies' boss Kevin Keegan knew the little magician's value and sweet-talked his boss into parting with his money to secure the transfer.

Any early doubts Sir John had about the veteran striker rejoining the Magpies were quickly dispelled by a series of eye-catching performances. Beardsley conjured more tricks and pulled more rabbits out of the proverbial hat than a seaside resort magician as Newcastle mounted a serious challenge for the Premier League title, pushing Manchester United to the limit. His vision, slalomed dribbles, slide-rule passes and a natural eye for a sensational goal not only justified the transfer fee but cemented his place alongside fellow black and white luminaries such as Hughie Gallacher, Colin Veitch, Jackie Milburn, and Len White.

Beardsley formed an almost telepathic understanding with striker Andy Cole before enjoying similar success with Les Ferdinand. With Beardsley, Cole, Ferdinand, and even later with Alan Shearer, they formed a formidable attacking force, striking fear into the hearts of every Premier League defender.

The Geordie-born playmaker enjoyed a glittering career with Liverpool, winning league titles and FA Cups, as well as earning over 50 caps for England while appearing in two World Cups. However, the humble striker insists that nearly winning the Premier League with his hometown club eclipses anything he achieved on Merseyside or for his country.

The Little Magician

Kevin said to me, 'I want you to come back and do what I did for Newcastle ten years ago. Make the youngsters better and make the club special again. Me, Chris Waddle, Kenny Wharton, Steve Carney and Wes Saunders, as young kids, had the pleasure of playing with Kevin as a player at Newcastle between 1982 and 1984. You cannot buy that experience.

In my first spell at the club, Kevin Keegan told me, 'Run around and you'll get noticed' and that's what I did and backed it up with goals as well. That's what makes football for me. Although football is a team game, it is also about individuals and what you do. I thought I brought something different to every team I played for. Kevin Keegan was a superstar, Terry McDermott was a superstar, Chris Waddle was a superstar but we all brought something different to the table, or the team. I'm not trying to be big-headed but I could do special things on the football pitch. When I go to bed at night and think back, I have some wonderful memories of playing football. No one can take those things away from me.

For me, it was always about wanting to play for Newcastle United, my hometown club. The pass by Terry Hibbitt to put Supermac (Malcolm MacDonald) through on goal to score in the semi-final of the FA Cup in 1974, was the best pass I've ever seen in my life. Terry Hibbitt was a superstar in my book. I've never seen a better pass to this day. My favourite player was "Jinky" Jimmy Smith. He, more than any other made me want to play for Newcastle.

I remember queueing up for tickets for the sixth round of the 1974 FA Cup against Nottingham Forest. My brother and I got the 365 bus to the Central Station and walked up to St James' Park and we camped out waiting for the ticket office to open. We didn't have sleeping bags. Think there were a few posh kids with a sleeping bag but not us. We eventually got tickets but then on the Friday before the game, my brother gave away my ticket to his best mate.

It was a blessing in disguise I suppose because there was a riot, supporters invaded the pitch when we were losing 3-1 and my brother was near all of the trouble. I battered him for weeks about it afterwards. He said, 'I saved your life. You could've been killed.' He then said, 'What are you worried about? You'll probably play for the team in the future.' I didn't think it was going to happen though.

I went to Vancouver Whitecaps in the North American Soccer League after playing for Carlisle United because nobody was interested in signing me. It turned out to be a great experience. I then went to Man United for five months and failed to make it but I wouldn't swap the experience for anything. I was in the reserves with Mark Hughes, Paul McGrath, Gary Bailey, Martin Buchan and Ray Wilkins. Man United had the most money back then. I returned to Vancouver for my last season after it didn't work out at Old Trafford.

I had a mobile phone in Vancouver back in 1983. Thought I'd won the Pools coupon. It was the size of a brick but I still thought it was special. My wife was out shopping in a mall while I was sitting in the car listening to the radio when the phone went. A guy on the other end of the phone said, 'This is Arthur Cox here, would you like to sign for Newcastle United?' Nothing else like, 'How are you doing?' I told him to 'fuck off!' Then, I put the phone down on him. I could see lots of Vancouver Whitecaps' cars in the car park and thought someone was taking the piss because between 1981 and 83 that's what happened. I got battered daily. It wasn't nasty, I wasn't offended, it was funny. That's just the way it was back then.

I played with lots of great British players at the time, such as Peter Lorimer, Leeds and Scotland, Johnny Giles, Leeds and Eire, World Cup winner Nobby Stiles, Man United and England, goalkeeper David Harvey, another ex-Leeds United man, and Terry Yorath. John Wile, who played for West Brom, Geordie Ray Hankin, Middlesbrough-born Dave Thomas, Alan Taylor from West Ham as well as others. We had a great squad of players. I would've been happy to stay there forever. It was a brilliant place and I thoroughly enjoyed it.

I'd never seen Arthur Cox on the TV, never heard him speak so I didn't know what he sounded like. There was no Internet back then so I couldn't do a quick search on him. That's why I thought someone was taking the piss. He rang back and this time he said, 'Can you give me five minutes of your time? How would you like to play alongside Kevin Keegan?'

I'm thinking, it might be Arthur Cox. He then asked how much I got paid and I told him £400 a week. He then offered me £300 a week. As you know, you don't go to another club for less if you're better than what's already at the club. I said, 'I get £400 a week.' He said, 'I can hear you but playing alongside Kevin Keegan must be worth £100 a week.' So, I said, 'OK.'

When my wife Sandra came back to the car from the shops she asked if anything had happened. I told her Arthur Cox had just rung me. She said, 'Who is Arthur Cox?' I told her he was the manager of Newcastle. She asked what he wanted. I said, 'He wants me to go and play alongside Kevin Keegan. She said, 'What do they want you for?'

A couple of weeks later, the season is over in the NASL and I'm flying back to Newcastle via Heathrow Airport. On the flight from London to Newcastle, Kevin Keegan is on it. I'm thinking, 'He'll not even know who I am.' I guess someone on the plane must have told him because as we were getting off the plane he approached and said, 'You're the little fella Arthur Cox was on about. I'll be at training in the morning. I'll see you there and you better be good.'

Sandra and I stopped in the County Hotel opposite the Central Station for the first six or seven months. It was handy for us to get around. Arthur picked me up the following morning and as we're going into Benwell training ground he's beeping the horn. I'm thinking what's going on? Then Kevin and Terry Mac came out with a few of the others whooping and cheering. It had obviously been set up by them all.

We trained at Benwell at the time and the pitches were awful. He said to his big mate, Terry Mac, 'I was on the plane with this fella last night. He's supposed to be good. He better be, we played for Liverpool and we're used to playing with good players. After five minutes of training, he went over to Arthur Cox and said, 'Yeah, he's not quite Kenny Dalglish but who needs Kenny Dalglish? He's decent.' From that day, he took me under his wing and he's been unbelievable for me ever since. He's the best football person I've ever met.

How did Arthur Cox discover me? Well, I was at Carlisle, first under former Newcastle skipper Bob Moncur but when he moved on Bob Stokoe took over as manager. What a lot of people forget is that Arthur was Bob's assistant at Sunderland when they beat Leeds United in the 1973 FA Cup final. It was Bob Stokoe who tipped off Arthur. I don't know if he ever saw me play. How could he? I was in Vancouver playing against the likes of Franz Beckenbaur, Pele, and Johan Cruff, and people like that.

To play with Kevin and Terry Mac was unbelievable because Terry Mac was also a superstar. When we played, Terry would just keep on bombing past me. I was like, 'Where's he going?' He then said to me one time, 'Any idea why I'm running, Pedro?' I said, 'I see you, but I'm not sure.' He said, 'Well, I'm hoping one day you might pass me the fucking ball!'

Kevin's last game for Newcastle was a benefit game, against Liverpool at St James' Park, for the club. The club got all of the gate receipts money. Liverpool had won the league and the European Cup but we managed to draw thanks to goals from Terry Mac and Kevin. The helicopter at the end was a great idea because he would never have got away. As he was getting on, he took his shirt off and gave it to some fella. When we got back to the Gosforth Park Hotel after the game, I told him it was a fantastic gesture. He didn't know what I meant. I said, 'Giving that fella your shirt.' He said, "I told him to give it to you." That fella, wherever he is, has my shirt and I want it back. So, if anyone knows him, can you let him know?

Scoring a hat-trick against Sunderland was pretty special. I also missed a penalty. I've still got the ball, it's in me loft. The good news is that no one knows where I live so they can nick it. I often blow it up, because it goes flat. It was 1985 you know. Aye, I blow it up and have a kick about in the loft. To be honest, I was shitting myself when Shola Ameobi got two goals against Sunderland. I didn't mind Kevin Nolan because he's not a Geordie, but Shola is. I'm still the last Geordie to score a hat-trick against Sunderland. Don't get me wrong, I love Shola but I didn't want him taking my record.

That time was special, playing with those guys but when Kevin brought me back it was a surprise. The surprise was more that Everton wanted to sell me. I don't want to sound big-headed but I was the best player there. They even had players like Martin Keown playing for them. That's how bad we were. Although it has to be said they were rubbish at the time.

Howard Kendal, the manager at the time, called me into his office and said he was going to sell me. I was shocked. I said, 'Why, I've been your best player for the last two years.' He said, 'I know. That's why I'm going to sell you. You're the only player I can get money for. I want to buy Les Ferdinand and you're the only player I can sell to fund that.' I said, 'I'd like to play with Les Ferdinand, I reckon I could help him.' He said, 'If I keep you, I can't get him.' I said, 'Who do you prefer?' He said, "He's younger, and there's clubs interested in you."

'Like who?'

"Derby County."

I thought, Derby fucking County! Then I remembered Arthur Cox was the manager. I love Arthur and still speak to him every week. He came to my house in Southport and offered me £1,000 a week more than I was getting at Everton, where I was getting £5,000 a week. He also said I could live where I was. There was no need for me to travel to Derby to live. He then saw me ponder and said, 'You're not coming, are you?' I said, 'No.'

Arthur replied, 'There's only one club I'd be happy for you to go to if you don't come here and that's Newcastle United.' I didn't even know Newcastle were interested at the time. I went back to Howard Kendal and told him I wasn't interested in signing for Derby. He then said, 'I've got one more card up my sleeve.' He then picked up the phone and rang a number and said, 'Kevin.' The guy on the other side said, 'No, it's Terry.' It was Terry Mac. Howard asked whether he was interested in signing me. Terry said, 'We want him.' Howard said, 'You don't know the fee yet.' Terry Mac said, 'It doesn't matter, we want him.'

I met Kevin in Wetherby in a hotel on the bend, just off the motorway. He said, 'I know what Arthur has offered you and I'm going to offer you £1,000 less but I'm going to give you a Rover car.' I was supposed to be the star catch if you like, and he'd done a deal with Rover to sponsor the players. They only agreed if I signed. Kevin then added, 'If we sign a player who gets more than you, we'll offer you the same.' Now you can understand why I never complained when we signed Ginola, Ferdinand, and Shearer. Others might have, but not me, I'm saying get them in! Kevin really looked after me. He is a God to me. Still is. He's the best man ever.

We got knocked out of the FA Cup against Luton and Kevin decided to take us away to Bournemouth for a few days. He told us when we got there, we could drink as much as we wanted but once we went to bed, that's it, no more drink that week because we had a game on Saturday. Terry Mac knocked on my hotel door and asked whether I'd seen Barry Venison, Steve Howey and Alex Mathie. He said if you do, warn them that the gaffer is looking for them because we were due to get on a bus at

2pm to go to Quaser Laser. The three of them are good lads but not very bright. Kevin waves us off and then him and Terry Mac go looking for them. As we're pulling away, we could see the Three Musketeers drinking in a pub across the road. We never told the gaffer but he marched straight across the road to the first pub and caught them. He then took them to the train station and was gonna put them on a train home. He would've done it until Terry Mac reminded him that if he did that, we would only have one sub for the game coming up.

Just before a team meeting the following day, Terry Mac came to see me and said he had some good news and I was gonna be made captain. I said, 'Who knows?' 'Me, you, and the gaffer.' I said, 'What about the captain, Barry Venison?' Terry said, 'He's gonna find out in an hour or so at the meeting.'

We all called Barry Venison, 'skip.' And later on, I walked past him and without thinking I said, 'Alright skip?' I don't have any malice towards Barry. He's a great lad and I still speak to him but being Newcastle captain was one of the proudest moments of my life. I loved looking after the lads, especially the younger lads like Clarky, Watto, Robbie Elliot, etc., it was special. I also got to help Andy Cole, who we signed from Bristol City. Now, Premier League players get a room to themselves. Back in my day, we had to share with someone. But when I came back to the club Kevin told me he was giving me a room of my own to sleep in because he wanted to send players to see me, especially the younger lads. Coley came the first time and asked, 'When do you want me to run? How do you want me to run? Where do you want me to run?
I asked him if could I give him the ball the first time as it was coming to me. If I can, get on your bike. I'll find you. It didn't always work, sometimes I'd lose it or misplace it but the majority of the time I'd find him. Andy is a diamond of a kid. He listened. You could tell because he did exactly as I asked of him. The same with Lee Clark. Should Andy

have kicked on and been a better player? Possibly. He was a lovely lad, very quiet and never in your face. In my opinion, he should have got more England caps. It gave me as much pleasure setting goals up for him, and others, as scoring myself. It still gives me a buzz now, thinking about the passes I made for others to score.

I wouldn't change anything in my life and if I was to be reincarnated, I'd like to come back as myself. It's really nice when people say 'I made Gary Lineker' and things like that. He (Gary) had to have a football brain to be in the places to take my passes. People have said I was perfect for him but he was a perfect partner for me too.

As much as I love Les Ferdinand, or Sir Les, as I call him and hopefully, he will be knighted in the future, one of my big regrets was not being able to be a number 10 to Alan Shearer. Alan would have scored 300 goals, not the 260 he has now. I'm not being cocky or big-headed when I say that. I just know it would've happened.

When Alan signed, Kevin told Big Les that Alan was going to wear the No.9 shirt. Les came to me and asked what should he do. He said he wasn't bothered about giving up the No.9 but didn't know what shirt to ask for. I told him to ask for 99. He said, 'What a good idea, Pedro.' He came back to me and said, 'I can't have 99. He said no one can have 99.' I told Les, Kevin was talking shit. He said, 'I can't very well go and tell the gaffer Pedro says you're talking shit.' I told him the former Real Madrid and Portugal goalkeeper Vítor Baía wore the No.99. He then took the No.10 and Lee Clark was devastated. Then Lee Clark takes No.20 and Alan Nielson is devastated.

KK then came to me and said he'd just solved two problems but there was one more thing, 'Alan wants to take the penalties.' I said, 'That's fine,' which surprised Kevin. He thought I'd want to take them but I didn't really care. I said I'd take them when he wasn't playing. It was great when he first signed because he couldn't travel with the first team. We couldn't get him insured so I had to travel with him. And Alan doesn't travel cattle class or business class, it's first-class. I loved it.

Ultimately, we failed to win the Premier League but did anyone ever see us going that close before Kevin came in? I didn't think so. In regards to the future, yes, I think we will see silverware at Newcastle sooner rather than later. People ask me all of the time why we didn't win the league that year. We had a way of playing that was a dream to play in and I imagine was a dream to watch. We just fell at the final hurdle.

We had some unbelievable players. Ginola, an absolute superstar. Tino, I loved him, the same with Big Les, Wor Al, Coley, Rob Lee, David Batty and Marc Hottiger. I still speak with Marc a lot. He was my favourite right back ever, don't tell Watto. We had an unbelievable atmosphere around the place. It was special. I'm not sure the club will ever replicate what we had or what Kevin created. And the noise that St James' Park generates, you can't buy that. It was a brilliant time in my life. I'd won the league with Liverpool but I would never swap nearly winning the league with Newcastle.

Chapter Twenty four: Malcolm Allen

Malcolm Allen joined Newcastle from Millwall on the eve of the 1993-94 Premier League season without having trained or kicked a football in anger with his new team-mates. It is fair to say the £300,000 signing was a surprise to everyone but the Welshman who believed it was his destiny to play for United.

As a teenage star for Watford, Allen captained and scored for the Hornets in the 1985 FA Youth Cup final against a Magpies side that included Paul Gascoigne and Joe Allon while Kevin Scott, who also played in the two-legged affair, was still at the club. Both Gascoigne and Allon netted a brace in the 4-1 victory at Vicarage Road after a 0-0 stalemate at St James' Park.

The former Lions' favourite was drafted in as cover for Peter Beardsley who had broken a cheekbone in a pre-season friendly at Liverpool and created a bit of history by scoring Newcastle's first Premier League goal at St James' Park in the club's first Premier League victory over Everton in a 1-0 triumph. Allen went on to score seven goals in only 12 games for United before injury cruelly brought his football career to an abrupt and premature end at the age of only 28. Although his time at St James' Park was brief, the United striker regarded it as one of the highlights of his career.

Destiny Calls

I knew Newcastle were looking at me while I was playing for Millwall. I'd scored against them a couple of times while we were in what is now the Championship. I was keen to play in the Premier League as I'd played most of my career in the top flight. Kevin Keegan was my hero as a kid as I'm a Liverpool supporter and then when he left Kenny Dalglish became my hero. North Wales was only two hours away but we couldn't afford to go to the games back then.

I'd just signed a new three-year contract at Millwall before Newcastle came in for me. We got so close to going up but lost in the play-offs. Mick McCarthy had signed for Millwall the same day as me and we were good mates. He then became Millwall manager. I was playing well, working hard and scoring goals and became a fans' favourite at The Den.

Mick rang me two or three days before the start of the 1993-94 season and said he'd just sold me to Newcastle and Kevin Keegan was going to ring me. I was shocked. Mick said they'd put a bid in and the club had accepted. Kevin then rang me, saying he wanted me to play in the first game of the season against Spurs at St James' Park adding I'd be playing up front with Andy Cole. I said, 'Where do I sign?' You have moments in your life that you never forget and that was one of them.

Kevin said there was a flight booked for me the next day from Heathrow and that I needed to be at the ground in the morning. He said he knew about my knee and needed a medical, and that my knee would be insured. He told me I wouldn't train with the boys but would see them an hour before kick-off. I flew up, passed the medical and everything was OK apart from my knee.

When I turned up on the Saturday, I thought this was absolutely fantastic. I always loved playing at Newcastle, right back to when I was captain of Watford and Paul Gascoigne was captain of Newcastle in the FA Youth Cup in 1985. We drew 0-0 up there and lost 4-1 at home after I opened the scoring. So, I always had this affinity with Newcastle. I always thought that something might happen and I'd end up at Newcastle. I knew it was a massive club with great support.

I got to the ground early on the Saturday before the Tottenham game and Kevin was there with Terry Mac, heading the ball against the wall while the players were coming in. It was, 50, 51, 52, 53 and then he stopped and said, 'The team sheet is on the wall, there's the formation and you'll be playing up front with Andy Cole. I'll never forget Kevin's team talk. He said, 'I've just been out there boys.

These supporters have worked their socks off all week and paid good money to watch you. Go out there and entertain them. All you need to do is score more goals than them.' That was his team talk. He made you feel like the best player in the world. We went out and lost 1-0 with my old teammate Teddy Sheringham scoring the only goal.

After a stuttering start, we went on to do well. I started pretty well and scored a few goals. I scored in a 1-0 win over Everton at home. I curled it into the top corner giving my Welsh teammate Neville Southall no chance. Not long after that, I tried to wind him up at a corner, telling him not to bother diving for those shots in the top corner. He kicked me up the arse. Imagine if we had VAR back then? So, I made a little bit of history, scoring the winning goal in Newcastle's first-ever Premier League home victory.

I retired from the game through injury in 1996 but people still come up to me and remember my time at Newcastle and say nice things. I did try my best and worked hard and I think people appreciated that. Although I didn't play much during the last year of my time, I still remember it fondly. It was a bit like a dream to be remembered from that time, with those players, most of who were better than me.

Kevin Keegan was a great manager and an even better man. He was a people's man and that's how he got those players to play for him. He always got to know the players and their families. He wasn't a great one for tactics, maybe in the way other managers were, but he improved the players and his team by getting to know them closely. He was such an inspiration and made you feel like the best player in the world.

The Monday night game against Sheffield Wednesday sticks out for me. I scored one and made another for Alex Mathie, who got the Man of the Match champagne after the game by the way. He came on as a substitute! Andy Cole scored the first after the goalkeeper spilt my shot. Andy was a great instinctive player and he could read how the game or where shots might spill. Yes, he missed a few but Andy had that Ian Rush clinical goalscoring side to his game. Andy was ruthless in front of goal. He would stand on his own man to score. Well, maybe not, but you know what I mean. I scored the fourth, a header but I almost scored the goal of the century in that game. I hit a 40-yard shot on the half volley that just missed the goal.

I've nothing but good memories with some great teammates. Brian Kilcline stitched me up one night. I love a curry and so did he. So, he took me out for a curry to the Simla, on the Quayside. We'd had a bellyful of lager before we got there. He'd obviously had more than me. Killer ordered a chicken phall. I like a hot curry. I usually have a madras but I was curious about Killer's dish. He said, 'Go on, have a taste.' My mouth was on fire for a week after just a spoonful. So, yeah, he stitched me up a kipper that night. He was a few years older than me and a few years wiser. Maybe this was a good life lesson and made me wiser for his experience.

I was a happy-go-lucky type of guy and I went out with Steve Watson and Lee Clark many a time. You could go out then without the worry of people taking pictures and videos with their phones. We had the best of times back then. We all had a great rapport and great teammates. There was absolutely nothing wrong with what we had. It was special, what we had, and I loved being part of it.

Peter Beardsley was head and shoulders above the others and we had some great players. He could see things we mere mortals couldn't. A ball would come to him at 30-40 miles per hour and he would hit it first time to someone else's feet. He had a picture in his mind before the ball came to him. You can't teach that to players, his vision and awareness, it was like he had eyes in the back of his head. I remember one game, it looked as if the ball was going out of play but Peter caught it and blasted it straight into the opposition's goal. Who does things like that? Peter Beardsley! He wasn't only a great individual player, he was a great team player too. He could gel and knit things together naturally and he played with a smile on his face. He was just on another level to anyone else and also part of that great Liverpool side.

Peter played a lot with John Barnes at Liverpool. I made my top-flight debut with Barnes at Watford, who Peter said was the best player he ever played with. Peter paid me a great compliment, saying I had one of the best first touches he'd ever played with. I thought maybe he was winding me up, given the great players he played with in his career, or just trying to boost my confidence. I retired three years later so that meant a lot to me. I played in training with Ginola and Asprilla but Peter was head and shoulders above everyone.

Newcastle was great trying to get me right when I was injured and I got good support from the physios, Derek Wright and Paul Ferris. They understood my frustrations and disappointments. Then Kevin called me before the 1995-96 season and said they'd called the surgeon, Mr Stainsbury, I think he was called, and said they'd done all they could. Apparently, the surgeon said no one else should go in there to try and fix it again. He said if I didn't want to end up in a wheelchair I should quit playing. Kevin was great with me. He said, 'Stay with us until the end of the season and do a bit of coaching. I said, 'OK.' I wanted to stay around and see us win the league. I couldn't have asked for anything more for me. The fans were great to me also, as was Sir John Hall and the board.

I think Manchester United just had more winners in their dressing room than we had. They'd been there before and got the T-shirt. They also had a manager who could get into people's heads. I wouldn't blame Kevin for anything because he was as good as any manager. They had the experience of getting results where they shouldn't have got them. The game we lost against Man United at St James' Park, with the Eric Cantona goal. I remember him coming into the players' lounge after the game and he had this aura around him. We had great players but he was a bit different. He seemed to thrive under pressure. They didn't seem to have any off days and every team has them. They just seemed to thrive on that pressure. We had players who had won titles in Beardsley, Bracewell, Venison and Batty but there wasn't enough to pull us through and get us over the line.

Chapter Twenty five: Darren Peacock

Darren Peacock became Newcastle's record signing when he arrived from Queens Park Rangers for £2.7 million in 1994. The Bristol-born central defender often cut a solitary figure at the back as United charged forward in a bid to plunder goals, leaving Peacock vulnerable to a counter attack. Yet the Bristolian played a pivotal role alongside Philippe Albert and Steve Howey in the team's rise to prominence in the Premier League during the mid-1990s.

Peacock believed 'it was only a matter of time before the Geordies clinched a major piece of silverware' and lamented leaving United for Blackburn not long after Kevin Keegan. The popular defender described his time at Newcastle as a once-in-a-lifetime experience, both on and off the pitch, adding the fervent support from the Toon Army and the camaraderie within the team made his stint at St. James' Park a "truly special time."

Last Man Standing

I got word that a few clubs were interested in signing me before QPR got a call from Kevin Keegan saying he would like to sign me. The club said if I was interested, I would have to put in a transfer request. This was because I had been promised a new contract at QPR. It was a bit complicated because the club were on the stock market and it seemed that they had forgotten about the contract offer. I put the request in to get the ball rolling and then next thing is I'm on my way to Newcastle.

Newcastle was playing Ipswich the night I signed and I think they won 2-0. I met the Newcastle hierarchy and then I met the gaffer, Kevin, at the Gosforth Park Hotel and signed. It was that easy. Things happened so fast that I didn't go back to my house in London for a month. I stayed in Newcastle because games were coming thick and fast.

Kevin was a bundle of enthusiasm when I met him, probably buzzing from the victory that night. He'd just broken the Newcastle record transfer fee of £2.7 million. It seemed as if the club were breaking the transfer record every week at that time. He didn't have to sell the club to me because everyone in the country kind of knew what was happening at the club. I reckon all of the players Kevin was after would tell you the same. Their mind was already made up. They didn't need persuading. He did tell me about the supporters and how important they were to the club. He also said we would play a 4-4-2 formation with five attackers and five defenders. He was very clear about that.

Training was something I'd never seen at a football club in my career before I got to the club and after I left. It was all fun and games. We always had the ball at our feet and it was all geared to making us better footballers. It was all five-a-side, six-a-side, eight-a-side and it was competitive. We had some fantastic players at the club who were great on the ball and there were players like myself who weren't as good on the ball. It was simple but it worked and I've never enjoyed training ever, anywhere else, since those days at Newcastle.

One Friday before a big FA Cup game, I remember Kevin walked us into Durham from Maiden Castle for a cup of tea and a slice of cake. It was such a relaxing thing to do. We didn't train that day. I've never experienced anything like it before or since.

The first time I went to training there were thousands of fans there and I thought, 'Christ, what's going on here?' Then in the school holidays, there was even more. Then the burger vans and ice cream vans started turning up. Kevin encouraged it and he also encouraged us to sign every autograph before we left to go home. There were three, four, 5,000 fans there. That's more than most League Two, some League One and non-league teams get. It was surreal at first but then we got used to it. I don't think it would be allowed now. When Kenny came in, he stopped it. I can't imagine another club where that would happen, where the fans would turn up in their thousands to watch us train, especially when it was belting down with rain. Getting cheered in training, was, well, it was mental. Team talks were so simple. Sometimes it was just 'same team, same subs.' Kevin would go around the players individually sometimes, and give them a pep talk to boost their confidence. There was no in-depth tactical talk or big boards with tactics on in the dressing room. Sometimes he'd talk about the opposition but it was very rare he did that because he had confidence in the players individually and as a team.

What we achieved in such a short time would be unheard of, getting a promotion and then finishing third in our first season in the Premier League. We qualified for the UEFA Cup and then we had a dip to finish sixth the following season but we had lots of injuries and our squad was pretty small compared to today.

The most memorable game would probably have to be the 5-0 win over Man United at St James' Park. After they beat us in the Charity Shield it seemed everything was geared up for revenge. Everything was so tense before the game for the supporters and the players. I've never played in a game like that before or since. Everything just clicked. We were smarting from that Wembley defeat and the gaffer just told us to go for it and we did. The gaffer also knew that we wanted to make amends for the defeat at Wembley. I was lucky enough to score in the game as well. Big Les knocked it back across the goal and I got my head on it and it managed to go over the line. Every goal after mine was stunning. They were good enough to grace any game, absolutely stunning.

There were a number of reasons why we didn't win the league. Man United had a very experienced manager in Alex Ferguson and the experience of their players helped them. Maybe we should have had something in place to learn how to defend as a team better. The players have also got to hold their hands up. Losing that sort of lead was unusual but it was one of those things. We players all talk about it every time we meet up. The gaffer's philosophy was just 'go out and play.'

The gaffer's so-called 'I would love it, outburst,' was nothing to what the media made it out to be. It was all blown out of proportion. It was his passion and commitment coming out. It was part of his personality and I don't see it as a big deal. The media jumped on it and saw it was a weakness and that we had a chink in the armour. We never did. It was passion and commitment and we were all behind him anyway.

Kevin leaving was a shock to everyone. We were all wondering if something had gone wrong behind the scenes. The players were disappointed he'd left. In fact, the families of the players were disappointed as well. Kevin was always welcoming of the wives and girlfriends, inviting them all down to training for a cup of tea etc. He'd sit down with our families and he'd want to know everything about them. It wasn't just on a professional level but also on a personal level. We were doing well at the time. What Kevin had done over the previous two, three years had set us up to do better and win things.

Pedro was the best player at Newcastle. Everyone would say he was two or three steps ahead of everyone but he was also a grafter, never mind his touch, vision and passing. If he lost the ball he'd graft to win it back. Even though we had great players coming in, Tino, Ginola, who had great technical ability but Beardsley was a one-off. Everything came so naturally to him. Some of his goals were amazing and he's done it all for club and country.

Phillipe Albert was great fun. He got it straight away. We had so many different colourful characters in our group but when Philippe delivered a joke it was even funnier because of the French-like twang to his accent. There wasn't one dominant character in the dressing room, we had several. Then you had Pav, who was quiet, but when he spoke, we listened, whether it was on the pitch or training ground. There were games where I wouldn't have much to do. I could kind of sit back and enjoy what was unfolding in front of me. It was the best seat in the house.

When I signed for the club and was unveiled at a press conference the gaffer mentioned that I needed to mention the fans because they are the lifeblood of the club, the area, and the region. He also mentioned that I would understand what he meant when I got to training. Then there was the fanatical away support which made our away games more like home games. We were moving so fast that we quickly became a nationally supported club and then a globally supported club. I lived in Horsley at that time and I was close to the supporters and understood what it meant to them.

Terry Mac was another great character at the club. He was like a buffer between the gaffer and the players. He had a great sense of humour and could defuse any situation if things were tense with a joke or one-liner. Terry knew the game inside out and he was especially good with the younger players. He was a bubbly person, very charismatic and he could reel off some fantastic stories from his days as a player. He could relate to everything we were going through and empathise with the players because he'd been through it himself at Liverpool and Newcastle. And, of course, Kevin trusted him completely.

It's a shame Kevin left because I reckon, we would have gone on to greater things in the next two or three years but it wasn't to be.

Chapter Twenty six: Ruel Fox

Newcastle United manager Kevin Keegan described Ruel Fox as "the best player in his position in the country" when he secured the Fox outside of the box's signature from Norwich City in early February 1994 for a then club record transfer fee of £2,250,000.

The fleet-footed right winger had the St James' Park faithful on their feet every time he forayed forward, helping himself to over a dozen goals during his time at United while setting up a lot more for the prolific Andrew Cole, the majestic Peter Beardsley and box-to-box man Robert Lee.

Fox was another pivotal piece in The Entertainers' jigsaw. He played in Newcastle's final 14 games of the 1993–94 season and scored twice as they finished third in the club's inaugural Premier League campaign to qualify for the UEFA Cup for the first time since 1977.

He then netted 10 league goals in his first full campaign, the 1994-95 season, as the Magpies finished sixth. Unfortunately, the signing of the equally fleet-footed Keith Gillespie and the arrival of dashing Frenchman David Ginola meant Fox had to move on as the United juggernaut gathered more steam.

Fox may have found himself surplus to requirements as swapped Tyneside and Newcastle for North London and Tottenham in the summer of 1995 but a little piece of his heart remains on Tyneside. The Ipswich-born winger recollects the seeming perpetual fun and frolics around St James' Park and Durham's Maiden Castle training ground and how he was bowled over by the charismatic Keegan and his white lies to get him to sign for the Magpies.

The Fox Outside the Box

My transfer to Newcastle was a bit strange. I played against them a month before my transfer. I was up against John Beresford. I got a call from the chairman, Robert Chase, asking me to go and see him before training one day. I didn't think anything of it at the time. It was about a new contract offer and I was pleased with what they were offering because I was happy where I was. Then he casually mentioned Newcastle had been in touch. He added that if I rejected the club's contract offer then I could talk to Newcastle.

I said OK, I'll speak to Newcastle. The chairman said, 'No, you'll have to go today.' It was weird. I thought I'd be going to training as normal, next thing I'm on an EasyJet flight to Newcastle to talk to Kevin Keegan and Terry McDermott. They were brilliant. Like a double act. They were joking saying John Beresford had come telling them to sign me because I was his most difficult opponent. Kevin told me that he knew there were a couple of other teams interested in me and that I could go home and think about it. But, when I got to the Gossy Hotel, they double-teamed me and wouldn't let me go. I ended up staying the night and they talked me into signing.

He told me that I would be getting twice as much at Newcastle than I would at Norwich. He still wanted me to go back to Norwich and get the money I was owed by them. I said it didn't make sense, going back to my old employees who I told I wanted to leave. Kevin said that was fine and that they had an offer for me and it would make me the highest-paid player at Newcastle. When I signed, I realised I wasn't.

At £2.5 million I was Newcastle's record signing. It only lasted two weeks because Darren Peacock came in for something like £2.75 million. I was sitting with Darren after he signed and he told me Keegan had told him the same thing, that he was the highest-paid player ever, at the club. It was quite funny and we had a giggle about it.

We were training at Durham at the time. Durham is a lovely part of the world. I had my three advisers (Lee Clark, Steve Watson and Robbie Elliott) pick me up from the Gossy Hotel and it took us about 45 minutes. My first memory was that training was cold and windy. The surface was quite flat but balls were flying all over the place.

It would be fair to say it was a bit different and something I wasn't used to because there were thousands of fans there watching us.

I thought my transfer from Norwich was a secret but when I landed at Newcastle Airport there were about 100 supporters there to greet me. It was amazing. This gave me an insight into how fanatical the fans were. The fact that we had open training sessions and the fans were watching was a great touch by Kevin, letting us mingle with them. At Norwich, I'd be used to training in front of no one.

I came from a family club, which was all about doing stuff in the community but at Newcastle it was that times ten. It was unbelievable. Kevin was very strong on us interacting with the fans. We used to do multiple events, talk-ins, going to the brewery and it wasn't a chore. It was a privilege to mix with them and they were so happy to have us there. It was very humbling and I loved it.

There was lots of banter at training. We'd get there early and have a kickabout in the hall at Maiden Castle before training started. There was a badminton court and we used to play head tennis. It was a mix of tennis and volleyball rules, keeping it up and knocking it over the net. We only had one touch each.

Keegan and McDermott would push their way onto the court and challenge us. Me and Watto (Steve Watson) were quite decent. We would beat them all the time. Then, after the head tennis competition, Kevin would pick some teams for five a side. Him and Terry Mac would watch and see who was winning and then join the winning team. The sessions were brilliant. There were loads of banter and loads of laughs and no one ever left training without a smile on their face. It was one of Kevin's things to make everyone relaxed.

Kevin wasn't one for tactics. You'd never see a clipboard for example, or him having a word about keeping an eye on a certain opponent. He'd just set us up in the right way, with a back four and the midfield and strikers etc. We all knew our jobs and what to do but he didn't go into depth about it. It was all about possession football and if we did our jobs the result would take care of itself.

Team talks were less than five minutes. He'd give a brief talk about the opponents, saying you know who you're playing against and if you do your jobs, it won't be a problem. He would fill us full of confidence before going out to play. Go do your best and play the way you know you can. It was quite simple but it worked.

Kevin and Terry were quite similar in a lot of ways in the advice they would hand out and we had enormous respect for them because of what they achieved in their careers as players. Derek Fazackerley was the coach and if anyone was giving out tactical advice, it was him. Terry Mac's advice was just as valuable because of his experience.

The atmosphere at St James' Park was unbelievable. You could feel it. The hairs on the back of your neck would stand up. I didn't understand the fanbase or the size of it until I arrived at the club. The first couple of games were away from home when I signed. The first one was against Luton in the FA Cup and we lost. I wasn't eligible to play but I got to see the fanbase for the first time. They'd travelled hundreds of miles to watch their team play. The away support was incredible. I didn't expect there to be so many of them and to be so loud.

I'd played in front of big crowds when we played away, such as Old Trafford and the big clubs. People talk about the 12th man, Newcastle supporters were more than that. They were like the 13th or 14th man, the amount of energy they gave to the players. It's hard to explain because it was so surreal.

My first goal was against Swindon in a 7-1 win. I'd been on the other side of those defeats in the past but there were days like that where we were untouchable. We'd knock it about and no one could get near us. I was desperate to score that day. It wasn't a great goal, it was a tap-in, but I got to celebrate with the fans, which made it special.

We got into Europe and I got our first goal in the second round of the UEFA Cup in the first leg at St James' Park which was also special. It was also nice to give fans something nice for travelling to all of those away games. We should have gone further in the competition but we had a small squad at the time and had a few injuries.

In the first round, we played Antwerp away and I set up a couple of goals for Rob Lee. That was a fantastic game to play in. The European campaign was the icing on the cake for me. That game probably stands out more than most for me. My best goal for the club was probably away at Ipswich in a 2-0 victory. Smashing in a 25-yarder was all the sweeter because they were giving me so much shit for 90 minutes for me being an ex-Norwich City player.

There weren't many games that I walked off the pitch and said to myself 'I didn't enjoy that.' So many memorable games: scoring the winner in a 3-2 win at Arsenal was special as well. Peter Beardsley set me up for my goal. There were times when Keegan and Terry Mac were screaming from the sidelines threatening to take me off if I didn't smile. It was amazing. A special time.

Another unique thing about playing for Newcastle at the time was that Keegan made us all socialise together. Generally, at a football club, you'd have one or two friends but Kevin didn't like clicks. I got on with everyone, like most of the players. In fact, it was the local boys, if anything, who were my best friends. Robbie Elliot, Lee Clark and Steve Watson looked after me and took advantage of me at times as well but that was all part of the craic. They were guys who showed me around the city, took me to restaurants, out for meals and drinks and the bright lights of the Big Market and Quayside. I was good mates with Andy Cole as well but maybe Lee Clark was one of my best buddies.

Andy Cole was like lightning and I struck up a great partnership with him on the pitch and off it too. We were from the south and both had our settling-in period and having another black person helped with that. He was a fantastic player, scored over 40 goals in one season beating the legendary Hughie Gallagher's record. It was my job to set up goals and it gave me great pleasure setting up goals for him and Peter Beardsley. I was privileged and fortunate to play with some great strikers in my career and Andrew was right up there with the best of them. Saying that, Peter Beardsley was the best player I played with at Newcastle. When you talk about players who have been there and done it and that's him and he was so humble with it. He would share advice with you and was happier to see you score a goal than him getting one for himself. He understood the game inside out and to play with someone of his class and calibre made my game so much easier.

When we were struggling, he was there for us. When we needed a leader, he was a leader. When you needed an arm around you, he was there comforting you. He would never rant or rave at a player he would just try and coach the best out of you. People talk about Andrew Cole and his goals but I think Beardsley was Keegan's best signing. How many goals did he set up for Andrew Cole? He did the same for me too.

I was flying when I first arrived at Newcastle. I was playing well, scored a few goals and got a Player of the Month award. Just after that, I got a call from Kevin asking me to go and see him. I thought it was a bit strange at first but then I got to his office and he asked how I was settling in. Told him everything was OK. He then said he was going to send me back home for a week because he was going to change the team around. I was shocked because I'd only been there a month or so.

I said I didn't want to go home but he insisted. I was fuming, got up, slammed his office door and went up to meet the lads for a warm-up. I thought this was a disgrace.

What the hell is going on here? I thought I'd done something wrong but I hadn't. All of the lads are in on it. They're pissing themselves when they see me, face like thunder. Kevin would pull those stunts all of the time to make you feel part of the club, and family if you like. He was probably the biggest joker at the club.

Keith Gillespie came to the club, who played in my position, I got moved over to the left, and sometimes I'd play up front and I scored a few goals but I didn't like it. I was thinking should I stay or go? If it was my choice, I would have stayed at Newcastle for the rest of my career but things change and move on. Keegan needed to sell some players so he could bring in others that were perhaps more expensive, which he showed with Andy Cole.

The sale of Andy did surprise me at the time but then you just get on with it and understand the dynamics behind it. It is the way you have to manage when the finances aren't there. The Cole deal allowed Kevin to bring in Keith Gillespie. I didn't feel as if my place was under threat, even though he played in my position. I still thought I'd get plenty of game time. I was very disappointed to be moved on because I had a fantastic season beforehand.

When Kevin told me Tottenham wanted to sign me, I felt the same as I did at Norwich, that I was happy to stay. I realised, however, that it was an indicator that the club wanted to sell you. I told Kevin I wanted to stay but said if you're not going to play me then I'm happy to go. It was quite an open honest conversation we had. I didn't push to leave. I was disappointed to leave and upset he didn't fight for me but on the other hand, I understood they were going to double the money they paid for me by accepting Tottenham's offer.

Chapter Twenty seven: John Burridge

John Burridge's career at Newcastle United was yet another colourful chapter in the story of one of football's most eccentric characters. Joining the club in 1989, as Jim Smith's Magpies tried to bounce back to the top flight for the first time of asking after relegation, Burridge, known affectionately as "Budgie," brought his larger-than-life personality to St. James' Park. Renowned for an extraordinary career spanning over three decades, Burridge is part of the exclusive 'more clubs than Jack Nicklaus' brigade, having played for an astonishing 29 teams during his career.

At Newcastle, Burridge's performances between the posts were marked by his enthusiasm and an unorthodox approach while his impact on and off the pitch was memorable. Burridge was also an early pioneer of dieting, long before sports food science gained prominence in the 1990s and 2000s. His dedication to fitness and nutrition was way ahead of its time. Often seen munching on raw vegetables, eating baby food and mixing smoothies before smoothies were a thing, Budgie often preached the benefits of healthy living to his bemused teammates.

Burridge's pre-match rituals of hanging from the crossbar and doing handstands to loosen up have gone down in football folklore much to the hysterics and bewilderment of his teammates, supporters and match officials. His eccentric behaviour and dedication to fitness left an indelible mark on the club and endeared him to the Newcastle faithful. The much-travelled shotstopper also made it known that former manager Arthur Cox made him 'mad' after jokingly suggesting he let in a couple of goals while playing on loan for Man City against Newcastle.

Budgie Perched

I got a call from Kevin to come back and help coach the goalkeepers when I was manager of Blyth Spartans. My wife took a call and she said, 'It's Kevin Keegan. He wants to talk to you.' I thought she was kidding. I was still living in Durham but playing for Hibs. I said, 'Hello, Kevin, do you want me to come back?' He said, 'Yeah, we need a goalkeeper coach. Budgie, you're 43 now, nobody will take you.' I told him I was still fit enough to play but he insisted he only wanted me as a coach. I told him I wasn't interested. He rang back the following day and said he would sign me a player-coach. I told him that was much better. Anyway, he saw how fit I was in training and I sat on the bench for about eight or nine games as cover after I came back.

I would coach Blyth two nights a week and then I'd look after the goalkeepers at Newcastle: Mike Hooper, Tommy Wright, Pavel Srnicek and Steve Harper. Shaka Hislop came later and he and Pav were both very good goalkeepers. Pav was the best shot-stopper as was Shaka. They were both good athletes but I think Pav was the better all-round goalkeeper.

Arthur Cox pulled me in training one day and said Man City have an injury problem with their goalkeepers and they need someone to sit on the bench. So, I went down and was sub a few times and then I was back to Newcastle coaching the goalkeepers. I then noticed Man City were playing Newcastle about five games before the end of the season and told Kevin. He was OK about it. I even travelled down to Manchester with the Newcastle lads on the coach on the day of the game. They were giving me all sorts of junk, telling me to let a goal in, and stuff like that.

Tony Cotton, the City keeper, went down injured in the first half. He managed to make it to half-time but when we were in the dressing room at the break, the manager Brian Horton told me I was in because Tony couldn't go on. As I was being introduced to the crowd by the announcer, Arthur Cox was behind me. He said, 'You better let in a couple of goals otherwise you're getting the sack.' It made me mad. I turned around and told Arthur, 'Right, that's it. You're not scoring.' Ruel Fox managed to get through and he was one-on-one with me. I'd seen him do this a million times in training so I knew what he was going to do, so I saved it at his feet. Andy Cole got up and headed it and I turned around the top corner. I ended up getting man of the match in a 0-0 draw.

I was asked to go up to the players' lounge after the game and Kevin was there. Everybody knows how good he is in front of the cameras but inside he wanted to win that game. He didn't expect me to come on. When I got in the room, I saw Kevin so I walked back out again. He came after me telling me to come back in. He was very nice to me to my face but I knew deep inside he didn't like it.

I made a £100 bet with Kevin when I was at Wolves, before I signed for Newcastle, that I'd play in a Superman outfit. It was when Kevin was still a player in 1983 and Newcastle was visiting Molineux. I was wearing it during the kickabout and Kevin said, 'I'll give you £100 if you play in it. I didn't think they would let me so I went to see the Wolves boss and he said he couldn't give a toss what I played in. The referee then said it was OK as long as I wore the Wolves shorts over my tights and it didn't clash with the Newcastle colours. The game ended 2-2 and fair play to Kevin, he put his hand in his pocket and gave me a 100 quid.

Jim Smith signed me but I knew my days were limited after he left and Ossie Ardiles came in. We had a bit of an altercation as players when I was in goal for Southampton and he played for Tottenham. We were winning 1-0 at the Dell and they got a corner with a minute to go. Ossie tried to block me. Some might know that because people used to stand on me at corners, I filed the back two studs in my boots so they were razor sharp. I looked around to see where the ref and linesman were and then I hit him. He's gone down screaming. I said, 'Get up you Argentinian bastard!" We won 1-0 and after the game, he was waiting for me outside the dressing room. I tried to walk past him but he gave me a right-hander. I grabbed him by the hair and threw him down the steps. And that was that.

We were at Maiden Castle when Ossie was announced as Jim's replacement. The chairman came in and introduced him to us. Everybody clapped but I thought, 'Oh fuck!' He went around everybody and shook hands with them, apart from me. He walked straight past me. I was summoned the next day to the secretary Russell Cushing's office and he told me Ossie didn't want me to come to training anymore. I was banned from the training ground and told that I wouldn't be playing again for Newcastle. I was handed a free transfer. Ossie wouldn't even talk to me or see me.

We were so close to going up under Jim. I remember saving a penalty from Phil Hardyman for Sunderland a minute before the end to earn a draw in the play-off semi-final at Roker Park. Mark Stimpson brought down Marco Gabbiadini. It was never a penalty. The referee made a mistake but I'd seen Phil take penalties so I did my homework and he put it to the same side and I guessed right. He then came and followed up by booting me in the face. I waited for him in the tunnel and dared him to do it again but he walked past me giving me verbals instead. Unfortunately, we couldn't get a result at home and Sunderland went up at the expense of Swindon who were penalised for financial irregularities. Mark McGee and Micky Quinn's goals dried up near the end of that campaign and I think I broke Newcastle's clean sheet record that season. Not going up was the biggest disappointment I had in football.

Derek Fazakerley was a bloody good centre-half at Blackburn Rovers and he was a great defensive coach. He had the defence coming out and going back as a unit. Kevin was an inside forward, a striker. He wanted goals, goals, goals. Had Newcastle hung on to Derek, they wouldn't have conceded as many goals but at the same time, they wouldn't have scored as many goals. I used to feel sorry for Pav at times because even his defenders were attacking like the big Belgian lad, Philippe Albert. So did Darren Peacock, John Beresford and Barry Venison.

The youngsters were super-duper at Newcastle. Lee Clark wasn't the quickest player or hardest tackler but he could run a game on his own. When he got on the ball he could see a pass very early. Steve Watson also went on to do great things. We had a great team back then with Shearer and Big Les up top, Robert Lee and David Ginola. We had players who could keep the ball and a little magician in the middle of the park called Peter Beardsley casting spells on players. Pedro was one of the best players I've played with or seen. He did things only other mere mortals could dream of and, he worked his bollocks off.

Kevin was all attack! Attack! Attack! Faz was more, defend! Defend! Defend! We lost a lot of games because the centre-backs were out of position. Darren Peacock was probably our only defender. Albert wanted to score a worldy every time he played. If I was the goalkeeper then I would've been fighting with everyone, even Kevin, who was gung-ho. People liked that kind of football to be fair. As a goalkeeper, you want a clean sheet and Newcastle didn't get many.

Kevin then went and bought big Les Ferdinand and my old mate from Southampton, Alan Shearer. I remember him as a kid. One time in training he's in on goal and I've dived at his feet and got the ball. He's jumped over me. I got up and grabbed him by the scruff of the neck and asked whether 'He was going to be a girl all his life?' I told him he couldn't kick me but it was alright to block. Anyway, a few years later and I'm in goal for Hibs, I think it was, against Kenny Dalglish's Blackburn. During the game, Shearer kicked me in the face. After the game, I go looking for him in the Blackburn dressing room. Kenny is telling me to calm down and take it easy. I said, 'Alan! Come here! Let's go and have a drink together.' I congratulated him.

The crowd at Newcastle is incredible. Newcastle is their life. It's not like that for fans in London. You know,

Newcastle does not get the good press it deserves. The two clubs where I was most happy were Newcastle and Crystal Palace. It was very sad to leave the club and even sadder when we missed out on winning the Premier League. One day, though.

Chapter Twenty eight: Marc Hottiger

Marc Hottiger's career at Newcastle United, though relatively brief, was memorable. Peter Beardsley is on record for saying the Lausanne-born defender was the best right back he had played with. Heady praise indeed from one of the greatest players ever to grace the hallowed St James' Park turf.

Hottiger joined Newcastle in the summer of 1994 from FC Sion for £525,000 after catching the eye of the United management team while playing for Switzerland in the World Cup in the USA. The Swiss international quickly became a fans' favourite for his marauding runs down the right flank as he joined the cavalry charge to support one of the most attack-minded teams in Premier League history.

Hottiger was one of the standout players in a difficult 1994-95 season where the Magpies were expected to kick on and better the previous season's top-three finish. Unfortunately, the squad was decimated by injuries to key players leading to a sixth-place finish in the Premier League, narrowly missing out on a spot in the UEFA Cup. Despite his eye-catching contributions, Hottiger's time at Newcastle came to an end in 1996 when he transferred to Everton. Nevertheless, his time at St. James' Park remains fondly remembered by those who witnessed his dedication and professionalism and his role in a memorable chapter of the club's history.

Pedro's Pet

I got a call from Terry McDermott after the World Cup in 1994. He said that he and Kevin Keegan had seen me play against Romania and the USA and wanted to sign me. I spoke with Sion, my club at the time, and then I came to Newcastle and signed. Kevin Keegan was a legend. It was an easy decision to make. When a man of Kevin's magnitude wants to sign you, it is incredibly flattering, especially for a small, unknown Swiss guy like myself.

I got a great first impression of Newcastle. A friend of mine told me about the place and how it was a working-class city. I was in a hotel near the sea when I first came to Newcastle. Training was so much fun under Kevin, Terry and especially Derek Fazakerley. Faz took most of the training sessions and of course, lots of fans came to see us train. I looked forward to it every day. I woke every morning wondering what I would learn today and couldn't wait to get started.

Training was all game-oriented and the spirits of the players were high. It was a great time in my life. All of the supporters at training were a surprise. In Switzerland we maybe had a few come along and watch but not thousands like at Newcastle. I think it was important at Newcastle for the fans to mix and bond with the players. They had a great relationship and it was a good experience for me.

Playing at St James' Park was special. I had never played in the English Premier League before and because of the relationship with the supporters, we had a good rapport and atmosphere exceptional, much, much more than all of the other Premier League grounds I played in. In Switzerland, we don't have this. It's a kind of fever. They live for the team and they work hard so they can buy tickets to watch the team. The stadium was great and the pitch was so green, like a golf green.

The young players we had were good for the supporters. I think it was good we had so many good young players in the side. The supporters love it when a local lad plays for the first team. I enjoyed playing with the local players. It was always a pleasure. I enjoyed all of my games at Newcastle but obviously, I enjoyed the two games where I scored: against Chelsea in a 1-1 draw at Stamford Bridge and in the FA Cup in a 2-1 win at Blackburn.

My first games were in a tournament in Glasgow. I had only signed two days before the competition. We played against Manchester United, Fiorentina and Glasgow

Rangers. The first game against Manchester United was special for me. Ryan Giggs was my opponent that day and I played well. We ended up beating them on penalties. Ten or 15 minutes into the game Peter Beardsley came to me and said, 'Keep it going, you're playing well.' This meant a lot to me and motivated me even more. The first game was important for me because I wanted to get off to a good start.

Philippe Albert was my closest friend at the club because we signed within a few days of each other and we stayed in the same hotel. We both spoke French so that helped me settle in. Then we moved into houses near each other in Jesmond but I was friends with all of the players: Lee Clark, Ruel Fox, Andy Cole, Robert Lee, Scott Sellars, all of them. We all used to go out to eat and drink something. It is hard to pick individual players out because the spirit was great between us all. I can't leave out Peter Beardsley, he was such a great guy, as was Pav.

It was a shock when Andy Cole was sold because he was such a great player for us. We can't blame Andy for leaving. He also had a great career at Manchester United. Kevin then brought in Les Ferdinand. But yes, Andy was a miss and it was a shame for us he left. Then I left soon after.

I was sad to leave Newcastle after such a short time. Kevin then bought Warren Barton and I didn't play so much in the second year. I would have stayed but I also wanted to play more games. Kevin said he wanted me to stay even though a couple of clubs had been in touch to ask about me. I also had a problem with my work permit and I needed to play a certain number of games so I could stay in England. Kevin couldn't promise me more game time. This is part of football, you know. It's a shame because if I had a choice I would have stayed. It was disappointing because I had such a good 1994-95 season. I also think Kevin maybe wanted a more defensive-minded right back and that's why he bought Warren Barton. I would have loved to stay like Fabian Schar who stayed over five years. This is my one regret in football, not staying longer at Newcastle.

It is also a regret Newcastle didn't win the league during my time. I think it was because they didn't have the experience of Manchester United. We lost too many games toward the end of the season while Manchester United kept grinding out results. The team had not been challenging to the title for such a long time and maybe some players didn't know how to cope while another few lost a bit of form. Newcastle didn't manage the games very well towards the end.

I used to come back to Newcastle and watch a game every season after I left, until a couple of years ago. Now I can't find the time, unfortunately. I hope to come back soon. I'm still in contact with John Beresford. Bez used to sort me out with a ticket. I remember the last time I wanted to come it was difficult because the owner made it hard for the ex-players to come back and watch.

I want to wish all the Newcastle supporters well. They were the best fans I ever played for. I hope they have every success in the future and hope they win something soon.

Chapter Twenty nine: Philippe Albert

Philippe Albert's left foot was so cultured it could compose a concerto, conjure a Renaissance portrait, and write sonnets. The Belgian international was unlike anything Newcastle fans had ever seen before. The Charleroi-born defender had a wand of a left foot, threading passes through the eye of a needle and conjuring goals only the greatest footballers could summon – just ask a certain Manchester United goalkeeper. He played more like a No.10 than a centre-half, such was his vision, skill, and passing ability. It is little wonder Albert was christened Prince Philippe by the fans, such was his majestic style of play.

The pull of Kevin Keegan was too strong for Albert, who had turned down Italian giants Juventus and Fiorentina before accepting to play for Newcastle. The Ex-Anderlecht defender was a big fan of the former Anfield No.7 and his all-conquering Liverpool side of the 1970s and 1980s. The £2.7 million signing hit the ground running and quickly became a cult hero due to his classy style of play and his surprising knack for scoring goals, a rare trait for a central defender. Newcastle fans also, subverted a well-known children's TV show, Rupert the Bear, to give the much-loved defender his own song

Albert's most iconic moment in a Newcastle shirt came during a match against Premier League champions Manchester United in October 1996. In a stunning 5-0 victory, he famously chipped Peter Schmeichel from 25 yards, a goal that epitomised the free-spirited and attacking philosophy of Keegan's team.

Albert's time on Tyneside came to an end, like many of The Entertainers, under Kenny Dalglish's management. The ball-playing defender confessed it was a wrench to leave Newcastle after spending what he described as, "The best five years of my life."

Everyone Knows His Name

After the 1994 World Cup in the USA, I was back in

Belgium training with Anderlecht. I was told there had been an offer from Newcastle. Kevin had been at the World Cup as a pundit and had seen two of Belgium's games against Holland and Germany, where I managed to score. Anderlecht agreed to a fee around the August time and I took a flight to discuss the move with Kevin and Terry Mac in Leeds. We met in Leeds because they wanted to hide from the press and fans in Newcastle.

We had a two-hour chat about how he wanted us to play football and I agreed to a four-year deal. It was very special. When Anderlecht said I had to meet Kevin Keegan and Terry McDermott, I didn't believe them. When I was a kid, I used to watch the great Liverpool side in their European conquests. Kevin and Terry Mac were fantastic players. I was not only impressed by their football abilities of the past but also as human beings. Kevin had so much charisma. You felt as if you were in the presence of greatness. He was a superstar. I was very impressed and the way he wanted us to play football was the way I liked to play. We had a very good relationship from the start.

We trained at Maiden Castle in Durham and during the school holidays, lots of kids would come down with their parents and grandparents. It was unbelievable around 5,000 people turned up. Kevin was very strict. He wanted us to train very hard and play some good football for the fans and then he would make us sign autographs for everyone before we went and had a shower. Sometimes we'd be signing autographs for two hours. I never experienced anything like it in my life.

My first game was away at Leicester City where we won 3-1 and then we had two home games against Southampton and Coventry where the atmosphere was unbelievable. There might have been only 36,000 inside the ground but it felt like 80,000 to 90,000. I played for the best clubs in Belgium but only 22,000 or 23,000 would turn up to watch us. I enjoyed every second of being at Newcastle.

We trained hard every day and Kevin and Terry Mac joined in a trained and played too. The players totally respected Kevin and Terry for doing the same as us. Kevin didn't like training twice a day so we did a long two-and-a-half-hour session in the morning. I never witnessed anything like the manager and his assistant joining in training so, total respect for them.

The young players at Newcastle had a great mentality and qualities. Steve Howey was a very good defender who could play football and use the ball very well. Lee Clark was a very good midfielder. Steve Watson could play in every position. Robbie Elliott was the same, he could play left-back or centre back. I have fond memories of the younger lads. They were very important to the squad.

Marc Hottiger joined the club at the same time as me so he was a good friend but I got on with everybody at Newcastle. Marc was good to me as he joined a couple of weeks before me and he could drive on the left, which was new to me. In Belgium, we drive on the right so it was very complicated for me. He helped me with my English which was not too good at the time.

I have lots of memories of games I played for Newcastle. At that time, we were the best team in England with Manchester United. I remember my first goals for Newcastle. I scored two against Leicester in a 3-1 home win. I scored two goals away at Maine Road against Manchester City in a 3-3 draw as well. Of course, the game most fans remember is the 5-0 home win over Manchester United. I was very lucky to score the fifth goal. Every goal from the game was absolutely superb. If I was pushed to pick one game that stood out it would be the 5-0 against Man U.

I had watched Man U a few times on TV and of course, I had played against them as well. I saw that Schmeichel would come off his line to reduce the angle. The two choices were to hit it hard or to chip and fortunately, I made the right decision and I was lucky it went in. I scored a lot of goals like that in my career but this one was very special because they were the best team in England and possibly Europe at the time.

I don't think we lost the title in 1996, Man U won it. I remember we had the second-best defensive record in the league. I remember the game in March 96 against Man U very well. I could talk about it for hours. We should have been 3-0 or 4-0 up at half-time and it would have been a true reflection of the game. Unfortunately, at that time we faced the best goalkeeper in the world who made some tremendous saves. Without Schmeichel, it would have been game over and we would have gone on to be crowned champions. Then Eric Cantona came back from suspension and scored some very important goals for Man U. There were games we should have won, like the one away at Nottingham Forest, where we drew. We were winning 1-0 at Blackburn and we lost 2-1. But I'm convinced that we lost the title in March because of Schmeichel. I still have many regrets over that season but overall Man U deserved to win the title that season.

Peter Beardsley was a fantastic player for us. David Ginola was another superstar and Alan Shearer was a fantastic goalscorer. Tino Asprilla also went on to play for us and Les Ferdinand. We had some fantastic players. We all signed for Kevin Keegan. He has to take the credit for putting together such a fantastic team. I didn't know much about Newcastle or the area or the mentality of the people from the North-East before I signed. The best five years of my life were spent in Newcastle and not only football-wise. It is a place in England where the people are just fantastic.

Everyone was very surprised when Kevin left. Nobody saw his resignation coming but we had to respect his decision. It was also tough for me to leave Newcastle. It was tough because I loved Newcastle but the new manager didn't like me and wouldn't play me. You don't know how disappointing it was for me to leave one of the best clubs in the world but I like to think positively and remember the five fantastic years I had at St James' Park.

Chapter Thirty: Keith Gillespie

Keith Gillespie will tell you that his career at Newcastle United was a high-stakes rollercoaster, filled with thrills, spills and some risky bellyaching bets. Joining the Magpies in January 1995 as part of the £6 million or £7 million deal that sent Andy Cole to Manchester United, Gillespie brought breakneck speed to the United touchlines, quickly endearing himself to the United faithful with his successful sorties down the wing.

The comparisons with fellow countryman George Best may be a bit unfair but the Northern Irishman willingly admits on occasion, like Best, he also indulged in a heady lifestyle of fast women and drinking. Nevertheless, it was his gambling habits that made the tabloid headlines. With a penchant for placing bets, Gillespie often found himself on the losing side of the gambling table.

His love for a flutter led to some sticky situations off the pitch but his performances on the pitch were anything but a gamble. His speed and crossing ability made him a key player for Kevin Keegan's marauders as they swatted away most that dared to play dice with them as United challenged for the Premier League title in the mid-90s. Despite the off-field antics, Gillespie's legacy at Newcastle United remains one of a talented winger who played with heart and passion, leaving fans with plenty of fond memories.

Despite being a lifelong Man United fan, the pacey Northern Ireland international had no regrets about moving to Tyneside, describing his time at Newcastle as the happiest of his career and life.

Bets Are Off

Kevin Keegan was an incredible person and certainly the best manager I worked under. You look at the managers I played under: Sir Alex Ferguson, Graeme Souness, Ruud Gullit, and Kenny Dalglish. His man management was just incredible. Some team talks with other managers could last 30-40 minutes. They'd go on and on and on.

Kevin's talks were about two or three minutes. Then he'd go around the players and have a chat, put his arm around you and within ten seconds you felt like you were the best player in the world and you'd want to run through a brick wall for him. This is what makes him unique. The other managers were massive names but for me, Kevin was top of those

I've said this many times: No one remembers who came second last season but ask anyone who came second in 1996 and they'll remember us because of the style of football Kevin had us playing. Going into training was an absolute joy. I know Kenny Dalglish wasn't popular with Newcastle fans but it would have been a tough ask for anyone following Kevin. It's the same at Manchester United. How many managers have they gone through after Sir Alex left? When Kenny got the job, we all thought, 'Wow!' I guess the fans thought they would take to him the same way as Kevin but then he dismantled Kevin's side. For me he was fantastic and you need to remember he helped get us into the Champions League. He was the manager when we beat Barcelona and he took us to an FA Cup final.

I was an apprentice at Manchester United when Newcastle got back into the top flight. They came to Manchester and Andy Cole scored in a 1-1 draw. The thing that stood out was the fans. I'd never experienced them before and they made a lot of noise that day. Then the following season I played against Newcastle a few times: in a pre-season tournament and then in (former Northern Ireland manager) Billy Bingham's testimonial. Then we played against them in the League Cup and then at Old Trafford where I scored.

Then I found out Kevin wanted to sign me. That was a massive thing for me. He could sell the club to anyone in 10, or 20 seconds. Before I went in to discuss terms, I had a 30-second conversation with him and he sold the club to me. The fact that he said the Andy Cole deal wouldn't happen if I didn't come, just shows the love he had for me. He was such an infectious character. It was a fantastic move for me to go to such a massive club as Newcastle. The only disappointment was that it was only four years because that was the most enjoyable time of my playing career.

I found out about the move while we were preparing for an FA Cup tie against Sheffield United. I played in the previous league game and expected to start again. The team was announced and the subs were named and I wasn't involved. Sir Alex pulled me to one side and told me what was happening and that Kevin wanted to sign me and didn't want me involved because I would be cup-tied. He told me to think about it. So, I watched the game and a lot was going through my mind. I grew up as a Man United fan. Then all of a sudden, I'm leaving. That is how quickly things change in football.

I spoke to Steve Bruce, Brian McClair and Bryan Robson. They all told me it was a great opportunity. Brucey was actually quite envious that I was getting the chance to play for Newcastle. I also had Andrei Kanchelskis in front of me as well but it was the best decision I made in my career. After the FA Cup game, Alex Ferguson and I jumped in a car and went to a hotel in Sheffield to meet Freddy Fletcher, Freddie Shepherd and Kevin. Alex did my deal, as in my wages, because I didn't have a representative at the time. I was on £250 a week at Man United. I saw Ferguson scribbling numbers down and wondering what that was all about. He then told the Newcastle guys I was on £600 a week. I looked up surprised at him. He just glared at me, so I didn't say anything. He told Newcastle that they should double that, and they did. I was on £1200 a week. The happiest people out of that deal were Ladbrokes in Gosforth. There were a few strange things about that deal because Alex didn't want me to go and then he's acting as my agent to get me a good deal.

My transfer to Newcastle was my decision, no one

else's decision. The proposal was put to me and Kevin said that the only way the deal would go through was if I agreed to it. I could've turned it down and stayed at Man United but I thought it was a great opportunity for me to play regular first-team football. Kevin did tell me his plans. He'd just sold his top striker but six months later he goes and buys Les Ferdinand. A year after that he goes out and buys Alan Shearer.

There was always a plan for what Kevin wanted to do. Obviously, the fans weren't happy he sold Andy Cole but there are not many managers out there who would've gone out on the steps to talk to the fans and explain why he did it. After the conversation, he had the fans' backing and he decided to take the club forward. It maybe didn't look like it at the time but he certainly proved it further down the line with the players he brought in.

Man United came back for me after they sold Andrea Kanchelskis. They bid £4 million for me six months after they sold me but Kevin turned it down and David Beckham, who was a central midfielder when we were playing for the youth team, moved out to the right side. Sir Alex rang and told me he was going to put a bid in for me. He asked if I wanted to come back. Obviously, I never said yes or no. How can you say no to a manager like Alex Ferguson? Newcastle never told me about it. I'm sure some players if they knew that, would have been banging on the manager's door demanding a move but I didn't. I wouldn't change anything about my career at Newcastle, apart from wanting to stay longer.

The 1995-96 season was eventful for more reasons than one. Everybody remembers Kevin's 'I would love it,' rant. I thought at the time, 'Fair play to him,' but I was also pissed off at the time because I scored the winner that night and nobody remembers it. Obviously, I had a gambling problem at the time, or too much time on my hands living in a hotel. I lived the first five months of my life in Newcastle at the Gosforth Park Hotel. Those were the days of fast women and slow horses. Joking aside, I got involved in betting at a very young age. I'd put bets on for lads at Man United, including the boss. It wasn't a big deal back then.

We'd train from about 10am to 12.30pm and then I'd head back to my hotel room. I needed something to relieve the boredom and that was at Ladbrokes on Gosforth High Street. I'll never forget my worst days, October 27, 1995. Two days before that we'd played Stoke in the League Cup. We'd travelled down to the game, had some lunch and then we were in our rooms. I'm sharing with David Ginola and he's sleeping after only two minutes of being in the room, or maybe that's just the effect I have on people. I was on the phone all afternoon putting bets on and I ended up winning three and a half grand. I was talking to this guy at the bookies and he's saying Newcastle's popular betting scores are 2-0, 2-1, 3-0 or 3-1. I put £500 on Peter Beardsley to score the first goal because he hadn't scored for about six games. Then I had £500 doubles with Beardsley scoring and 2-0, 2-1, 3-0 3-1. After about 20 minutes Peter scores and I've never run so fast in my life to kiss Peter Beardsley. Then we score again and it's 2-0 at half-time and we're sitting there quite rosy. In the second half, I had a cross-shot which the keeper saved but Big Les is on hand to knock it in for 3-0. There were about 25 minutes left so every time I got the ball I was either shanking it into the crowd or going into the corner to keep the ball.

Then Paul Peschisolido gets a run in on goal and I'm saying to myself, 'Score, you bastard, score!' He didn't score but my bet was still safe. Then with six or seven minutes to go, Darren Peacock wandered forward. I wasn't too worried because it was Darren Peacock. Somehow, he ends up in the box and he rifles it into the top corner to make it 4-0 and everyone is jumping on him because he didn't score many. It was at that time I realised his middle name, Darren 'Fucking' Peacock! He's just done me out of £52,000 and he knew nothing about it.

Two days after that game I lost £47,000. I didn't know that until I went to the bookies and he told me. I'm thinking, 'Oh, fuck!' The day after that I tried to recoup some of the money and I lost another £15,000 while we were on the way to Tottenham on the coach. I had a good game. Don't know how, given I'd lost £62,000 over two days. On the way back we were having a drink and playing cards and Kevin came to the back of the coach. I was sat next to Peter Beardsley and Kevin pointed at me but was talking to Peter Beardsley and said, 'He could be the best player in the country at this time.' I'm thinking, 'If only he knew I'd just lost £62,000.'

The Sun got wind of the story so I had to go and see Kevin. I had dinner with him and his family and he sorted the whole problem. I was due a signing on fee money so, the club forwarded it to me so I could pay the bookie. That was the end of it. I didn't get any help or anything and I stayed off the gambling for a few months after. I was always going to go back to it. Kevin was brilliant about the whole thing. The hardest part was telling my mum a story was breaking in the paper. I phoned her and she said, 'Och, son.' She asked, 'How much, £20,000?' I said more, she said. 'Och son.' And then I kept going until it was £47,000 and every time she would say, 'Och son.' She was pretty devastated about it. I still gamble today but it's not silly money. I once put £4,500 on a horse and it won. It's about £20, £30 every weekend betting on the football results. It doesn't matter whether it's £4 or £4,000 you still get that same buzz. It was a very steep learning curve.

As for the fast women. There was this time when Newcastle tried to sell me to Middlesbrough when Kenny Dalglish was the manager. I was pretty pissed off about it to be honest. So, I went out this Friday night and ended up in Julies nightclub. I lived in Whickham back then and went home with these two young women. We dropped one off and then the other girl asked if I wanted to go inside. So, I went inside and we kind of got it on. I was pulling my trousers on around 2.30am the door went and I'm thinking, 'Who the fuck is that at this time?' The girl I'm with says, 'It's my boyfriend.' I don't know why but I ran across the landing and I went into the nearest room, which was the kid's bedroom. I jumped on the top bunk and pretended to be asleep. I heard these footsteps coming up the stairs. A minute later the door opens, the light goes on and I pretend to wake up. The boyfriend goes, 'Fucking hell! It's Keith Gillespie! You been shagging wor lass?' Next thing, we were fighting, swapping punches and falling down the stairs like it was the movies. I then realised I had to go home before 3am because my girlfriend was at home. So, I eventually got out and ran home. I'd lost my keys so she had to let me in.

I got home and I've got a split lip. My girlfriend asks what happened and I said I got jumped on outside the chippy. My girlfriend has got the TCP out and the next thing, the police have turned up outside my house because the boyfriend told the police I'd assaulted him. The police are going through this story and my girlfriend is giving me daggers. I said I only went in because they had some posters of me on the walls and I had to sign them. My girlfriend must've believed me because we later got married. Although I am divorced now.

I did play a bit of football outside the women and horses though. I got injured in our charge towards the Premier League title. I was out for about five weeks and I was kind of rushed back in one sense and maybe didn't hit the heights I did before that. In terms of balance to the side. Tino was brought in and Peter Beardsley was moved to the right wing. Peter was an unbelievable player, one of the best I've ever played with but he's not a right winger. Everybody knows that. He wasn't going to get down the line and cross balls for Les Ferdinand like I was. This is all hindsight. Fair play to Man United, they went on an unbelievable run. It was demoralising every week. We'd come in after our game and ask about their score and it always seemed to be 1-0, Cantona. They just kept clawing back that lead.

We had so many disappointments towards the end of that season. The big one was losing to Man United at home. We win that, and we deserved to win it, and we go on and win the league. We go to Anfield and score three goals and don't get anything. We're 1-0 up with less than ten minutes to go at Blackburn and we don't get anything. Looking back there were some factors but it was an incredible season for the fans. Look at our home form: 17 wins, one draw and one defeat. The defeat was where Peter Schmeichel was man of the match, which tells you another story. It was sad we didn't get over the line because if we had won the title that season, with Kevin in charge, we had the capabilities of being a regular top-four side. Kevin would have demanded more.

I loved playing with Big Les, he was an absolute dream. He could make bad balls look good and he was the best header of the ball there was. Put the ball in the box and more times than not he would be on the end of it. I loved playing with Warren Barton. He was a great athlete and he just fed me the ball. If he knew I had the beating of the full-back he would constantly give me the ball.

Peter Beardsley was incredible though. I think he was about 32 or 33 when I came to the club and after seeing him close up in training and in games I thought, 'How good must this guy have been six or seven years ago?' He just seemed to get better and better. I got along very well with Peter and in most players and fans' eyes, he was the No.1 player who had ever played for the club. He was a genius.

Tino was arguably the most skilful player in my time at Newcastle, although Ginola was superb. That move where Bez would play the ball into his feet with the full-back up his arse was something else. He'd take a touch, feint one way and then go the other way. It was phenomenal but with some of Tino's tricks in training, you'd be left thinking, 'How did he do that?' There are probably times when Tino probably didn't know how he did it. Well, that was the feeling we had. Tino was great to play with and a joy around the dressing room and in training. He always had a big smile on his face and that was the way he played football.

I would say Kevin got the best out of me as a footballer because the style of our play was suited to me. There were times when I tried to track back and help the defence but Kevin encouraged me to stay up ready to be on the front foot when we next went on the attack. It was disappointing to get injured for a while during the 95-96 season because I was playing the best football of my career. I was providing plenty of goals and popping up with the odd one now and again.

Had you asked Newcastle fans at the beginning of the season whether they would take winning or losing the title on the last day of the season and they would have said yes. That is why it was disappointing to throw away that 12-point lead. It's a big regret for all of us not winning the league. It is something that will haunt us forever.

Chapter Thirty one: Warren Barton

Warren Barton became the most expensive defender in English football when he left Plough Lane, Wimbledon, to move to St James' Park, Newcastle, for a record £4 million transfer fee. The defender-cum-midfielder had already been capped by England when Kevin Keegan came calling and would be capped a further two times by the time he'd joined up with his fellow teammates ahead of the rollercoaster 1995-96 season.

The highly-rated defender had the pick of the Premier League's finest with his beloved Arsenal favourites to win his signature while newly-crowned champions Blackburn were also in the race. Barton's signing, if anything, encapsulates all you need to know about the enormous pulling power of Kevin Keegan. He could sell coals to Newcastle, sell sand to the Arabs and talk the birds down from the trees, such is his charisma.

It's fair to say Barton had a chequered start to his career on Tyneside but with some grit and determination, he eventually won over the boo-boys with some wholehearted displays to become another fans' favourite.

The Londoner confessed he loved his time on Tyneside and likes nothing better than reminiscing over playing in front of "the best fans in the world," and how his big mate Rob Lee has yet to buy him a pint despite spending over ten years with him as a player.

Centre Parting

I first heard of Newcastle's interest in me in the season before I signed, 1994-95. I'd already spoken to Celtic, Blackburn Rovers and David Dein at Arsenal, Sheffield Wednesday and Man City. I was actually at a game on the Bank Holiday Monday, watching Blackburn against Newcastle. Alan Shearer scored for Rovers in a 1-0 win at Ewood Park. He got above John Beresford at the back post to head it home while Blackburn was going for the league. Kevin Keegan came down to London to see me. I was sitting in reception at Wimbledon when he passed me on the way to meet the Wimbledon chairman. As he passed, he said, "Come and join a big club." Kevin had loads of charisma.

I was in the England squad at the time with Les Ferdinand. We were both linked with a move to Arsenal and Blackburn. We were kind of a double act, wanted by the same clubs. I'd also spoken to Peter Beardsley when we were in the England squads to get to know about Newcastle.

I'd played at St James' Park earlier that year before I signed and the atmosphere was unbelievable. I turned to one of my friends, 'Imagine playing in front of this lot all of the time.' Lo and behold, I was there six months later. It was quite an easy decision to make when Kevin Keegan wants you.

Training at Maiden Castle was surreal. I played for the Crazy Gang and we might have got only four or 5,000 supporters to watch a game. There were 5,000 to 6,000 watching us train at Maiden Castle. We used to get in early to sign autographs and pose for pictures. The pictures have just started to reemerge recently which made me feel really old. It was amazing to experience all of that passion, excitement and intensity.

One time I remember Terry Mac and KK sitting on top of a burger van having a cup of tea and a sausage roll watching us train. It was an amazing experience. All the local lads: Lee Clark, Watto, Robbie Elliott and Steve Howey made me feel really welcome. Then Big Les came in with Shaka (Hislop) and David Ginola and we hit the ground running.

It was surreal, all those supporters watching us whether it was raining, snowing or sunshine. It kind of made you realise how important the club was to the fans. Sometimes it would take 45 minutes to get out of your car, sign the autographs and pose for the pictures before you got to the changing room. Great times, happy memories.

Training was intense. We'd do the warm-up and passing drills and do some shadow play but we used to train how we played, with intensity. Particularly, Peter Beardsley would set the tone for how quickly we would train. I remember talking to Les one day, asking him whether he'd touched the ball yet. He said he hadn't touched it for about three weeks. The ball was fizzing around everywhere. It was one-touch, two-touch and very intense.

Sometimes it was difficult to adapt and you were afraid, sometimes, that if you didn't train well or had a bad session, you wouldn't get picked for the team. It didn't matter whether you were a £4 million, a £6 million signing or you'd arrived at the club on a free contract. Training was always fun as well. It fostered team spirit among all of the big characters. It was everything I wanted and loved every minute of it.

I was a big money signing back then and the transfer fee put a lot of pressure on you but I couldn't do anything about the fee. I got told I was too small to make it when I was younger and then I became the record transfer fee for a defender at £4.5 million and Newcastle's record transfer fee. Thankfully, I didn't have that burden long as Les Ferdinand came in two days later for £6 million.

I could have stayed at Wimbledon and had a comfortable life but I wanted to come to play for Newcastle, try and win something and compete under pressure. It was hard at times. When you didn't perform well, you'd get some stick but that came with wearing the black and white shirt. It was a nice pressure.

Big Les was probably my best mate at the club at the beginning. We used to live next to each other, room together and would drive into training together. I was close with Rob Lee, John Beresford and Peter Beardsley too but I got on with all of the lads. I played with Rob Lee for over ten years and, I'm not saying he's tight but, he never bought me one drink. Tell you another thing: I won't get in a limo with him again.

It was a big blow and a big disappointment for us to

lose Les after only two seasons. He'd scored something like 50 goals for us. It was heartbreaking to lose him, Kevin and Ginola all in the space of a few months. Then Gary Speed came in and he was my roommate for the rest of my time at the club. I'm probably more in touch with Shay Given than the others now. He is a great fellow and was a great player but there were a lot of great guys at the club at the time. I'm still in touch with Nash (Lee Clark) now his son (Bobby) is doing well. I'm sure if I saw any of the other lads, we'd just hit the ground running again.

Terry Mac was great for us. He'd be there when we were asking questions about certain things without having to go to Kevin. Kevin was so passionate and emotional. He wanted the team to do well so passionately. Terry was great to bounce ideas off and if we needed stuff like tickets etc. When you spoke to him about the game, he was brilliant. He knew his place. He knew his role. You don't work with people like Kevin Keegan, Kenny Dalglish or Graeme Souness if you don't have anything to offer. He was brilliant for me and my family when I first got there and he always had that cheeky Scouse one-liner for everything.

His heart was in the right place and he wanted us all to do well. He was exactly what we needed at the time. He made everything move a lot smoother. His one-to-ones were brilliant. He'd offer you advice and you'd think, 'That's brilliant, where did he get that from?'

It's hard to pick a favourite game because they were all great but my debut was memorable, against Coventry City at St James' Park. We won 3-0 and Les got his first goal for the club. Before the game we were warming up and all I could see was a sea of black and white, everywhere. The 5-0 win over Nottingham Forest stands out as well. It got us into the Champions League. Les got a couple of goals, Tino scored and the Mackems and Smoggys got relegated which was the icing on the cake. The Barcelona game at home springs to mind as well. We beat them 3-2 and Tino got a hat-trick. You can't really beat that game, against Barcelona, one of the biggest clubs in the world, in the Champions League. It doesn't get much better than that, playing against the likes of Luis Figo and Luis Enrique.

There were loads of memorable games though. I didn't play in the first 4-3 game at Anfield when we were going for the title but I played in the second 4-3 game the following year under Kenny. We were 3-0 down at half-time and we were crap. Kenny made it clear in no uncertain terms that he wasn't happy. I managed to score but don't ask me what I was doing up there. I managed to get on the end of a long ball and poked it between David James' legs. Unfortunately for us, we switched off again and Robbie Fowler sneaked in to break our hearts again to score the winner

The first game was sensational. It was 1-0, 1-1, 2-1 and kept going on and on and on. Playing at Anfield is a great experience for players and the second game was a game of two halves, to coin a cliché. It cost me £250 because I volleyed the sky microphone behind the goal. We thought we'd snatched a draw only to be robbed at the end. It was a rollercoaster of a game and that was what it was like at the time at Newcastle. We had so many highs and lows in my time at the club.

My favourite goal was probably scoring the only goal of the game at home to Tottenham. Again, I don't know what I was doing that high up the pitch but I managed to get my left foot on the ball and ram it home for the three points. I grew up an Arsenal supporter so that was quite nice. I've got so many great stories of my time at Newcastle, I can't tell most of them because it'll get us all into trouble. Playing golf with Steve Howey in Marbella springs to mind. He's coming down the 18th hole of this course dressed, not in golf attire I can tell you. I'll let Steve tell you that one.

Nobby on his trumpet always caused a stir. He'd call

you at 11pm and play his trumpet down the phone. Alan Shearer's first night out with us, we had to put him in a taxi home. There are a lot of funny yarns. I remember we'd gone to Sheffield Wednesday and won 2-0. Peter Beardsley scored an outrageous goal. After the game supporters were waiting outside for him and they put him on their shoulders and marched him down the high road. It was a marvellous time to play for Newcastle.

Peter Beardsley was the best player I played with at Newcastle. Alan Shearer was the best goalscorer, and Ginola was unbelievable. He was something I'd never seen before in my life. Rob Lee said the same thing. We played Hearts in a pre-season friendly and he terrorised them. Pedro was unbelievably consistent. He trained like he played so you can imagine how he was. Him and his wife Sandra were great to me and my family.

Kevin's "I would love it" outburst gave us immense pride. We could kind of feel it coming. The pressure was building and he bit, which was what Alex Ferguson wanted him to do. Kevin was in a bad mood for a few weeks after Fergie's comments about us playing at Stuart Pearce's testimonial at the end of the season and us having to go to Nottm Forest to play them before the end of the season. I was proud of Kevin for standing up to Fergie. It was an outrageous thing to say, that maybe Forest would go easy on us. I wish we could have won the title and rammed it down their throats after it but it wasn't to be.

We didn't win the title that year perhaps because of a lack of experience, pressure and we changed our system a bit. Think it was a little bit of all of that. And, we lost our momentum. We were box office at the time so we were always playing the sky games, on Sunday or Monday night. We were the last team playing on a weekend. Man United would be playing at 3pm on a Saturday and they knew what to do before we played.

In the game we played Man United at home when Cantona scored, we were brilliant in the first half. Peter

Schmeichel was making save after save from Big Les and Tino. In hindsight, maybe we could have managed the game better and just tried to avoid losing. A draw would have been a good result and they would have been nine points behind us. At half time we came in a Kevin said, 'You've killed them. Go out and do it again.' We got done by a sucker punch, a counterattack.

After that game, we couldn't get our momentum back. We started to change the formation and tinker with the system. There isn't a day that goes by when I don't think about it, not just for the missing medal for my mantlepiece, it would have been great for the club and the city of Newcastle. Leicester won it, Blackburn won it, Liverpool and Chelsea, etc. It would have meant so much to the city to win it.

I was shocked and devastated when Kevin left, even though I wasn't in the team at the time. I'd lost my place. I felt let down at the same time because all of us, or most of us, had gone to the club because of him, his dream and the vision he had for the club. I think the only player he told was Alan Shearer. We were shocked. We didn't know until we were driving into training. We'd heard the rumours on the radio, TV and press but it wasn't until Terry Mac and Arthur Cox told us.

It was a surprise as well because we'd just beat Spurs 7-1 and we thought, 'We've got another chance this season.' We felt we had let Kevin down the year before, Alan was with us now and we wanted to make amends this year. Kevin was so passionate and felt as if the club wasn't going in the direction he wanted.

The fans are the heart and soul of the football club and the football club is the heart and soul of the city. I got a bit of criticism a couple of years ago for saying a team like Newcastle should not be ticking along (as Steve Bruce said) when we had a different manager and owner. Newcastle is not a club that just ticks along and survives. That's not what the fans deserve. They were great with me and my family and kids. The fans love their club.

For years it was soulless, ten years. I had friends who had given up their season tickets. You couldn't get tickets when I played. That's how precious they were. When the fans are behind you there's no better feeling for a player. Seven and 8,000 would regularly travel away as well if they could get tickets. At home, there is no better feeling than to go down those steps and then emerge onto the pitch and hear that roar, the passion and build-up to what they've waited all week for was amazing. Kevin would tell us, 'They've worked hard all week, now go out there and entertain them.' And that's what we'd do.

They're the best in the world. They took me to their hea rts, which was something special, especially for some-one like me and Rob Lee, who aren't from the area. They loved you if you tried for the shirt. They'd give their right arm to be in our places and we tried to let them live their dreams through us. We thought it was our responsibility to do that for them. I still miss it but I did it 220 times and it was a pleasure to play for those loyal supporters.

Chapter Thirty two: Les Ferdinand

Affectionately known as "Sir Les" for his majestic performances on the pitch and his chivalry off it, Les Ferdinand is universally adored by Newcastle United fans and players. Arriving from Queens Park Rangers in 1995 for a princely sum of £6 million, Ferdinand soon established himself as a club legend while donning the iconic No.9 shirt.

When he wasn't smashing up a Blue Peter TV set in a bout of playful exuberance, the burly striker was smashing the back of the net - 25 times in his first Premier League campaign at St James Park and 29 in total - with a little assistance from David Ginola's wing-wizardry on the left, Keith Gillespie's speedy supply from the right, while Peter Beardsley was conjuring more assists and tricks than a fairytale wizard.

The popular Londoner then formed a formidable partnership with Geordie legend Alan Shearer in his second season on Tyneside, feasting himself on another 21 goals as United finished runners-up to Manchester United for a second successive term. Fast, fearless as a lion, and as strong as a Marvel superhero, witnessing Sir Les leap like a salmon and hang in mid-air was a sight to behold - especially when mere mortals could only jump like a tin of tuna.

Ferdinand's time at Newcastle may have been relatively brief but his impact was profound and he justifiably stands shoulder-to-shoulder alongside the club's greats.

Sir Les

I'd had a decent season at QPR, scored 26 goals in all competitions at the end of the 1994-95 season. I heard Newcastle were interested but it was Aston Villa who put the first bid in for me. That kind of got the ball rolling if you like, and Newcastle then showed their hand. I spoke to Aston Villa first and then I went to talk to Kevin Keegan. A few clubs then came in for me but after I spoke to Kevin, I knew that was my destination and where I wanted to go.

When I was growing up Kevin Keegan was the face of football. I watched him play football for Liverpool and England and watched him on Superstars. I always said to myself if I was going to leave QPR it would be only to better myself and going to Newcastle, with the squad they had at the time, I knew I was going to better myself. And, with Kevin being there, I was going to learn from him, who was a top striker in his playing days. I was in awe of Kevin when I met him yet given his star-studded career and reputation, he came across as very humble.

I worked with some great coaches in my time like Gerry Francis and Don Howe but when I went to Newcastle everything was so much faster. The ball moved quicker and everything was done at match tempo. That is what Kevin wanted, whether it was in training, five-a-side or even a friendly. He wouldn't let the tempo slip in training and it just mirrored the game on a Saturday.

I was quite close to Warren Barton as we signed at about the same time but Lee Clark and Steve Watson took me under their wings. I'm not sure it was the right wing, however. They both looked after me when I arrived. Warren and I were both from London so we could understand what the other was saying as Geordie was difficult to understand at first and we were good mates. Joking aside, we had a really tight-knit group and everyone got on with each other. That was what stood out for me, the camaraderie in the squad was brilliant.

I had always known the No.9 shirt was special before I came to the club. Kevin said to me, 'I'm giving you the No.9 shirt because you're big enough to wear it and it won't be too heavy for you.' Saying that, I only fully realised how important it was when I scored on my debut against Coventry City. The reason I remember that goal more than any of the others is because had there been a roof over St James' Park that day, it would have come off because of the noise the supporters made when I scored. I realised then, that this is the most iconic football shirt at this football club.

Kevin knew his stuff. If he thought you were confident enough to take a free-kick and bend it in the top corner then he'd let you get on with it. It was the same with corners, etc. We didn't really have a designated taker of corners. If you wanted to take them and you were confident then you would take them. I remember leaving the dressing room after one of Kevin's team talks and said to one of the lads, 'I feel like a million dollars.' He said, 'You should do, he paid 6 million of them for you.'

The Geordies in the squad were vitally important. They helped us understand the city and what the football club meant to the fans. Down south, I've seen young players buying a flash car for themselves after they've done well and they've been slaughtered by their fans for being flash, At Newcastle that never happened. If Newcastle fans saw one of their own in a flash car they would applaud and encourage them for doing well for themselves. The local players were revered by the fans.

Peter Beardsley was a wonderful player. My only regret is that I didn't get to play with him earlier in his career. He was still an exceptional player when he came back to Newcastle for his second spell. I always think about what he did for me as a player and what he could have done for me if I'd played with him earlier. Everyone he played with in his career benefitted from playing alongside him. Despite being a wonderful player, I thought David Ginola was probably the best player I played with at Newcastle. In that first season, I thought he was going to be crowned European Footballer of the Year. Then we had Robert Lee. He was a much better player than I ever imagined until I got to play with him at St James' Park.

There was always something happening at the football club, surprises. Kevin pulled me to one side just before we were boarding a flight to go on a pre-season tour and told me he was going to sign Alan Shearer. He said, 'We've agreed a world-record transfer fee and we're trying to get the deal done today.' I'm thinking, 'Brilliant! We could do with another striker, although I guess many people were probably thinking we didn't need one. I think most people probably thought we'd need another defender given that we shipped a few goals towards the end of the season. For me, I wanted another striker because it would mean we'd score more than the other team which was our motto. Kevin told only me at the time because he said, 'When the media get hold of the story, they'll speculate that you're on your way out of the door.'

Terry Venables, the England manager at that time, famously said that he didn't think me and Alan could play together. Keegan said, 'I'm not trying to prove anybody wrong, I just think you two can play together and you'll be successful.' The last thing he said was, 'Alan asked for the No.9 shirt.' I said, 'What did you say?' Kevin said, 'I'll ask Les.' He then added that Alan has worn the No.9 all his life, at Blackburn, Southampton, England.' I said, 'So have I.' Then I thought, 'I'd never been the guy that stood in the Gallowgate or Leazes End and supported the guy wearing the No.9. Alan had done that and it was a dream of his to wear the famous No.9 shirt. Keegan, at the time, told me that he thought I could wear and carry the number when I first signed. In the end, I said, 'You're the manager and if you want Alan to wear the No.9 then that's what you've got to do.'

I've been fortunate to play at Wembley for England on numerous occasions but playing in the Charity Shield at Wembley when we lost 4-0 to Man United is probably the worst I've ever felt. Apart from not winning the league the season before that is the worst I've ever felt in football. The supporters stayed to the end and clapped us off the pitch, despite us being humiliated. I always knew Newcastle supporters were special but this brought home how great they were. That is why the 5-0 victory over them at St James' Park later that season was payback for the supporters, not for us.

I think that was the best result I had in my time at the club for the supporters. Kevin's team talk before this game was, 'You owe these supporters.' That was it. Nothing more, nothing less. No tactics, you do this or you do that, and there wasn't a player in that dressing room that didn't believe we owed the supporters. Every one of us knew we did.

I actually think we played better in the 1-0 defeat at home the season before. It was just one of these games. We could have been playing up until today and we wouldn't have scored. Every team has those games but you never want it to be against your biggest rivals. Philippe Albert hit the crossbar from a free-kick, the rebound fell to me but I put it over the bar. Then I was put through on goal a few times and Schmeichel came out and sprawled. It's not like he saved them, the ball just hit him because he'd made himself so big. On another day I score a hat-trick. It was just one of those games.

The same could be said about the 4-3 game at Liverpool. I remember one of the lads went down with an injury and Big Del (Derek Wright) came on to attend to him. I took a bottle of Lucozade out of his bag and thought, 'Those at home will be watching a hell of a game of football.' It was no comfort that it was voted by Sky as the Greatest Premier League match of all time. I always tell people that I was lucky to play in front of probably the best football supporters in the world and the team that rivalled them would be Liverpool. Playing in front of both sets of those supporters in a midweek game under the lights was probably the best game I ever played in.

We were all disappointed when Kevin left because we felt as if we were onto something. We felt as if we were close to winning something and he was the captain of the ship and when you lose your captain it's going to set you off course. That is exactly what happened. Certain people say we bottled winning the title but that wasn't the case. When we started the 1995-96 season, we were playing free-flowing football that everybody was loving. When I went home to London and I'd bump into different people they would say they weren't Newcastle fans but they would rush home to see us play if we were one of the Sky games because we were fantastic to watch. We just went out and played. Everyone believed in one another. Then around Christmas time or just after, everyone was talking about us winning the league and that's when we used to think about it. I don't care what sport you play, the minute you start thinking about it you cause yourself a problem.

It's like when you play golf. You play at your best you're not even thinking about it, you just play. When you start thinking about it too much, such as is the ball in the right position? Have I got the right club? When you do that, things go wrong. It's because you're trying to make things perfect. Then your reactions are slower. We started overthinking things. We can't do that, we can't do this, we need to stop the opposition. That's when the free-flowing football stopped. Obviously, we never thought about that before.

Kevin told me that the club had come to him and said we needed to raise £6 million. Kevin had said there'd been offers for me. Kevin was a bit cheesed off. He said to them, 'Do you want me to sell Les? We've been offered that for Les.' Apparently, they said, 'We're not selling Les.' Kevin said, 'OK, then let's put this to bed.' That was Kevin's way. Then Kenny Dalglish came in and they started saying the same things to him, 'We need to raise £6 million.' Then offers for me came in and I left.

Had Kevin still been there who knows what would have happened? I was disappointed to leave. There was unfinished business as far as I was concerned. I had two of the best years of my career at Newcastle. I scored 29 goals in my first season and 21 in my second season. That is not a bad return. So, to be shown the door was pretty disappointing.

Chapter Thirty three: David Ginola

Kevin Keegan had a knack for unearthing special players and there weren't many as extraordinary as David Ginola. Like Philippe Albert, he was unlike anything Newcastle United supporters had ever seen before. Where mere mortals flourish with time and space the Frenchman relished games where the opposition tightly man-marked him or tried to close him down mob-handed. Ginola could conjure time and space in a broom cupboard, charm the broom cupboard mop into tackling his marker before putting the fullback in his coat pocket.

Ginola's left foot was so cultured it could quote Shakespeare, his right foot so erudite it could split the atom while possessing all the style and grace of a Russian ballerina. Like several of Kevin Keegan's Entertainers, the £2.5 million signing from Paris St Germain reluctantly left Tyneside because of a change of manager but he left some wonderful memories and like us all, gets nostalgic about the Keegan years.

KK's Pièce de Résistance

When I signed for Newcastle, I was living in Woolsington, next to the airport. Tino lived about 300 yards away from me. Kevin asked me to make sure Tino was home by 11pm every day. I'm not sure I succeeded with that. Tino would often call me at midnight and ask me to come over because he had some problems. So, I get in my car, wearing my pyjamas, and drive over to Tino's house. The lights were on in every room. Cars were parked all over the place, on the lawn. I opened the door to music blaring and between 60 to 70 people dancing. He says, 'David, I can't get rid of these people. Can you tell them to get out, in English?'

It was a very enjoyable time to play football and important that we had several Geordies in the side. My English wasn't particularly good at that time so understanding the Geordies in the dressing room was, as you can imagine, pretty tough. I am from Saint Tropez, and as you can imagine, the weather is 'shite' (he said in Geordie) and always cold (he laughed). The Geordie fans are great, and very passionate about their side. There was always a lot of talk about my transfer fee and wages but I hope I justified my price tag and my salary and gave something back to the Newcastle supporters during my time at the club.

I remember we won 2-0 away at Sheffield Wednesday and I scored my first goal for the club. Everyone was happy with our start. I like to have a cigarette and a glass of wine after a game and my smoking surprised the lads. I got on the team bus, went to the back of the bus, and lit a cigarette. The players all turned to me and said, 'David, you can't smoke on the bus.' Kevin said he didn't mind me smoking as long as it was outside the bus. No, I didn't smoke at half-time, like a Sunday morning pub player, as some people have suggested.

I've never seen a manager in my career like Kevin Keegan. He was loved and so close to the people. It was a love story between him and the fans. I remember one time we were leaving the training ground on the team bus from Durham on the way to Southampton. As the bus was pulling out of the car park an old lady, between 70 and 75 years old, had come to wave us off. Kevin stopped the coach and went down to see her. He gave a hug and kiss and chatted for a minute or so with her. I thought, 'Wow.' This is something you don't see every day. In today's game, you never see that and I think we should get closer to the fans. The players are too detached from them now.

We were fighting for the title against Manchester United and Liverpool. At one stage, as everyone knows, we were 12 points clear of the rest. We went to Anfield to play Liverpool who were a great team at the time. We were flying and they were trying to catch us. We went to Anfield determined to win. We wanted to show everyone we meant business and that we could be consistent every week. The game was quite special on one hand because we had the game in our hands. We scored three goals and scoring three goals at Liverpool is quite good. We lost two goals in the last few minutes which shocked us. I think maybe that planted a seed that teams could beat us and we started to lose confidence. I feel ashamed we lost the title for the fans. The fans deserved to win something. We made some silly mistakes and lost concentration at the back and Kevin was annoyed. We needed to be more consistent to stay at the top of the league. It was no consolation to be involved in such a great game.

The following season when we played Manchester United at home, the game was a joy to play in. It was a joy to score and see all the happy faces around the city after the game and how proud they were to be Newcastle United fans. I'm sure the fans had a great week after that.

Barcelona tried to sign me in 1996 and Kevin told Sir Bobby Robson, 'No!' I was back in the South of France for my summer break in 1996 when I took a call from someone with a Geordie accent. He said, 'Hello David, this is Bobby Robson, I want to sign you for Barcelona.' I thought it was a joke at first. Bobby added that he was going to call Kevin and make an offer. Then I got a call from Kevin two hours later. He told me Barcelona had offered £7 million, which was a lot of money in 1996. Kevin told me he was going to refuse it. Barcelona then raised the offer to £12 million. Kevin came back to me and said, 'I don't want you to leave. You're doing very well for us. The fans love you and if I let you go, they will kill me. So, you're staying here.' It was a nice story because I'm a Latin guy. I love olive oil and sunshine and girls in short skirts but I was happy to stay here and play for you guys in the freezing cold, wind, and rain (he laughed).

My son had friends around in my house in London not long ago and he asked if I had some videos he could show his friends from my playing days. I told him he would find some of my goals on YouTube, and the one against Ferencvaros in the UEFA Cup was there. It's funny, because when you play you are generally in a bubble. You block everything out around you, the noise, the players, everything. Then, when you score a goal like that it's like you've escaped the bubble and everything comes alive around you. That's how I felt after that goal. I miss those moments in my life now. That is why you have to enjoy them when they happen.

When I was playing for Paris Saint Germain, we had a very strict dietician. We could only eat pasta, olive oil, rice, chicken breast and fish. When I came to Newcastle it was such a culture shock. On the team bus travelling to an away game, we had Only Fools and Horses on the video, Del-Boy, Rodney, and Trigger. It was so funny I bought the whole series. Then we had Sid the Sexist. I didn't understand a word of it other than 'Tits oot!' Everyone was laughing on the coach, so I laughed too, even though I didn't know what they were laughing at. We also had jellybeans and chocolate bars on the bus. Not only that, on the way back Terry Mac was going down the bus with a piece of paper making a list, asking the lads, 'Fish and chips or chicken and chips?' It was incredible. We stopped in Wetherby, at the Wetherby Whaler. The food was wrapped in newspaper, dripping in grease, covered in salt and vinegar, and we had to use our hands to eat it. I thought, 'This is something special.' But I loved it. Ta, very much.

I always had a great relationship with the fans of every club I played for. I played in Paris for four years and I was called 'The Prince.' The Paris chairman said he couldn't let me go because the fans would go crazy but I had to leave. It was the same at Newcastle. I spoke to Sir John Hall as well, who was my hero at the time. Still is. He told me about the city, the players, the language, and the culture of the city. Newcastle was a special time for me but so was Tottenham. I was voted Players' Player of the Year in 1999, the year Man United won the treble. This was special because I was recognized by my fellow professionals.

I have so many fond memories of my time in Newcastle. I went to Bamburgh Castle. Walking around the Metro Centre with my family and trying a Sunday roast in a Whitley Bay pub. I went to Whitley Bay because Derek, the physio, told me I would enjoy it with the family. I drove there with my family, and parked the car. It was a lovely sunny August day. While we were walking, I saw people playing volleyball in the sea. One of my kids said, 'Come on daddy let's go,' so. I put on my swim shorts and went for a walk on the sand. The sea was about 300 yards away from the sand. I thought the water must be really nice because the people were splashing about and laughing, having fun. I got to the water and it was freezing. I say, 'Hey kids, let's go play volleyball closer to the shore.

After that, we went to a really nice pub. The staff were really friendly. They told me about the roast beef and Yorkshire pudding and French beans. I don't know why they call them French beans. It's mange tout. They asked how I liked my meat and I said, 'Rare.' I could see they tried hard. The food was laid out fantastically well on the plate, except for the meat. It was rock hard! The waiter asked how it was and I said, 'Fantastic! I love it.' I remember going down the Big Market and, it wasn't that nice. Well, not at 2.30am on a Sunday but it was pretty special.

What did I think of Kevin's 'I'd love it rant?' I loved it! Some of us were still in the dressing room and we heard the noise outside, all of the shouting. We then ran out of the dressing room, thinking it was a fight and we wanted to help. We then saw Kevin pointing at the monitor shouting. We were like, 'Gaffer, what are you doing?' All fond memories.

I met Lee Dixon in person on Match of the Day the week before I got sent off for elbowing him in the face. He was always a tough opponent. It's OK, there's no bad feelings between us. I saw him recently and he said he lost a tooth from when I elbowed him. After the game, all of the Arsenal players went out onto the pitch looking for it.

It was strange to come back and play against Newcastle. The first time I came back with Tottenham I was in the away dressing room and I thought I was in the wrong dressing room. I didn't want to play at first. It was a strange feeling. I mistakenly went to the home dressing room, much to the merriment of the players. They were saying, 'David, wrong dressing room. You're next door now.' It was complicated because I knew everyone. I knew the doorman, the kitman, and everyone. I loved these people and had great relationships with them all. That is the downside to football when you leave a club.

I didn't want to leave the club but when Kenny Dalglish took over from Kevin it was a shock and it just wasn't the same anymore. I argued with Kenny and he didn't play me much after that. He tried to get rid of all the foreign players Kevin signed. I was frustrated at the time and I said something in the newspapers that if things don't change, I will have to leave. The following day we had a row. He told me I couldn't go to the newspapers and say these things. I said, 'You treat me like I'm having an affair with your wife.' He said, 'How dare you talk to me like that.' I said, 'At least I'm talking. You never look at me or talk to me.'

He wasn't the guy to take us to the top, as it was proved. He didn't make the most of the players we had. Under Kevin, it was such a pleasure every day in training and every Saturday away and at St James' Park, where the atmosphere was magnificent. I miss those days. One day, those happy days will return.

Chapter Thirty four: Faustino Asprilla

Faustino Asprilla was yet another "Wow" Kevin Keegan signing. The tale of Tino's red wine glugging before a spectacular cameo at the Riverside has gone down in Geordie folklore. Almost twisting the head off Middlesbrough defender Steve Vickers, the enigmatic Columbian found the head of local hero Steve Watson with a precision cross to level the scores before Les Ferdinand wrapped up a 2-1 victory on Teesside with a scuffed shot from 18 yards that went under Boro keeper Gary Walsh.

The Colombian forward's brief sojourn at Newcastle United was memorable on so many right and wrong levels, on and off the pitch. Signed in February 1996 for a reported £6.7 million from Parma, Asprilla's arrival was seen as the final piece of Keegan's jigsaw as he closed in on the Premier League title. Known for his flamboyant style, incredible skill, and unpredictable nature, the St James' Park faithful quickly took him to their hearts.

Asprilla could conjure the sublime and ridiculous, as well as displaying a couldn't care a less attitude but when he was on it, it was poetry in motion. Strangely, Tino saved his best for Keegan's replacement, Kenny Dalglish, on the grandest stage in the 1996-97 UEFA Champions League, when netting a hat-trick against Barcelona. United utility player Steve Watson described the performance as "the finest he's ever seen." High praise considering he played alongside two Premier League legends Alan Shearer and Wayne Rooney.

However, Asprilla's tenure at Newcastle was not without its challenges. His unpredictable nature often led to disciplinary issues, and his form could be erratic. Despite these issues, his talent and charisma left a lasting impression on the Geordie faithful.

100% Columbian

Kevin Keegan told me that the fans were fantastic and that Newcastle was a great place to play football. I got off the plane and it was raining. It was cold and then it started snowing. I thought, 'What the hell!' Kevin told me not to worry about the cold because he said there was a beach in Newcastle.

It is obviously very difficult to adapt to any foreign country when you arrive because of the different language and culture but when I was on the football pitch there was only one language, football, so I felt at home out there.

Fabio Capello signed a pre-contract with Parma and one of the conditions was for me to leave because he didn't like me. In the end, Capello went to Real Madrid, a team who also wanted to sign me. Davor Suker was Newcastle's first choice and had I gone to Madrid, Suker would have gone to St James' Park. Capello stopped that. I should've shagged his wife!

When Newcastle showed interest, I was curious. I had achieved a lot of things and I wanted a new challenge. Kevin Keegan sold the club to me. I loved his passion. When I stepped off the aeroplane, I thought I'd got the wrong plane. I thought I was in Siberia. It was freezing and I couldn't see ten yards in front of me for the snow. Just as well I was wearing my fur coat. Someone said, 'Tino, you look like a pimp and a porn star.' Newcastle was bizarre. I had heard of Newcastle but had never seen them play. There were so many people chanting my name. Even now when I see those photographs of the snow, I feel cold.

I was signed in early February 1996 and before I knew it, we headed to the Riverside Stadium for the Tyne-Tees derby with Middlesbrough. Kevin introduced me to my teammates and, after I'd quaffed a glass of wine with my lunch, he asked whether I'd be up for playing. I thought, this is crazy, but hey, I like crazy so agreed to go on the bench. With 20 minutes to go we were losing 1-0 and KK told me to go on. It was great fun. I wasn't match fit but nutmegged one player and sent the Boro centre half for an Evening Chronicle, setting up Super Stevie Watson to equalise. I also had a hand in Big Les's winner. Peter 'Pedro' Beardsley also set me up to score with a header but it was saved. It's fair to say it was a memorable cameo and I was knackered after my exertions.

I started at West Ham and played well but we lost in that game. I scored my first goal for the Magpies in a 3-3 draw with Manchester City. City's centre half, Keith Curle, was a dirty player and must have thought I was a softy because I had skill. One elbow to his nose and a head butt later, he was squealing like a girl! The FA didn't take too kindly to that and I got a one-match ban and a £10,000 fine.

I scored two more goals for Newcastle in my first season, one at home to West Ham in a 3-0 victory and in a 4-3 loss to Liverpool in what has been dubbed the Greatest Premier League game ever. Many people blamed me for United losing the title that season but the truth is, I wasn't fit. I hadn't played for six months because I was in dispute at Parma.

I was confident a good preseason and Newcastle supporters would see the best of me but then KK signed Alan Shearer for a world record £15m and I fell down the pecking order but I was still enjoying being at the club. I loved my teammates, even though they were always cutting up my socks and my favourite Disney t-shirts. We had plenty of parties back at mine. I also wrote off my club car, a Range Rover.

The guys were always bringing their favourite videos for the bus journey such as Only Fools and Horses and Auf Wiedersehen Pet so I thought I'd bring a video of my girlfriend, Petra Scharbach, in one of her films. I thought Kevin Keegan was going to have a heart attack. He was screaming at the bus driver to turn it off. A shame because she was so beautiful.

An injury to Shearer and I got a run of games and scored two in the UEFA Cup against Ferencvaros. We won 4-0. I also scored twice against Metz to take us into the quarter-finals and celebrated by putting my shirt on the corner flag. I got booked and suspended and missed the game against Monaco.

It was sad when Keegan resigned in January but when he left new manager Kenny Daglish started playing me up front in a three with Les Ferdinand and Shearer. I had a free role in a front three and it worked a treat. We were unbeaten for the last ten games, and finished second to get into the Champions League. It was strange when I first met Kenny. I wondered what language was he speaking.

Everything was going well in England but I always seemed to attract trouble every time I went home. I was sent off for fighting with Paraguay goalkeeper Jose Luis Chilavert after he spat in my face. A policeman tried to make a name for himself in Columbia and tried to throw me out of a concert in Tulua, so I nutted him. He'll think twice next time.

I started the 1997-98 campaign brilliantly. I scored twice in preseason at Juventus in Italy, repeated that in the opening Premier League game of the season at St James' Park against Sheffield Wednesday. I also scored in the Champions League qualifier at Croatia Zagreb to send us through to the group stage.

The most memorable moment and the highlight of my Newcastle career came when I netted a hat-trick in a 3-2 win over Barcelona in the Champions League group stage. My teammate Keith Gillespie was superb and provided two great crosses for my headed goals and I scored a penalty after the keeper brought me down to score the opener. Ironically, Daglish wasn't going to let me play because I had come back late from Columbia and he was angry, so I went to see the Barca players in their hotel before the game to say hello. I also had sex with my girlfriend before the game, something I never did because I thought it was unlucky. I never prepared for the game properly. Who knows what would've happened if I did, maybe I would have scored six goals. It was the first time in 20 years Barcelona had lost the first leg of a European tie.

I loved Newcastle and my favourite two players were Alan Shearer and Peter Beardsley but towards the end, I didn't feel the love reciprocated. I felt Kenny destroyed all of the good work Kevin did, selling our best players and not signing better players. Parma wanted me back and offered me a four-year contract. I asked for the same contract for the same money from Daglish but he wouldn't give me it, so I left with a heavy heart. Daglish accepted the £7.5m fee from my former Italian side. At the same time, the fans of Parma were not very happy with Carlo Ancelotti and something had to be done to appease them.

It is a shame I left Newcastle because I loved it and I keep coming back to see the fans because I feel a lot of love from the supporters but not so much from the weather because every time, I come back I catch a cold. Fans ask if I can still do a summersault? Unfortunately, not anymore, only with my girlfriend.

Chapter Thirty five: Alan Shearer

Alan Shearer's goalscoring exploits are legendary. Not only a great goalscorer but a scorer of great goals. The Newcastle-born marksman fulfilled a Boys' Own dream by joining his hometown club from Blackburn Rovers in 1996 for a then-world-shattering record transfer fee of £15 million. Shearer's insatiable appetite for scoring goal after goal cemented his place as the greatest striker in Premier League history.

Shearer's debut season saw him plunder 25 league goals, earning the Premier League Golden Boot and helping the Magpies finish second in the Premier League. Known for his Roy Race-esque rocket shots, timely heading ability, and clinical finishing, Shearer terrorised top-flight defences and consistently found the back of the net. Over his ten years at the club, he scored 206 goals in 404 appearances, making him Newcastle's all-time leading scorer.

Despite never winning a major trophy with Newcastle, Shearer captained his team in several memorable campaigns, including UEFA Champions League and FA Cup runs and became a legend to the Geordie faithful. Shearer's legacy at Newcastle endures, with his iconic No. 9 shirt and a statue outside St James' Park, symbolising his immense contribution to the club. Shearer's career at Newcastle is a testament to his loyalty, talent, and enduring status as a footballing icon.

Shear Class

As a kid, I just wanted to be a footballer, like my hero, Kevin Keegan. I was no different to any kid growing up in Newcastle. My dad threw a ball at me as a bairn and bought me a Newcastle strip and that was me away. I did the same to my son, here's a ball, here's a strip, get on with it.

My old man used to watch Newcastle every week. I was the same as a kid and my son is the same now, he goes home and away to every game. My son is like any other Newcastle fan. He, and they, go to work every week to make sure they have a good time every weekend. They spend a lot of that money earned on Newcastle United whether it is going to the games, watching in a bar or buying the club merchandise. I've been all over the country and, when I've walked through the towns and cities, I've never seen the mams and dads, brothers and sisters, grans and granddads, all wearing the football club shirts as they do in Newcastle. Newcastle is their life!

If it wasn't for my parents, I wouldn't be in the position I am in now. We lived in a humble, three-bedroom council house in Gosforth. They worked hard and gave me whatever they had for football boots, strips, travel and everything else. They gave me great advice and told me to do whatever I wanted to do, emphasising that as long as I worked hard, I would get my rewards. They didn't force or push me into anything. They just wanted me to have a right good go. It wouldn't have mattered if I didn't make it as a professional footballer. I do the same now with my kids.

It was tough to leave Newcastle for Southampton as a 15-year-old boy. I remember my mother standing on the platform of Central Station, tears streaming down her face. I couldn't imagine letting my kids do that but it was the best thing I could have done and that was the way it was back then. I signed for Southampton on schoolboys' forms at 14 and then I signed apprentice forms when I was 16. It was a tough dressing room I walked into with some really hard pros there: Mark Dennis, Jimmy Case, Russell Osman and it was a really volatile dressing room.

I went to West Brom, Manchester City and Newcastle on trial as a kid. I had a couple of offers, including Newcastle, but I looked at Southampton's youth set-up and saw the kids that had come through the system and thought I stood a better chance at the Dell than anywhere else. I also thought I would grow up better down there. I had a few friends who were exploring some dark areas and I could have easily been led down that path. So, to leave was one of the best decisions I ever made.

I remember coming to Newcastle for the first time to play at St James' Park with Blackburn. I got a call from my dad and he said, 'You better not score today.' I'd just come back from injury so I was on the bench and Kenny put me on with about 30 minutes to go. I did manage to score and I didn't get a well done off my dad that night, funny enough.

I'd just signed a new contract with Blackburn the year we won the Premier League. I wanted a clause in my contract that if a club came in for me and offered a set amount, I'd be free to speak to them. Jack Walker, the Rovers' owner, said he wouldn't put the clause in but said, 'My word is my honour, if you want to leave then you come and speak to me and you can leave.' We finished sixth the year after we won the Premier League title. I knew there were a number of clubs interested in me: Newcastle, Man United, Liverpool etc. I went to Jack and said, 'The time has come where I'd like to speak to other clubs.' He said, 'OK, you can talk to them but it will be a world record fee of £15 million from Newcastle and Man United and I want it in cash, up front.'

Back then transfer fees were generally spread out over the length of your contract and not all upfront in a lump. I told Jack that he was making it impossible for me to leave because no one had that sort of money back then. Jack then agreed it would be £7.5 million on signing and another £7.5 million 12 months later.

I went to see Kevin (Keegan) in the morning at David Platt's mother-in-law's house in Cheshire before a Bryan Adams concert and then Sir Alex Ferguson in the afternoon. Sir Alex asked whether he was the first to see me. I told him I'd seen Kevin first to which he replied, 'That's me fucked, then.' The talks with Sir Alex went well and I was impressed with what he had to say. I asked if I could take the penalties and he said, 'Eric (Cantona) is on them.' I said, 'I know but can I take them?' He just looked at me with those steely eyes of his as if to say, 'I'm not telling or asking Eric that.' It was such a difficult decision to make. One minute I was going to Man United, the next it was Newcastle. At one stage I'd decided to sign from Man United. I'd driven around Manchester and I was going to buy Graeme Souness' house.

Two days later I got a call from Kevin, asking for another half an hour with me. It was just before Newcastle were going to fly off to the Far East for their pre-season trip. He drove to Manchester to meet me in an airport hotel. After the chat, I thought, 'You know, it's ten years since I left Newcastle. I want to go home and wear the famous No.9 shirt and score goals for the supporters.'

I rang my Mrs at home in Formby, which is in Merseyside, and said, 'I've made the decision, I'm going home. I need you to pack me a bag and call me a taxi to come pick me up at the hotel in Manchester. The bag arrived the next day and I never went back to that house. I flew out to the Far East with Kevin. Out of respect to Sir Alex, I thought I should ring and tell him my decision. I rang him once, no answer, I rang him again, no answer and the third time he didn't pick up again so I left a voice message. He didn't ring me back, which I understand. I think somebody must have told him I'd signed for Newcastle.

I should have known what it would be like after watching all of the fuss about Kevin when he came as a player but I was still unprepared. I was like those kids following him around wherever he went. He was the Pied Piper and I followed him. Then, when I was introduced at the Leazes End in the pouring rain to 15, 16, 17,000 or whatever it was, I thought, 'This is madness.' I loved every minute of it. I looked out across the sea of black and white and thought. 'Why are you lot not at work or school?' It was bonkers but so great to be back. I didn't feel any pressure from the price tag. I loved the fact I was the world's most expensive player. If there was any pressure, that was on the club because they'd paid that money. It was a privilege for me, and I enjoyed the 'most expensive' tag.

Obviously. Les Ferdinand was wearing the No.9 shirt when I signed but I asked Kevin whether I could have it. He said he couldn't guarantee it but said he would speak to Les. Les said to Kevin, 'But I've got the No.9 shirt.'

'I know, but Alan has asked for it.'

'Does that mean you've given him it?'

'No, but he has asked rather nicely if he can have it.'

Les is one of the nicest people you'll ever meet and he didn't want to give it up but he kind of knew what the shirt meant to me, and the people of Newcastle. Anyway, he gave me it and he took the No.10. We scored, I think, 49 goals between us and I missed two or three months through injury and he missed six or seven weeks. That is a phenomenal number of goals between us considering we missed all of that time through injury.

One of the worst decisions this football club has ever made was to sell Les. It was made by another of my idols, Kenny Dalglish. The club agreed a fee of £6 million with Spurs on the eve of a pre-season tournament at Goodison Park, Everton. They told Les and of course, Les didn't want to leave. Subsequently, I broke my ankle in the game at Goodison Park and Kenny, Freddy Shepherd and others went and tried to do everything they could in their power to stop the deal going through. Les being Les, refused. He said, 'You wanted rid of me and that's it, I'm off.' And rightly so.

While we're on the subject of people leaving, Kevin leaving surprised and hurt me. I was disappointed because he'd worked so hard to get me here. I didn't sign for Kevin, I signed for Newcastle but Kevin was my hero. He is a great talker, has great passion and to this day still loves this football club. You can imagine how hard he was trying to sell the football club to me. Although he didn't have to sell my hometown club to me. I knew what it was all about. So, for him to leave after six months of my coming here, after making a huge decision to turn down Man United, where I was guaranteed to win trophies, yes, I was angry and disappointed. I still don't know the full reasons why Kevin left, whether it was as far as he could take the club or the club wanted to go in another direction.

My first meaningful game for Newcastle was the Charity Shield where Man United thumped us 4-0. My second game was Everton away, where we lost 2-0. I thought, 'What the hell have I done here?' Things got better though and come October we beat Man United 5-0 to gain some revenge for the Charity Shield defeat. Everybody remembers the great goals by Ginola, Les' header, Philippe Albert's chip, and Man United were such a great side at the time. It was such an iconic game. Everybody on the day had a ten out of ten performance. And after 20 years the Man United fans are still singing that song about me. I love it!

I thought Kenny Dalglish was an ideal replacement for Kevin at the time, having worked with him at Blackburn where we won the league. He created a great atmosphere at Ewood Park and he won the double as a player-manager at Liverpool. I thought with that experience, coming to a massive football club like Newcastle, and following a huge personality like Kevin, he would be ideal. I still don't know whether it was his decision or the club's decision to sell Les and replace him with Jon Dahl Tomasson or Andreas Andersson. Then there were the John Barnes and Ian Rush signings on top of that. Kenny did sign Nobby Solano, however, which was a great signing.

We got to an FA Cup final under Kenny and the atmosphere at the semi-final against Sheffield United at Old Trafford was unbelievable, as was the semi against Spurs the following year. My family were in one stand and they said it was rocking and moving because the Newcastle fans were that loud. For us as players, it was incredible. Then we got to the final, played terribly and got told we had to do a bus parade from the Gosforth Park Hotel to the Civic Centre: It was embarrassing for us because played so poorly. There were hundreds of thousands lined up cheering us. Can you imagine how good it would be to finally win something?

The irony isn't lost on me that I was a ball boy in Kevin Keegan's last game from Newcastle in 1984. In fact, I was there in 1982 for his debut against QPR, where he scored in a 1-0 win. I never thought in a million years I'd play for the club never mind get a testimonial. It was one of the proudest moments of my career. It was just a shame I couldn't play the whole game against Gordon Strachan's Celtic. I came on to take that staged penalty. That night was everything I hoped for and a hell of a lot more. The easy part was to give the money from the game to charity. The hard part was which charity. So, I set up a charity, a foundation on the A69. It makes me proud every time I pass the Alan Shearer Centre, which short break provision offering respite care and activity centre for children with learning disabilities. Bringing up kids is hard enough but try and imagine how hard it is to bring up a kid with a disability.

Everyone talks about Kevin and The Entertainers because he gave the city and the fans a bit of hope. I heard and read that the club can't attract players from abroad but Kevin could. And who wouldn't want to play in from of 52,000 fans? If they could build or make St James' Park bigger, the fans would still fill it every week. It would be great if the club could do all of that now.

My Newcastle career was everything and more. I scored my first goal against Wimbledon on my home debut at the Leazes End. I grew up in Newcastle and I wanted to play for the football club. To end up as the club's record goalscorer, beating the late, great Jackie Milburn, having a statue outside the ground and enjoying the relationship I have with the supporters is special. I have to thank the Shepherd family for the statue, by the way, they funded it, and also to the council for putting it where it is.

I wouldn't change a thing. I know I didn't win any trophies with Newcastle. I know I would have had a shed load of trophies had I signed for Man United but I had an amazing ten years here.